A MAN AT ARMS

Memoirs of Two World Wars

FRANCIS LAW
A portrait by Raeburn-Dobson
painted in 1947

A Man at Arms

Memoirs of Two World Wars

Francis Law

COLLINS
8 Grafton Street, London W1
1983

William Collins Sons and Co. Ltd.
London · Glasgow · Sydney · Auckland
Toronto · Johannesburg

British Library Cataloguing in Publication Data

Law, Francis
A man at arms.
1. Law, Francis   2. Great Britain – Biography
I. Title
941.082'09'24   CT788.L

ISBN 0 00 217057 4

First published 1983
© Francis Law 1983

Photoset in Ehrhardt by
Rowland Phototypesetting Ltd
Bury St Edmunds, Suffolk
Made and printed in Great Britain by
William Collins Sons & Co. Ltd, Glasgow

To comrades
fallen in two world wars
and in gratitude to Rosemary
whose love and companionship
have sustained me
for over half a century

Preface

These memoirs, originally written for my family, tell a
story of personal experience. Such judgements and
opinions as they contain are therefore entirely personal and make no pretence to be anything else. The
accident of age – I was nearly 18 in August 1914 and 43
in September 1939 – enabled me to see active service
in both wars. In that respect my experience was I suppose unusual but except in the sense that everybody's
life is unique I make no such claim for my own.

Acknowledgements

I would like to thank those of my family and friends who have encouraged me to persevere in the writing of this book. In particular, Peter Cochrane, DSO, MC, Ronald McNair Scott, Richard Ollard, Alan and Maureen Trotter. I would like to thank Verity Anderson (Mrs. Paul Paget) and Lord David Cecil for their kind permission to quote from *The Last of the Eccentrics* and from *The Cecils of Hatfield House*, also Macmillan publishers for my references to Rudyard Kipling's *The History of the Irish Guards in the Great War*.

Contents

A Farewell to Arms

His golden locks time hath to silver turn'd:
O time too swift, O swiftness never ceasing!
His youth 'gainst time and age hath ever spurn'd,
But spurn'd in vain; youth waneth by increasing:
Beauty, strength, youth, are flowers but fading seen;
Duty, faith, love, are roots, and ever green.

His helmet now shall make a hive for bees:
And, lovers' sonnets turned to holy psalms,
A man-at-arms must now serve on his knees,
And feed on prayers, which are age his alms:
But though from court to cottage he depart,
His Saint is sure of his unspotted heart.

GEORGE PEELE 1558–97

Chapter One

An Irish Childhood

Outside swirled the snow, driven by the wind upon the window panes. Inside the comforting warmth of my father's house, wrapped up to the point of suffocation and scarlet-faced, I held my first court, taking a dim, unfocused view of the denizens of a new world gathered about my cot. My parents welcomed me, were loving, thoughtful and indulgent and remained so throughout their lives. The year, 1897, was that of the Queen's Jubilee. Victoria, queen and empress, sat securely on her throne, aged, remote, and venerated, titular head of a great empire, built somewhat haphazardly, upon which 'the sun never set'. Sunset was alas even then not far distant. Few were alert to its stealthy approach, none to the final eclipse. Britain's future looked serene, prosperous and in every way secure.

My birth took place in Dublin at the end of January within a stone's throw of my grandfather's house in Fitzwilliam Square, where my father had been born. In early spring we moved northwards. Our country home was in County Donegal on the shores of Sheephaven Bay. The 'Big House', known as Marble Hill, was Georgian and of modest size for those days. Nonetheless it sheltered us all comfortably, including frequent guests, a housekeeper and staff of ten. About a quarter of a mile from the house stretched a deep sandy shore roughly three quarters of a mile in length; between house and shore lay grassland with apple and quince trees whose blossom was enriched by a sea of daffodils. Bordering the avenue was a steep bank, massed with flowering shrubs, rhododendrons, azaleas and hydrangeas, mostly deep pinks and blues. There were two large gardens with high sheltering walls. In spring the slopes were carpeted with primroses and later by abundant wild strawberries. Beech woods formed the background and behind the main garden stood a plantation of splendidly tall Scots firs with their red trunks.

Views from the house were superb, for the main rooms looked over the waters of the bay. Beyond the further shore stood line upon line of hills, the lower and nearer green or heather-clad, those beyond blue and purple. The very clouds, ever changing, were a delight. No one could possibly have enjoyed a happier childhood, for wherever I looked beauty and things of interest encompassed me. It was in such idyllic surroundings that my early years were spent, and it was to them that in adolescence and later I could so happily return. It was a paradise for a growing boy fond of the outdoors and encouraged to be interested in all about him.

Our lovely home was remote. The nearest town of size was Londonderry, nearly forty miles away, so that we had to be largely self-supporting. From an early age all animals were known to me as friends, as indeed they were, to be treated kindly, including horses, milking cows, sheep, poultry of all varieties, even pigs. Dogs there were of course, though my mother only allowed a favoured few to live in the house; the rest were in kennels. Those that I remember best were a pair of white West Highland terriers, with us for years before they vanished into the sea and drowned. Another was an Aberdeen terrier bitch called Kelpie, a tremendous character, and a most patient one, who would sit for hours above a rabbit hole and pounce unerringly on anything that emerged. Yet another was a vast Irish deerhound, shaggy, splendid and friendly, called Lomair after some legendary Celtic hero. My father took Lomair with him when riding. Often after dining we invited this great dog to demonstrate his agility. My parents stood at each end of the dining room, I in the centre holding a long stick horizontally over which Lomair leaped with astonishing ease, to be rewarded with biscuits, then promptly went to sleep in front of a blazing log fire when we moved over to the drawing-room, and stayed dreamily immobilized till bed-time. The little dogs, including spaniels, could get all the exercise they required chasing rabbits through the woods and out of the rhododendron clumps.

My mother's influence in those formative years was paramount. This was natural enough, for my father was often away. Her influence was wholly beneficial and has guided me unconsciously throughout my life. My mother taught wordlessly, by example and encouragement, the value of self-discipline, of physical fitness and control. Few things were forbidden. On occasion I was encouraged to be adventurous and to take risks though cautioned against foolhardiness.

Thus by the age of six I learnt a degree of self-reliance, and if by poor judgement or over-optimism I came to grief and suffered damage, it was all good training for life, unbelievably good training for what was to come only twelve years later, when I found myself in army uniform.

All I cay say of my father at this stage was that he was gentle, generous and had a lively sense of humour. His manners were exquisite, belonging to the eighteenth century rather than to the first years of the twentieth. He held that good manners, where not entirely superficial, sprang from the heart and should reflect thought and respect for others in whatever walk of life. He was highly sensitive and wholly trusting, his trust sometimes misplaced and occasionally abused, but he was warm-hearted and forgiveness came easily to him. This was largely lost on me in my earliest years when my mother appeared to be the dominant character, since she was always there. I do remember an occasional gentle reprimand for swinging on rather splendid dining-room chairs, appearing for a meal with hands unwashed or for leaving every door open, encouraging cold draughts. My father was allergic to draughts, looked askance at grubby hands, and did not appreciate needless destruction of furniture, to which his thoughtless son and dogs contributed. He was a romantic – alas, where are they now? He would sing to himself in his bath or out of it such charming songs as Handel's 'Where'er you walk'. He had a pleasant restful voice. In short, he was a civilized human being. A species rare at any time, now fast becoming extinct.

I was yet to discover what a sad and lonely childhood he had endured. His mother had died when he was four, his father when he was ten. He was devoted to his father as some charmingly touching letters to his little son reveal. My grandfather's death from pneumonia was sudden and totally unexpected, for he was only fifty-eight. He had gone for a fortnight's salmon fishing in Donegal, caught a chill and died within days to everyone's consternation. He had been Member of Parliament for Londonderry for many years and three years earlier had been appointed Lord Chancellor of Ireland in succession to the veteran Lord O'Hagan. He had previously held a variety of important judicial offices, and could have expected to have given many more years of service in high office.

Because my grandfather's duties required him to be constantly away from home in Parliament and at the Irish Office in London, the child was much alone, deprived of a parent's love, care and guidance.

For a sensitive intelligent boy this amounted to deprivation. His death was a disaster for his family and friends and must have come as a devastating blow to his small son. A sad sense of loss remained with my father throughout his life.

My father's loss could easily have happened even earlier, in 1882; after a meeting at Viceregal Lodge, the Lord Lieutenant, Lord Spencer, the Irish Chief Secretary, Lord Frederick Cavendish, and my grandfather came down the steps together. My grandfather's carriage had drawn up. He invited Lord Frederick to drive with him to the Chief Secretary's Lodge where he would drop him off. Unhappily Lord Frederick decided to walk the short distance unescorted. He was ambushed and murdered by terrorists. It was a tragic affair, for of the many Chief Secretaries appointed, he was the one thought the most likely and the most determined with his deep interest in Irish affairs to do all he could for Ireland and in every way to ease the lot of its people. My grandfather was terribly shocked by Lord Frederick's murder. Both Members of the House of Commons, they had known one another for years and had become friends, admiring each other's abilities, sympathies and aspirations.

From the age of ten therefore my father was brought up by stern, elderly and rather unimaginative cousins, governesses and tutors until he went to school in England, then on to Rugby following the footsteps of his elder brother, fifteen years his senior and already in the army. I got the impression later that though he did well academically at both his schools, he had little affection for either.

He came into his own at Oxford where he made many lasting friendships and enjoyed himself, for it was his first taste of freedom. He had at last been given a generous allowance. His minority had been a long one and funds had built up, so that at twenty-one he found himself relatively well off for those days. He hunted occasionally and kept a very elegant gig with a lively, well groomed horse between its shafts.

He took an active interest in the arts, especially the theatre. He played the Cheshire Cat in a performance of *Alice in Wonderland* in 1894 in the garden of Worcester College in the presence of 'the elderly Christchurch don' Lewis Carroll. Nigel Playfair, afterwards a great friend, produced the play. Years later my father and Nigel Playfair planned jointly to launch *The Beggar's Opera* but the advent of war in 1914 put a stop to this. After the war Nigel Playfair produced

The Beggar's Opera at Hammersmith: an historic success.

My father read history and having got his degree left Oxford and promptly married. An account exists of an Irish bicycling tour in 1895 that reads: 'Rosslyn went off to Downhill, from whose gale-swept colonnades he, the Bruce twins, Hugo Law and four sporting young ladies of County Derry headed inland. All tyres were solid and all pedals fixed, allowing no free-wheeling. The girls, wearing knicker-bocker suits and outsize cloth caps secured by hatpins, let rip downhill with their toes resting on the steps each side of their front wheels. The only means of stopping was the sharp application of a front-wheel brake which could well result in the rider going over the handlebars. The gayest, wildest, prettiest and most universally adored of the four was Lota Stuart, whom Hugo soon afterwards married'.

When in due course I appeared Rosslyn Bruce agreed to become a godfather. He was a brilliant eccentric to whom my parents were devoted, as he to them. At Oxford Rosslyn had made his mark in many spheres, especially as a startlingly witty speaker, also for his entertaining prose and poetry. His love and admiration for animals caused him to be nicknamed Francis d'Assisi at Oxford, which saintly name my parents decided to bestow on me.

My godfather was also known as 'the Honourable Member for Dogs', for he was never without one throughout his life. In his last year at Oxford he got his degree in classics but did badly in theology. His treatise on David had ended 'Notwithstanding the tribute which we should assiduously lay at the shrine of the great Hebraic king, he was essentially a man one could not introduce to one's sisters'. His examiner was not amused. However, Queen Victoria was, by a Skye terrier that Rosslyn had bred and sold to her. Amongst a host of friends and admirers was J. M. Barrie, who, it has been claimed, 'may have found in Rosslyn Bruce – always so full of fun and mischief – the boy who never grew up'.

The household at Marble Hill (so called from a long-vanished marble quarry nearby) consisted at that time of a housekeeper, 'Ellen the cook', a kind but formidable personality who had been sent to London for training, and two maids in each department – eleven all told including a laundry maid and a butler called Bingham. They were a happy lot who got on famously together, were efficient, hard-working and a delight to have about us. A character, Mr B. was an imposing figure with mutton chop whiskers. He was an enthusiastic sportsman with rod and gun. This passion in the end led to his undoing. I was ten or eleven at the time. When off duty he would vanish on his bicycle, no one thought to enquire whither. It came to light when he was caught in the act of shooting at salmon as they leapt to negotiate obstacles on their passage upstream. A complaint was lodged by a neighbour and Mr B. was spoken to by my father. Our neighbour consented to overlook the offence on Bingham's undertaking never to repeat it. Alas, after some years of undetected crime Mr B. could restrain himself no longer, made a foray into enemy territory and was caught afresh. This time there could be no reprieve. He was an excellent butler and everyone missed him when he had to go.

My eldest sister was born when I was three and there was rejoicing. I have no recollection of feeling jealous when she became the centre of attention. Perhaps this was because there had already been implanted in my infant mind a certainty that my mother's love and devotion was wide enough to embrace us both, and that the nursery staff would never fail or desert me. In another three years a further sister was born. After that I enjoyed the luxury of a room of my own. Supervision was relaxed and I took advantage of my new-found freedom to get up to any mischief that came to mind.

There was plenty of scope, for adjoining the house was a walled area known as the Upper Yard. Though both big gates might be locked I found I had a way into it through the kitchen and laundry rooms and spent happy hours there. A dovecot stood in one corner where pigeons were constantly harassed by sparrow hawks and kestrels and devoured by an occasional peregrine falcon, all three nesting nearby. On another side stood the coach-house, loose boxes and stalls for the horses, harness-rooms full of interest with saddles, harnesses, shining brasses and bits. A long and very heavy buff-coloured overcoat hung there with silver buttons embossed with the family crest. There was a hat with a cockade, which I tried on but it not only slid over my ears but blotted out all vision. Like the coat, this hat was no use for dressing up, a frequent play-ploy. There was a machine for loading shotgun cartridges with measures of powder and shot, empty cases for loading, and cartridge wads. I must have loaded a lot of cartridges with adequate skill, for no one who used them blew up. Actually the machine was little used until the stock of cartridges ran low, for I remember splendid wooden boxes supplied by Eley, each holding 500 or 1000 cartridges at about £1 a hundred. There were very big lofts above full of hay and fodder, access by ladder, where I spent a lot of time out of sight. In the coach house, used in part as a garage, stood an enormous red Packard, beside one or two horse-drawn carriages. This car, of formidable size and construction, was built on the lines of an early Dreadnought battleship. Why it had been bought was a mystery as it was seldom used.

Another happy hunting ground was the Lower Yard which lay below the Upper, with generous and varied accommodation for all forms of livestock other than horses and dogs. Here cows were milked and animals fed. When old enough I would find my way there to get into everybody's way, yet those busy and competent ones were kind and patient and appeared delighted to have me around. I tried my hand at milking but made little of it and was twice knocked off a milking stool by an infuriated cow. This yard was always full of life of one sort or another. Besides cattle and pigs, poultry of various kinds were to be found there – turkeys, ducks and hens. With a choice of free range for the hens, collecting eggs in and outside the yard was a welcome and useful occupation. If I trod on a hidden nest or broke a few it did not matter.

Built on to one side of this yard was yet another long low barn full of animal feed and hay, against the wall of a well stocked fruit and vegetable garden. My father had enlarged it by raising the roof and creating a large room above to be used for recreation on wet days, for country-dancing, fencing, and modest theatrical performances, for which a stage at one end was frequently in use. When the family was at home dances were given at least once a month for the country people, most of whom walked for miles. Great urns of tea and plates of food would be carried from the kitchen to refresh the dancers. This made much more work which was not resented, on the contrary there was never trouble or unpleasantness. Local fiddlers and concertina players gave sound. Guests staying in the house were expected to join in with us for an hour or so. It was all very friendly and widely appreciated. Dancing ended when the last couples, faced with a five mile walk, thought it time to go and this was seldom before daybreak.

The ripening fruit in the garden below the windows of the dance room became a source of temptation and I sought like the blackbirds means of relieving overburdened strawberry plants of their produce. There were also tempting-looking cherries under netting on the walls. There were two doors into this garden, both securely locked – keys hidden. The walls were too high and the drop too great from the dance room windows for an assault from without. Then one day quite by chance when playing about in the barn below I fell through a loose pile of straw and found myself facing the top section of a barn door. To my joy it was unlocked but as it opened inwards I had to remove much straw before I could tug it open sufficiently to squeeze through. At last I was in forbidden territory and taking full advantage of this gorged on luscious strawberries for many a day. My guilty secret I kept to myself, covering up my tracks with straw before leaving.

Operations against fruit in the main garden were much more difficult, though the rewards for success were correspondingly greater. There were four gates or doors into it, all but the main gate kept locked and that was in full view of the house; in addition, that garden was very seldom deserted. However successful raids were carried out, particularly when my sisters were old enough to take part in them. They always contrived to look unspeakably innocent and so made splendid collaborators.

An unusual feature in both gardens was that many paths were lined with strawberry plants rather than with boxwood so that there was always a superabundance of this fruit to be used for jam made in enormous quantity, whilst dessert strawberries were grown under nets near the greenhouse in which grapes and peaches flourished. Apples, pears, cherries and red currants were grown espalier fashion against the walls, netted against the ravages of birds.

Soon after settling down at Marble Hill my father had built a charming lodge at the gates, to replace whatever had been there before. The architect had been one of the two talented Scots brothers Lorimer, one the artist and Scottish academician, the other an architect of distinction. In this lodge lived our head man and his splendid family, which in time built up to six. The eldest boy, some two years my junior, became a close friend and constant companion. His father was an outstanding personality, immensely strong physically yet gentle in all he did or said and a man of complete integrity. He was a paragon of virtue though he would himself have denied this strenuously. He had a fine sense of humour. It is difficult to imagine what as a family we owed to this one man, for during my father's frequent absences he had to look after everything about the place. He only had three men to help him in this, though the gardens were splendidly kept and produced more vegetables and fruit in season than even our hungry household could consume.

My parents hated the winter cold so we moved in November to London or to Paris, generally in alternate years. The first London house I can remember was in Kensington Square. Later with the arrival of my sisters and a rather larger staff to look after us, my father bought a charming house in Cheyne Walk, Chelsea. Close by lived an elderly eccentric. He was fond of children, gave frequent parties and showered gifts upon them. He had two menservants, who to our delight often appeared in Highland dress. He was an enthusiastic Jacobite, quite mad about the Stuarts. Somehow he knew that my mother was a daughter of that illustrious, ill-fated house. On meeting he would always bow and insist on kissing her hand even in the street. Unwilling to hurt his feelings, perhaps touched by his devotion to a lost cause, she accepted the old man's veneration with smiling dignity and grace. We children were impressed and intrigued as to what caused so venerable a man to behave thus.

I still remember from about this time my first meeting with Peter Scott, now renowned for his interest in and knowledge and paintings of wild fowl, the inspirer of the Slimbridge Wildfowl Trust and like ventures. I had wandered into the drawing-room to be confronted by a very little boy walking about stark naked, whilst my mother and Kathleen Scott were deep in conversation. Many of us are prone to be rather prim when we are young, and my first reaction was one of mild shock. Mrs Scott (later Lady Kennet) seemed determined to bring her son up toughly so that he might measure up, physically at least, to the standard of endurance of his gallant father who had perished nobly in Antarctic snows. For myself I was more than content to be warmly clad.

About this time I became enthusiastic about the theatre though my taste for melodrama was not shared by my parents. I was therefore dispatched to view the most dramatic and sensational plays then running, with 'Ellen the cook' as my guardian, before whom when roused the bravest might quail. Our outings were nearly always to matinees, for Ellen would be required to cook dinner, sometimes an elaborate one when guests were expected as they often were. On such occasions I would rendezvous in the kitchen, though expected to be asleep upstairs, and enjoy such titbits as Ellen thought fit to bestow. She was a faithful, not to say resourceful, ally.

Some years we went to France; Biarritz, Arcachon and St Jean de Luz I remember vaguely. Strangely enough it was in Paris that I first learnt to swim, under my mother's instruction, so that when we moved to the coast of Brittany I took to the sea like a duck to water. Once we spent the whole year abroad, and it was then that two incidents occurred, stamped on my memory.

My sisters and I had been left for some days in a pension whilst our parents went to visit friends. We were watched over by our governess and a nurse who had a furious row with the landlady over food and sanitary arrangements. Fed largely on mushrooms by our frugal hostess, we all became ill. Our parents were recalled and we were at once removed to more salubrious quarters. Reproached on the score of sanitation the landlady made the splendid reply, 'Mais il y a toujours la forêt'. That became a family jest, for appropriate occasions.

Another time I was sent to a French school, much to my indignation and disgust to start with, but I got on well and was rather spoilt as the odd man out. The headmaster, who was young, rode a motor bicycle and towed my bicycle about with it at the end of a rope. He introduced me to a type of small boat I had never seen before, propelled by underwater paddles worked by one's feet. Indeed one way and another much more time was spent in play than in learning. This suited me fine. One morning, bicycling along the shore on my way to school, I was astonished to see vast numbers of small fish coming to shore on an incoming tide. This was altogether too much for me, so casting away my books in order to make use of the basket that had held them I dashed into the shallow waters of pools, scooping up what fish I could on to the sand, then into my basket. I had not been long at this before a number of locals arrived with all necessary equipment and one kind woman with a net soon had my basket filled to overflowing. I looked round for my bicycle and books of which there was no sign, all had disappeared under the waves. The bicycle was at length recovered, but not the books. This episode did not seem to discourage the French schoolmaster. His youth was not far behind him, he had a fellow feeling for the young and thoughtless.

At a very early age at Marble Hill I was encouraged to ride, and I was furnished for a time with a particularly idle, obstinate, overfed donkey. He was happy to graze by the wayside, was never in any particular hurry to go anywhere, and as a steed though amiable was a heartbreak. When about two I sat in a sort of miniature howdah, a wickerwork chair upholstered in red leather fitted as a saddle, my steed led by a man in slow and stately fashion. I was soon promoted to a pony, which answered to the uninspired name of Johnny. Though no 'bronco' he was a much livelier mount, and when required to do so suffered the indignity of being put between the shafts of a pony trap.

About this time I was presented with a curragh, a boat built of wood and tarred canvas with ribs of hazel rods. It had no keel and capsized with the greatest of ease, but it was unsinkable. At its launching I christened this craft the *Good Hope* after a battleship of that date. It was put to many severe tests and twice had large holes torn in its bottom when carried by waves on to barnacle-encrusted rocks. Each time it was salvaged, stripped and the three layers of tarred canvas replaced. The final indignity came when I decided to turn the *Good Hope* into an ocean cruiser for which she was in no way fitted and furnished her with a half deck, a mast and sail, which I hoisted in a light wind. At once, having no keel, she rolled over. So we learn as we go along. Off came the decking, out came the mast, and back to the job for which she had been fashioned, which was fishing with long lines and lobster pots.

At nine I was presented with a .410 bore gun and let loose upon the countryside but not before being trained in its use and much cautioned 'never, never let a gun, pointed be at anyone' etc. My early victims were innocent rabbits of which there seemed to be unlimited numbers. There was however a most unlucky snipe who chose to come out of a clear sky and settle itself in or behind a pin-cushion of a gorse bush in a bog. I stalked this tiny bush and let fly in the centre of it, up went the snipe, then down to earth. It was the most unsporting shot that I have ever made, but at the time I was thrilled. Shooting became a passion and there were few days when I returned empty handed. One day a large flock of wild geese (greylags) settled nearby. I had tried many times unsuccessfully to stalk them and get within range. Somewhere I had heard that if an approach were made by farm cart one could hope to get to close quarters, so I hastened to harness Johnny into the pony trap. All went according to plan, the approach march looked like succeeding though it was difficult for me and my young companion concealed in the trap to judge distance with accuracy or to control our excitement. At last we were spotted by the ever vigilant geese and they rose as one. To cries of 'Shoot between the pony's ears, Master Francis, shoot between the pony's ears!' I complied, the geese flew off undamaged, Johnny took to his heels and the pony trap, out of control, bounded away.

My sisters, now aged about seven and four, working together, would raid the cook's larder, despite being extremely well fed. It was a large one and always well stocked. There was a fair sized window cut in the door for ventilation over which a sheet of perforated zinc had been tacked. The door itself was always locked. However, we were not easily defeated and food, as for all puppies, was always a draw. I found a means of easing the zinc back on three sides, hinging it on the fourth. Only the youngest was small enough to get through this window, so sister Ruth was hoisted through it head first, with her little arms stretched out before her. Holding her legs I would let her slowly down until her small hands had gained contact with the flagstoned floor. It was then up to her to select whatever delicacies were to be found and to pass them in great haste to us. If interrupted the drill was for me to press the zinc quickly back into position, for Ruth to hide under the marble slabs, and for sister Mary to look innocent, allay suspicion by entering into animated conversation with and draw off our interrupter. When all was clear, Ruth would be hauled out head first, gauze re-attached, our haul recovered from the boot hole – a small room under the stairs where shoes were cleaned – and away to feast in some distant loft. I remember a craze for tree climbing and for clambering over roofs, both discouraged by our elders and very much so by nursery staff and governesses.

These splendid sisters were later to help with my long line fishing. The object was to catch sea trout, though we got very few, for those we may have caught were destroyed by dogfish who then became hooked themselves. Hauling in these lines was always a noisy affair, what with laughter and sisters' shrieks as dogfish and very large skates with their spiked backbones and lashing tails, both evil looking creatures, came over the side and leaped about our bare feet, until knocked senseless and returned to the sea. Another sport was catching large crabs from rocks at spring tides. There were masses and they made very good eating. We also caught sand-eels. These are really small fish, and made only tolerable eating, but excellent bait for sea trout. In hot weather they threw themselves out of sand banks and could be quickly grabbed, but the best method of catching them was to draw a long knife through the sand the blunt edge foremost, bringing the sand eel up to meet the disengaged hand. In this way on warm days at low tide, when sand banks were exposed, a great many might be caught. Yet another diversion was spearing flat fish, plaice and the like. This was not at all easy to do. They had to be spotted then stalked cautiously and slowly, finally the actual spearing carried out swiftly and accurately, allowance being made for distortion in the water.

Vast numbers of large mussels grew on rocks in the estuaries. A small proportion of them held little pearls. Very occasionally we would collect some of these, boil the poor things, then look for the pearls. We collected a few, but the yield was always below expectations so that we gave it up.

Sea bathing was superb, the water so clear whether bathing off beaches or more generally in deep water off rocks. One favourite bathing place was known as Harry's Hole. We never learnt who Harry was or if he had been anyone at all. The attraction of this particular place was that it was a long narrow gully with clear, green deep water whatever the tide. With its flat shelving rocks, most of them quite free of barnacles, it was ideal. With deep water, diving from any height was in no way a hazard. There was a cave at the landward end that could be explored at low tide; even when the tide was full one could swim into it and admire the multi-coloured stones, rounded and polished by the action of the sea over untold years. In summer we took to the sea sometimes thrice daily, and occasionally when older enjoyed moonlight bathes from the shore. Even now I remember the cool sensuous feeling of the closely mown grass edges of the avenue on which we would run barefooted on our way to the beach.

Below the house was a small pond with a little stream flowing into it, where my father sometimes hatched brown trout, for restocking Sessiagh lough. Into this pond every year our thirty-foot centre-board seaboat was put to expand its timbers following its winter's rest on land. I had been forbidden to play about in it, but being of an age when it is easy to forget instructions I clambered aboard, was spotted by the woman at the lodge who set her small son to watch me. He was not as alert a sentry as he should have been, for I got out of the boat unobserved and went off in search of other business, quite unaware of the commotion my disappearance was to cause. A whole troop headed by my mother was soon collected and dived about in the water in search of my small body. Having abandoned the search they all came trooping up dejectedly to the Big House to be greeted when just short of it by a small boy on his bicycle-horse, ringing its bell and singing loudly. My obvious astonishment at the sight of so many dripping figures proclaimed innocence of evil intent and somehow banished any idea of punishment, for in their relief they found it in their hearts to forgive and laugh at their own discomfiture and assumption of disaster.

I remember having a marked aversion to water (except salt water) between the ages of six and ten. Perhaps most small boys feel the same? Earlier, in the nursery firm hands would soap, wash and dry me in front of a blazing fire, whether I liked it or not. Thereafter, free from a nurse's attention, I went to great lengths to avoid a bath. I cannot now understand why, for after ten I was hardly ever out of one. However, at that early stage morning baths were definitely out of favour. My deception plans were well rehearsed. Water sprinkled generously on bath mats, rather less on surrounding carpet, towels left crumpled lying in a damp heap, bath water soapy, an odd wet foot print thrown in as convincing evidence of successful ablution. Indeed I am ashamed of all that subterfuge considering the toil of maids carrying upstairs great cans of hot water in which I was expected to splash about in front of a warm fire. If I refused to wash at least I enjoyed the fires, especially at night when, reviewing my day's misdeeds, I slid unrepentant into bed to watch the flickering light of the fire reflected on the ceiling. I found this warming and comforting, and it led me with not a care in the world swiftly to deep untroubled sleep. So the spoiling days slid happily away, and were gone for ever.

It must have been about this time that my father spent much time abroad. Urged by a Victorian sense of duty and by an entirely laudable wish to alleviate distress, my father would travel to distant lands to introduce to tyrannical governments some sense of compassion in their treatment of neighbours as also of their own people.

'Britannia ruled the waves' all right, and indeed a considerable land area of the world as well, bringing great benefit, justice and order to large segments of it; but alas not to all. Unfortunately there remained areas and peoples not greatly influenced by liberal thought, even less by Christian ethics – notably the Turks. For centuries it had been a national and profitable pastime for them to massacre Armenians and Greeks who were established in their territories or in neighbouring lands. Particularly vulnerable were those – in contrast to the Turks – unwise enough to work hard and grow rich, attracting thereby envy and attention to themselves as ripe for plunder. One of my father's humanitarian expeditions was to Constantinople in an effort to dissuade the Turks from butchering the Armenians or from encouraging the Kurds to do so on their behalf, in the most revoltingly wholesale, cruel way. At the Sublime Porte he met with every civility. These matters, he was assured, would be looked into, excesses discouraged or proscribed. But of course the massacres soon continued, the massive pillage and booty resulting from them being far too valuable a source of income to be abandoned for any abstract ideal.

Another jaunt with an Oxford friend, Noel Buxton, was to North Africa. This time it was designed to persuade the Moors to display a greater degree of humanity to each other and to their neighbours. Alas, as was only to be expected, the mission failed. North Africans continued to be exploited, extorted, imprisoned, executed, hands severed for trivial offences or for none, ears cut off, and eyes gouged out. Such engaging methods of ensuring and maintaining order or for discouraging incipient revolt had been practised for centuries. Liberal thought, likely to undermine the authority of those who held sway, was extremely unwelcome – so unwelcome that Noel Buxton was shot in the jaw for propagating it. He had to grow a beard to hide his wound and the scar later resulting from it. My father, to keep him in countenance or because his razors were blunt, grew one too.

The bearded traveller returned to Marble Hill with a number of trophies, amongst them an enormously long Moroccan gun, its stock heavily inlaid with ivory and mother o' pearl, and a leather powder horn generously encrusted with brass studs. Both were for a time hung in the hall. As for the beard, it barely survived an hour, my mother demanding its instant removal. It was always wise to obey her command.

My third sister was born after I had gone to school and was much the youngest of the family. As a small girl she was a tomboy, very athletic with a passion for horses and dogs. She rode a lot as a child, and as a young girl whenever she could, the speedier and more unruly her mount the better. Though very slim she was strong and had 'good hands', so that she never had a serious riding accident. She always groomed her own horses and enjoyed doing it. Of the four of us (times having suddenly changed with regard to the education of young women) she alone went to university and got a degree, of which, like many other girls, she took no obvious advantage. Like her elder sisters she had good looks and vivacity and all three were in due course to marry soldiers, whose careers took them to many parts of the world.

At about nine, having worn out a number of governesses – none actually driven to suicide – I went to school ten miles north of Dublin. It was run by two brothers, Scotts of Willesborough, who were distant cousins of my mother; their father had been British ambassador to St Petersburg in Tsarist days. The house itself, known as Baymount Castle, was large, cold and bogus, and had originally been built by a magnate of solid means and little taste. The grounds were spacious and provided excellent playing fields, they were sheltered by thick belts of trees. I was only beaten once. It had been a 'fair cop'. I was discovered doing a balancing act in the open window of my dormitory with a drop of fifty feet on to a paved path. The caning I thoroughly deserved, if only for showing off to my young companions. It did me nothing but good, was not resented and did not really hurt much. It drew my attention to the fact that the 'beaks' acting *in loco parentis* had a duty to return me to them if possible in one piece.

Steep grassy banks facing the sea led down to the main road to Howth and to the village of Clontarf which many centuries before had been the scene of the battle in which King Brian Boru with his wild and formidable Irishmen had scattered the invading Danes, slaughtered a goodly number, and driven the survivors into their boats and out to sea. The grasses on these banks grew high and harboured a fabulous number of different species of colourful butterflies and moths, never seen today.

I was reasonably attentive to my work, but glad when it was over, for the lure of the playing fields was soon irresistible. By and large I enjoyed my school days. I was confirmed with others in St Patrick's Cathedral in Dublin – where my father had installed a charming window in memory of my grandfather. In due course I passed the not very exacting examinations for entry to a public school in England.

My parents came to develop a craze for highbrow intellectuals, some of whom came to stay. There were writers like Belloc, also active politicians who had something to say about improving the world. They spoke with conviction and distinction but where in the end did it get us? We children hated the sight of them, though no doubt we should have profited greatly had we been older, interested enough or invited to listen to what they had to say, for they talked incessantly. Bingham, the butler, shared our disapproval, and went so far as to write to my uncle, then serving in India as an ADC to the Commander-in-Chief: 'You would not believe the sort of people who come here these days', and then went on to tell what sort of people! Delighted, my uncle sent the letter back to my mother with brotherly jests. G. K. Chesterton was an exception. A bit of a child himself and reassuringly untidy, we approved of him.

As a small boy I always enjoyed visits to my Stuart grandparents at their house not far from Londonderry. Being the eldest and for a time the only grandson, I suppose I may have been indulged to some extent.

My grandfather had a tidy mind and the rides and walks cut in his woods (unlike ours) were kept clear of undergrowth and overhanging branches by what he called his 'gang of workmen'. He was an enthusiastic naturalist and had a vast number of nesting boxes fixed to trees. He enjoyed watching badgers emerging from their setts in the evening with me on a seat at his side finding it hard not to fidget or chatter. He was the kindest of men, had been a good athlete and was still very agile and most competent in a boat. When he came to stay at Marble Hill it was a joy, for he was never happier than when sailing up and down the bay whilst we children and any others who were with us caught large numbers of mackerel on lines with weighted lead sinks and spinners, one side of the boat competing against the other.

When staying with him and big enough to handle it, I borrowed a 12 bore gun with hammers and barrels of Damascus steel. My early quarry was wood pigeon and rabbits, for there were a great many of both.

The main garden was extremely well kept and productive. I remember particularly the masses of succulent gooseberries of several varieties on which I gorged without restraint.

My grandparents, always loving and generous, fed me on all the rich food I craved, particularly chocolate in many forms. My departures were occasions for charades. These were the days of gold coinage, and suitable coins would be thrust into my not very resisting palm and if I put up a mock show of resistance, then into a pocket. Either way I won. I remember being struck by great sheets of postage stamps hung up in a small writing room off the main hall, free for all who had a use for them. I of course had none, but it struck me even then as a thoughtful gesture.

I remember too the holding of morning prayers, in the library. They were attended by everyone in the house; first we would gather there, then all the servants trooped in. This was a daily ritual. It was not done to dodge it. It was soon over and off we went, no doubt uplifted, to a large and very satisfying breakfast. My goodness, what breakfasts they were in those days, tables groaning under the weight of such variety of good things. No silly ideas about slimming.

We did not have the daily ritual of morning prayers at Marble Hill, probably because all the servants were Roman Catholic except Bingham. The little church that served our needs was about a mile away. It was in those days well attended. We had a splendid family pew at the back with tall wooden walls; the seating ran round three sides of our little fortress. Steps led up to its only door. No one, unless he were tall, could see out and certainly with the door shut no one could see in, not even from the pulpit. This being so, we children took advantage and depending on who was in charge of us would read, play or talk in hushed tones. We had to pull ourselves together when we heard footsteps of a man approaching the door bearing the collection plate into which we would put our modest offerings if we could find them. On occasions when we could not, financial assistance was sought from the escorting adult.

When I was about twelve, having had ample time and opportunity to have shot someone or myself and failed, I was presented for my birthday with a 12 bore gun. This was indeed promotion. My little .410 bore gun was laid aside and with this formidable weapon I ranged far and wide. It was not long before I had shot my first pheasant, my first grouse and mallard drake, all three heads and breasts were mounted on small wooden shields as tokens of my skill and prowess, and many another was to follow. Rather sad little relics they seem to me now, and had I the power to do so life would at once be restored to those beautiful creatures, that they might fly about the clear air as was their birthright. To a thoughtless boy of twelve, however, they were prized trophies of the chase.

As I grew older and stronger, I used to set myself 'tests' when I was out shooting. When I came to an obstacle like a wide field drain, which was frequently, I would throw my game bag and cartridge bag across and force myself to follow by leaping over it with my gun – ostensibly to save time and cover more ground. Sometimes it proved too wide for me, and I had to slither across to the far bank, getting very wet before clambering out.

A much more serious hazard had to be negotiated at the edges of ponds or small loughs, overgrown by water weeds and surrounded by an undulating green carpet, treacherous, for it could easily give way. But such places harboured snipe and it was hard to avoid taking risks. Once, when as usual I was shooting alone, I went clean through such a carpet, but luckily managed to pull myself out – very slowly, for struggling would have plunged me deeper, and for good.

As a family we were fond of music and our tastes were catholic. Though my mother played the piano adequately she was insufficiently practised to do justice to the classics. To say that we were fond of music was not to say that it took a first place in our lives. How could it? The world was a place of wonders and appreciation of music was only one of many. So too was the incredible bounty and beauty of nature all about us. From the sky with its unnumbered stars, its sun and moon, to the deep blue green of the seas. From the sublime to the ridiculous. From the jack snipe, the kingfisher and tiny wren to the tall giraffe. Was there any end to it? We did not think so. Returning to music, my father thought fit to buy a most efficient instrument called a pianola which, attached to a piano, allowed anyone other than a half-wit to play the most ambitious music with confidence. All that was required of the 'pianist' was a minimal attention to the music scroll as it unwound. I remember with delight my father's enthusiasm. Perched on a high stool he played frequently with tremendous feeling, swaying backwards and forwards and from side to side as might the great Paderewski himself, transported by the rhythm and beauty of sound.

Both my parents were dedicated readers, so that my father would sometimes remain closeted in his small library for hours on end. My mother read avidly when free from her multifarious household duties. My own reading as a boy was spasmodic and largely confined to authors such as G. A. Henty, Ballantyne, Rider Haggard, Scott and Stevenson. I enjoyed animal stories, though many were sad and when they ended disastrously and cruelly for the animals (as they had a way of doing, at human hands) the book was cast aside before its pages became sodden with tears. Later I came to enjoy poetry with heroic or romantic themes, and learnt many poems by heart. Henry V's Agincourt speech, 'The Burial of Sir John Moore', 'The Battle of the Baltic', 'Breathes there the man with soul so dead', 'The Charge of the Light Brigade', 'The Armada', 'Horatius' and so forth – good lively stuff. Later my taste widened.

Encouraged by friends, my mother took to painting in oils, mostly landscapes, occasionally still life. She had considerable natural talent. When in London she would visit schools of art. Her feeling for our countryside, for its rivers, lakes, boglands and mountains was truly deep and was reflected in her painting. There came a day when she decided that she must have a studio in which to work undisturbed. She soon realized this by building a very small cottage on a ridge above the main woods, yet sheltered by them. The building went up in a trice, as the stone for its foundations and walls lay just below the surface and could be quarried on the spot. Once some stunted trees had been cleared from the site she had from her long windows an uninterrupted view over the waters of Sheephaven Bay to the hills beyond. This was the first of a number of houses (five in all) of varying size to be built on the place to her design in the course of her reign at Marble Hill. The first little house became a favourite retreat not only for my mother but for us children and for certain favoured guests. George Russell (A.E.) a close friend, painter, mystic and poet, spent many peaceful hours within its walls, and painted tall angelic figures on each side of the big open hearth.

My mother admired the country folk who were our neighbours, and always did what she could to help them through difficulties, sickness, bereavements, and to alleviate distress when it lay in her power to do so. She was able for example to help a poor woman who had arrived at the lodge one night in a state of collapse, perished with cold and soaked by rain. This stray had made her way on foot from Galway or from Connemara – her parents having died in the potato famine years before. The lodge at once contacted my mother. The wanderer was brought up to the house, dried out, fed, put to bed and was looked after by the maids with great kindness; my mother, touched by her story, had a very little house built in haste that was to be hers for life. Being an unusual character with strange tales to tell, she became in time quite an institution and visitors in ever increasing numbers would journey to her door, bearing gifts of every kind, so that her tiny house was soon furnished with all that she required.

On my last visit to the old lady to take leave of her before going out to the war in France in 1915 I was in process of clambering over a stile when a pair of metal tongs came sailing through the air and struck me on the ankle. I looked back in astonishment, about to protest, when she explained to me that this strange custom was reserved for those about to embark on long journeys who might require good fortune, to bring them back safely.

Two other old women of quite different characters lived alone in our neighbourhood. One, Biddy Diver, was reputed to be a witch. She certainly looked like one to my childish eyes. She lived in a little heather-thatched cottage in the middle of a hazel wood above an estuary from which at low tide she could gather cockles and mussels. She fascinated me as a child and from time to time I visited her out of bravado, drawn by an irresistible impulse to test her powers of magic. Happily I never left her door in the guise of an otter, a hare or a magpie, but it was always thrilling to contemplate the possibilities and to flirt with the supernatural.

The third strange woman was said to swim about the rocks and with her toes dislodge lobsters from their crevices, and catch them. Perhaps she was half a seal? There were many about our shores following the mackerel shoals out of the deep Atlantic water. Who could say? Anything is possible in childhood, for imagination runs free, and that is part of the charm and delight of our earliest years.

The time was approaching when a decision had to be made to which English school I should go. Various people were consulted, an aunt who had had two sons at Eton pressed me to be sent there. My soldier uncle for whom I had a great respect had done well at Shrewsbury. Rather unfairly, it was left to me to choose. Having been brought up 'in the bog', far from those seats of learning, I really had no knowledge of either. Certain factors tipped my decision in favour of Shrewsbury, these were first my uncle's success there, second that I knew and liked a neighbouring boy who was already at that school, finally Dr Cyril Alington, an Oxford friend of my father's, had some years earlier moved from Eton to Shrewsbury as headmaster, and would welcome me if I joined him.

By and large I enjoyed my school years. In my first year of settling in I actually did some work, even secured three elegant prizes,

Homer's *Iliad*, *The Oxford Book of English Verse* and its companion *The Oxford Book of Ballads*, all richly and magnificently bound. Sad to relate after this promising but quite unnatural burst of academic exuberance, the lure of the playing fields took over, and my enthusiasm for learning waned. Blessed with a 'good eye', helpful in most games, always fit and strong for my age, and abounding in energy, I played all games with much enjoyment. I even managed to play cricket and row, a combination that needed some planning and was not always possible. We played a lot of Eton fives in winter and spring. I won my school colours for cross-country running and athletics early on, which brought certain privileges.

I liked my housemaster, an Oxford rowing blue, and my headmaster who would from time to time invite me to breakfast and less frequently to an evening meal. His kindly, cheerful red-headed wife was a Lyttelton and his young family then consisted of a son Giles and two daughters, one of whom years later married Lord Home, who first met her when Cyril Alington returned to Eton as its headmaster. He had two greedy dogs known as Eggs and Bacon. Dr Alington was an outstanding personality, he had a charming voice and his sermons in Chapel were brilliant and compelling. He had great sympathy for the young and was quite prepared to discuss any problem with remarkable patience.

For example, when about fifteen I sought a satisfying explanation of 'the human situation', for the glaring inequalities of treatment meted out to hapless individuals. How could it be that our Creator and God of love, as we were taught, would countenance terrible sufferings and privations, ghastly accidents and mutilations, blindness, deafness, deformity and so many other crippling ills that appeared to fall haphazard on the outwardly innocent? That line of thought led me to consider that the only justifiable explanation was that to achieve ultimate perfection a long process of trial and error was called for requiring many lives in which we were to overcome our passions, infirmities of mind and heart – eradicating bit by bit all that was evil. It was all very confusing and I sought clarification at the hands of my headmaster who listened patiently to my arguments but turned down the conception of re-incarnation. He was I think surprised that one of his less intelligent pupils had turned philosopher, a seeker after knowledge and profound knowledge at that. We had several discussions, but he stood firm against re-incarnation, yet advanced no argument to convince me that no such possibility existed.

Being far from my Irish home, my occasional days off were enlivened by visits of kind friends living within reach. Two I remember especially and with gratitude, an aunt, Violet Bryce, who welcomed me at her lovely house in Bryanston Square, whenever I could get to London, and Nellie Hozier, later Mrs Romilly, a sister of Lady Spencer-Churchill. Both kind and generous, they made these rare outings memorable.

Aunt Violet and others were extraordinarily kind to me throughout my boyhood for which I was, and still am, lastingly grateful. Though taught that it is 'more blessed to give than to receive', being at the receiving end had its charms. Was it not likely that something of the kindliness and generosity experienced would rub off on a recipient? I hoped so. One fine day I was happy to welcome a large wooden box which held four splendid trays of delicious chocolates. It even had a lock. It had come from Washington whither my aunt had gone to stay with her brother-in-law, at that time our ambassador to America. Life was then full of pleasant surprises. The rough days, unforeseen and unsuspected, lay ahead.

Of many friends in my house Bobby Shaw was one. He was the son of Mrs Astor (later Lady Astor and the first woman MP). With him I paid the first of a number of visits to Cliveden. I remember this occasion well, for it was a lovely summer's day and the gardens looked glorious. So did my hostess as she raced up the steps – two at a time – to greet us on the terrace above, she looked so young, slim, and elegant. Her welcome was warm and unaffected and I thought her quite enchanting. That afternoon there was a garden party with the regimental band of the Coldstream Guards in full dress playing on one of the terraces. This was my earliest introduction to that most splendid regiment with which, though at the time there was no inkling of it, I was to have the closest and happiest of contacts. A large house party of distinguished guests such as Arthur Balfour was there for the weekend, but being young we spent most of it shooting water rats on the banks of the Thames and only met our elders at dinner. Never finding it easy to be on time, I was impressed by Mrs Astor's tact in always coming downstairs after the last of her guests had assembled so that no one should be embarrassed by being late. She must have had a bell in her room to be rung when everyone was down, for she arrived looking radiant on the heels of the last arrival.

At Shrewsbury the only major clash I had with authority was over non-attendance at our corps' annual camp. It arose year after year, the commandant complaining to my housemaster and headmaster alike that I would not abandon a fortnight of my summer holiday for camp or for any form of soldiering. Very few boys at that time took service in the corps seriously, though we enjoyed field days during the term, learning very little from them. We fired off blank ammunition, occasionally making prisoners of those opposing us who were even more idle and unalert than we. I so loved my Irish home and all it had to offer that I saw no compelling reason to give up a single day, said so, stuck to my guns, and got away with it. My impression was that all but the commandant were amused, even impressed by my intransigence.

When about thirteen I paid my first visit to Switzerland and learnt to ski. Thereafter such visits became annual events. A natural good balance from 'bog trotting' helped in skiing as in skating. Like all beginners I had my share of trouble and suffered minor damage. On my earliest visit I took part in a friendly mixed ice hockey match that gave rise to some merriment. Intent on scoring a goal, my enthusiasm far in excess of my skill, I charged the goal mouth and unable to stop carried all before me. The goalkeeper, a very substantial woman, the goal itself and I disappeared from the rink ending up a tangled mass in the deep snow bordering it. Later my skating improved. I was able to win a formal race against a rather older Canadian boy, who had unwisely and openly claimed invincibility. It was a popular win, for most people enjoy the triumph of the under dog, and look sourly on the boastful.

About this time my parents were introduced to a distinguished Spanish artist, Mathilde de Cordoba, who had painted portraits for the Spanish royal family and other Spanish notables. She was invited to stay at Marble Hill and in due course arrived slightly embarrassed by her experiences in Londonderry through which she had had to pass. It was her first visit to Ireland and the date was the 12th July with Orangemen in bowler hats and yellow sashes marching through the streets. She had brought with her a fine green flag in her innocence and, stirred by the music of the bands, waved it furiously. This friendly demonstration was met with scowls, ill humour and threatening shouts that surprised her greatly. Soon her driver implored her to curb her enthusiasm lest both be lynched by a humourless, outraged Orange mob. She spent nearly a month with us during which time she painted a number of charming small portraits of my sisters and others. She was to pay us visits in later years so that we all came to know and like her greatly. Apart from small portraits in oil she produced a number of quite excellent copper-plate etchings of various members of the family including two of my Stuart grandparents, that of my grandfather being an extraordinary resemblance to Van Dyke's portraits of Charles I from whose house he claimed direct descent – the same forehead, nose, eyes and small pointed beard.

My mother was a great walker and would go off alone to cover miles and miles of country. She had tremendous poise, held herself splendidly and always moved with ease and grace. None could compete, and few tried, though there was one big walk in which a number took part, covering some thirty miles of tough going and the scaling of four substantial hills in the course of the day. We were driven to the foot of Errigal (2466 feet), part of the Derryveagh mountain range and its highest peak. Racing ahead I had got a little short of the top when I lay down exhausted to be told by my uncle, roughly I thought, to get on with it, and having got my second wind led for the rest of the day. The view from the top of Errigal was magnificent. Rank heather waist high in the valleys between hills made the going hard, but we got to the summits of Alton Beg, Alton More and Muckish mountain (2200 feet) with a final walk into the village of Creeslough where cars met us. It was a memorable feat, a day long remembered.

So our lives went on most happily amongst friends in lovely and comfortable surroundings. I was allowed as I grew older to spend what time I wished in London with the Bryces, and with them at Glengariff in County Cork, where they were turning a small island in Bantry Bay into a garden paradise. Pretty well anything can be grown there. The island was dominated by a Martello tower built with many others against the threat of Napoleonic invasion. This tower was to have been replaced by a great house of size and splendour, the plans of which I had been shown in London. As things turned out the house was never built owing to the outbreak of war. Slipways, garden walls, a gardener's cottage, and a number of small and charming buildings to the design of Harold Peto were completed, the materials, marble and other things, brought from Italy by sea. The island and its gardens were left in due course to the Irish nation. They are now visited by large numbers of people drawn by their exquisite beauty and by that of the countryside.

During my summer holidays in 1914, when I was seventeen, war was declared on Germany on the 4th August. All was peaceful in Donegal and troubles distant. My parents were paying visits to friends in the west, when a telegram arrived for my father; in his absence it was handed to me. It was from my uncle, now a senior staff officer in the War Office, to say that if I were willing to accept a regular commission he could arrange for me to go to the Royal Military College as a 'gentleman cadet'. This was indeed a surprise and a challenge. I had hoped to go up to Oxford, was looking forward to this and had actually very belatedly decided to turn over a new leaf and get down to serious work for my last year at school. In leaving, sacrifice had to be made of envied prizes now ready to fall into my lap. However, after some thought, I replied accepting the proposition. My parents on their return were much upset at the news, but soon got over the shock or appeared to do so.

So ended a childhood that had been very happy, uncomplicated, but never dull. The 'slings and arrows of outrageous fortune' had not yet caught up with me. A sterner, more testing life lay ahead, I realized this but it failed to weigh me down, for I hoped that, whatever trials I would have to face, I should meet them with resilience, confidence and such courage as I could muster.

Chapter Two

Sandhurst to the Trenches

In September 1914 I found my way to Sandhurst where I was posted to 'C' Company in the new buildings. My company commander was a major in the Rifle Brigade, his second-in-command a captain in a Scottish regiment. They were both admirable as was our senior staff sergeant Cahill of the Irish Guards – later to be RSM of my 1st Battalion in France. He was a splendid creature standing well over six feet with a magnificent voice which could be clearly heard in Camberley when he was drilling us.

We were worked very hard as was only to be expected, for casualties in France had been heavy and a steady flow of trained young officers was required to replace those lost in battle. Our days started early and there was little time for games, though when there was we played vigorously. It was a tough but healthy life and being strong and fit I certainly enjoyed it, though a few broke down under the strain.

Our training apart from drill was simple but strenuous and severely practical. The aim was to teach us speedily all that was thought necessary for a young platoon commander to know, that he might lead and inspire men in battle, and look to their welfare at all times. We took part in simple tactical exercises, map-reading, compass work by night, patrolling and shooting on the range. On the whole those of us who survived the first two months, and most of us did, learnt a lot, were reasonably competent and had gained an increased self-confidence.

Geoffrey Holmesdale was our company's under officer. In due course he joined the Coldstream and as it turned out he and I were both gazetted as captains on the regular establishment of our regiments on the 13th March 1918; we were said then to be the youngest captains in the Brigade. We were both lucky to have got through our training at Sandhurst in about four months and to have survived the rigours of four years of combat. I made several wonderful friends at Sandhurst though alas many perished.

About a month or so before we were likely to finish our training we were required to fill up forms indicating the regiments of our choice in order of preference. We were allowed three choices, but with no guarantee that we would necessarily be gazetted into any of them. My choice was the Irish Guards, followed by the Black Watch, a splendid regiment with so romantic a name. In the event my first choice came up, and in early January 1915 I was commissioned. With one other from Sandhurst, Stephen Christy, who became a dear and close friend, I travelled to the reserve battalion of the Irish Guards at Warley Barracks in Essex. Determined to do my utmost, I felt that matters of survival and success were largely beyond my control. They were in the hands of others seen and unseen, in whom I had unshaken confidence and trust. As to the unseen Power, I was and still am ready to support the view of the prophet Job who said 'Though he slay me, yet will I trust him'.

The Irish Guards was then the 'youngest' regiment in the Brigade (the Welsh Guards were raised in 1915). The regiment had been raised in April 1900 by an army order which stated 'Her Majesty the Queen, having deemed it desirable to commemorate the bravery shown by the Irish regiments in the recent operations in South Africa, has been graciously pleased to command that an Irish regiment of Foot Guards be formed. This regiment will be designated "The Irish Guards".' At that time we were a one-battalion regiment, with the reserve battalion acting as training unit; the 2nd Battalion was formed during 1915.

The old, condemned barracks at Warley, near Brentwood, were built round a square. The men's barrack rooms and administrative offices formed three sides, the officers' mess and living quarters the fourth. Stephen and I arrived there, nervous, but proud of our new uniforms and at first a little self-conscious when returning salutes directed at them.

Our reception was kindly if not overwhelming. There was none of that tiresome childish business of totally ignoring a newcomer, said to be a practice in some regiments.

We settled down happily and were given plenty to do. Though we had been trained for it, the command and responsibility for some fifty or more grown men was a challenge. The older and more experienced responded generously to our youthful enthusiasm, as good men always do. I was a conscientious young officer so I opened a ledger giving details of every man in my platoon in order to know about his family background and any problems.

The reserve battalion was then well over 1200 strong; with few exceptions the NCOs and men were reservists recalled for the duration of the war. Few were to survive it. Warley furnished drafts for our 1st Battalion in France, which had suffered grievous losses, especially among officers. Having had three lieut. colonels, two majors, and seven captains killed, we were obliged to ask other regiments of the Brigade to send us any retired officers they could spare. My first company commander was 'Bingo' Pakenham, seconded from the Coldstream, and RSM Kirk was also on loan from them. Our officers varied widely in age and experience. The older ones averaged about thirty-five. These we considered senile. Wisely they tucked themselves into a secluded haven away from the chaotic noise we revelled in. We were allotted a large room at the end of a passage in which to romp. Romp we certainly did, for we were a very young, fit, happy and riotous lot. Our ages varied from just under eighteen (as in my case) to twenty-four. An early commanding officer was Lord Kerry, later Marquis of Lansdowne, who was charming and had in consequence a happy battalion.

Food in our mess was expensive and superlative. Most of it came from Fortnum and Mason. Delicious paté and hams, gorgeous chocolate cakes and delicacies in abundance. We were always hungry and tucked in. Salmon and game in season arrived from relations, friends and well wishers. Such bounty was never to be seen again. If we lived well, why not? Our lives were most unlikely to be long. The average period of survival for a subaltern in the line was even then thought to be about three weeks before he became a casualty. Many were killed or wounded much sooner; others survived for months; very few, with charmed lives, for years.

Our training was largely confined to route marching, drill and weapon training. About once in ten days the whole battalion was paraded en masse and required to carry out a number of drill movements. Impressive they certainly were, with twelve hundred bayonets flashing. These splendid parades were held outside barracks, for the square could not possibly contain them. They never failed to provide comic relief, the one justification in my eyes for holding them. Back to the Macedonian phalanx on a grand scale is suicidal today. Some platoon commanders in the close-packed ranks could be relied on to give a wrong order when the whole mass was on the move. This would generally produce a gorgeous 'box-up', giving those in authority a chance to shout themselves hoarse, adding to the confusion. Our second-in-command, Gerry Madden, had been a cavalryman and seemed unable to adjust to infantry drill. He got tremendously excited and would dash about on his horse bellowing incomprehensible orders. Large, dark and fierce looking, he was in fact a kind man.

Stephen and I, having just had a thorough grounding in drill at Sandhurst, survived but most of our contemporaries had not had this advantage and some never got things right. It was all good fun but useless.

When free of duty most of us would go to London. The journey was a short one and the fares cheap. The battalion had an elegant Irish jaunting car with a well groomed horse between its shafts, and shining harness. It plied between barracks and Brentwood station. It met most London trains, and we made much use of it. The Guards Club was then situated near Marlborough House, close to St James's Palace and everyone rightly had to belong to it. The building was small but comfortable, and frequently used for luncheon. Life in London, despite the war, provided gracious living. People were very kind, showing us generous and even lavish hospitality.

Soon after joining all 'young officers' were required to pass a simple written examination covering subjects as diverse as the histories of the Household Brigade and of the regiment, correct modes of address, and how when in plain clothes to wear a Brigade tie! As all the world knows, this tie is of royal racing colours – dark blue and red. Any civilized being will realize – lest the world collapse about his ears – that the blue stripe should be uppermost. There were many famous dos and don'ts long since forgotten. To be seen carrying a parcel or getting into or out of a bus was shaming and definitely taboo. Junior officers, regardless of age, were referred to as 'young officers' – some were over thirty. You went to London, never to town, you saluted and took orders from anyone senior to yourself on parade and called him sir. Ten minutes later, off parade, you called him whatever came into your head. This was generally something rude unless he happened to be larger and stronger. Then insults were best cloaked in honeyed words, the sting concealed, taking its time to sink in – time to gather a defensive phalanx of friends and to place massive furniture to obstruct any onslaught. Stephen being large and strong was splendid on riotous occasions, while little Johnny Kipling (Rudyard Kipling's only son) was very small, a useful ally who fitted neatly under a table, shooting out a leg with admirable timing to leave attacking giants sprawling on the floor.

In April some of us were sent to a course at Chelsea Barracks. As I debouched afoot from Lower Sloane Street one morning, Johnny Kipling did so too, but at speed in his little yellow Singer car and charged into a battalion of Scots Guards, taking them in flank. They scattered like starlings before continuing on their way, affronted no doubt, but happily undamaged. Next day came a justified complaint from Birdcage Walk calling for disciplinary action. We were all interviewed and confined to barracks until one of our number should own up. A day or two passed with no relief. We looked sourly at one another and searched for Johnny who happened to have been laid up at home. When told of our plight he at once informed authority that he alone was responsible.

About this time Harold Alexander, or Alex as he was known to everyone, and Eric Greer, both of whom had been slightly wounded in the opening phase of the war, returned to duty with the reserve battalion. They were great friends and outstanding athletes, being mile and quarter-mile champions of Ireland respectively. They went for training runs through Thornton Park nearby. Hearing that I used to run cross-country they asked me to go with them. I was flattered and often plodded along, an ugly duckling behind two elegant swans. Alex had a true athlete's frame, slight and well built. He was rather fair in those days, and his moustache wasn't yet the splendid affair so well known in later years from a multitude of photographs. This was my earliest meeting with Alex (then a subaltern) who was to have a profound influence on me and for whom my admiration grew with the years.

In May I was posted to the 1st Battalion in France. I set out with Vyvian Harmsworth and Dickie Tisdall, unencumbered by a draft. Friends and relations came to see us off at Victoria Station bearing gifts; gas masks, safety razors and charcoal-burning hand warmers. My mother, fearful that I might have to lie out wounded suffering desperate pain, brought a phial of morphia with instructions how to use it. All these presents were given away or lost. The gas masks were to be removed unceremoniously by our experienced quartermaster who furnished the latest official issue; a horrible contraption, but necessary since the Germans had first used gas in April at Ypres. The day was lovely, the crossing to Boulogne calm. The train to the front did not start before nightfall, so we bathed and baked on the beach; it was then necessary to wear a bathing dress and the only ones we could get were striped horizontals, black and yellow from neck to knee. The night journey passed in sleep and at rail-head we were met by horses and grooms. I remember the ride towards the distant sound of guns, a sound that so many had wished to hear in days not long before when the cry was 'it will be all over by Christmas'. We young really had a crusading spirit. Unsophisticated we accepted the sentiment prominently displayed in the chapel at Sandhurst, 'Dulce et decorum est pro patria mori'. Mercifully we gave it no serious thought, as few who had shared my time at Sandhurst were to be spared.

The 1st Battalion had gone to France in August 1914 as part of the original BEF, and with it had taken part in the retreat from Mons, the battle of the Marne which flung back the German advance on Paris, and the 'race to the sea' when each side tried to overlap the other. The battalion had distinguished itself in the desperate fighting to hold Ypres and prevent the Germans reaching the Channel ports, and had spent that winter, and the spring of 1915, in and out of the trenches in the Neuve Chapelle – Festubert area, roughly the centre of the British line from Ypres in the north to the Somme in the south.

The battalion, part of the 4th Guards Brigade, was out of the line in rest billets when we reported for duty. The commanding officer, Jack Trefusis, was a kindly man and, as I was to learn later, a good soldier. I was ordered to join No. 1 Company, and in turn was introduced to my new platoon. My company commander was Monty Gore-Langton, a tough character, dark and powerful, and utterly fearless; he had left the regiment and gone to Canada, returning on the outbreak of war. The company was at full strength – four platoons of some sixty men apiece, four platoon commanders, a second-in-command as well as the company commander – for throughout the war the great gaps caused by casualties were regularly filled by fresh drafts from Warley.

There was little time to get to know the men of my platoon, for forty-eight hours later we returned to the trenches, where one very quickly got to know people through and through. I hope I was still a conscientious young officer, but I made no attempt to start another log book with every man's particulars: in or out of the line there was simply no time for it, apart from the impossibility of carrying such a thing around.

The section of the line then held by us was known as the 'Brickstacks' in the area of Cuinchy, near Givenchy. This area had long been the scene of desperate fighting, and beyond our parapet the ground was littered with unburied dead. Some bodies had been built into our front line trench. One German was embedded with his feet sticking out, boots and all. The men saluted him from time to time and wished him good day. He was still in position when we were moved to another sector. This sounds revoltingly callous, but at that time there was no alternative. Parapets had to be built or repaired at speed and always in darkness so that the living might live a little longer. The dead had ceased to care.

It was in this sector that Michael O'Leary had won his Victoria Cross some months earlier. The Germans had held a series of sandbagged positions astride a narrow valley between the tall brick-stacks and the embankment of a railway that followed the line of the La Bassée Canal. Fierce and costly attacks had been made up this narrow valley to dislodge them. In the last of these, O'Leary clambered up the embankment and shot down the opposition at each barricade from a flank. Effective of course, all enemy eyes being directed down the valley to their front. Most spectacular too, as he was silhouetted up there on his own. I had him as a second sergeant in my platoon for a time until he was posted home to be used for recruiting purposes accompanied by ballyhoo. Artists drawing for the *Sphere* and *Illustrated London News* made him the hero of the hour.

Monty Gore-Langton sent me on a night patrol within twenty-four hours of my joining him. In charge of a sergeant and six men, I had to examine a large mine crater in No Man's Land, see whether it was occupied by the enemy and if so to bomb him out of it. It was a pretty disgusting mission because of the numerous long-dead bodies over which we had to make our silent way in pitch darkness. Returning I found one man missing, so set off again to bring him in. My sergeant was furious and when we found the man who may have gone to sleep he struck him a vicious blow on the bottom with an entrenching tool handle.

It took a little time to grow accustomed to the trenches, although by 1917 we were more used to life in the trenches than life above ground. They varied from sector to sector, depending on the lie of the ground, the nature of the soil, how close they were to the enemy line and hence how thoroughly they had been dug and repaired. The Germans were usually on a line of their own choosing, invariably higher ground than our positions, which perhaps accounts for the superiority of their trenches. On low ground, and in wet weather, the trenches of course became a gigantic system of ditches and land drains.

Normally there were three sets of trenches, front line, support and reserve, linked to one another and to the rear areas by a network of communication trenches. Front line trenches were never dug in a straight line; to minimize casualties from shelling and to avoid an entire trench being at the mercy of an enfilading machine gun, they were zig-zagged with traverses, which made communication difficult. Ideally, the trench was dug well below head height, perhaps seven or eight feet deep, with a ledge as the firestep from which one could observe and fire over the parapet. It was a frightful problem to revet these trenches to stop them falling in; constant enemy shelling made it worse by blowing in the sides, smashing the parapets and blocking all passage. They were wide enough to let two men pass, just; stretcher bearers had the utmost difficulty in getting casualties away, particular round the right angles of the traverses. In those early days, dugouts and latrines were simply scraped out of the side of the trench, with a completely un-shellproof roof of a sheet of corrugated iron covered with sandbags. Here and there short saps led forward from the front line trench to listening posts.

Repair and improvement of trenches was a never-ending job in the line. Much of the work of course we could only carry out at night up on the parapet, hoping that the enemy wouldn't choose that particular moment to open up. I can still see in my mind's eye the figure of one of my best sergeants, Hugh Carton, a magnificently built man, outlined against the night sky as we filled and laid sandbags, to patch up the shell-shattered parapet. Carton was a superb NCO, vibrant with life and energy – like so many more he was killed a year later on the Somme. Filling sandbags was one of the many tasks that we all, young officers, NCOs and men, did together. Anything we could scrape up in the dark went into those sandbags, which often in the Cuinchy sector included pieces of dead bodies. A unit was always judged by the standards of repair and of hygiene in which it left its trenches. Needless to say, all units grumbled at what they considered the poor state of trenches or billets which they took over from somebody else.

Trenches were all named – Piccadilly, Regent Street, Charing Cross and so on – because apart from the front line trench they all looked alike and clear identification was essential. Without it the entire trench system would have been a bewildering maze; even so, occasionally guides would lose their way coming up the communication trenches. As a result, there would be congestion and serious delay to reliefs, supply parties and the evacuation of casualties. Since all these activities were carried out in the dark, within the narrow confines of a trench, any halt to the free flow of movement led to chaos.

We suffered casualties daily and accepted them with regret and resignation. Sudden death being no stranger, we soon learnt to live with it, and whilst it saddened us it held no terror. Mutilation was another matter, it was sickening. It did scare us when we had time to give it a thought. I was very young and naive in 1915, and though I hope I did not lack imagination or sympathy for those whose lot I shared, I fear that I took everything as a matter of course. This, I thought, was how grown-ups behaved; I certainly accepted a way of life that I recognized as disagreeable, dirty, very uncomfortable, sometimes dull and often dangerous. I felt for the dead and was much concerned for the wounded: otherwise I got on with the job. There was always something to be done, night or day. No time for deep or philosophic thought.

Accepting casualties did not mean inviting them, and I did all I could in my platoon, and later my company, to keep them to a minimum by sound training, alertness and example. The wounded who could not walk were carried by our company stretcher bearers back to the regimental aid post for treatment. The dead were often put on stretchers, covered by a ground-sheet, and left at the junction of a communication trench with the front line, to be collected for record and burial.

Strangely, I have never forgotten a young Grenadier, perhaps eighteen, large, pale and very fair, lying on a stretcher, not covered with a ground-sheet, awaiting collection. I had paused for a moment before going on my way, and thought about the waste, sadness and loneliness of this last journey, for there was no one else to keep him company. He was not one of mine, and this sad experience was nothing new to me, but I must have been in a reflective mood, for this picture has been with me for over half a century.

Trench routine had become standardized. The day began with 'stand to' one hour before dawn when every one manned the line ready to repel an attack, for this misty half-light was the favourite time for both sides to take offensive action. Troops stood down at full light, except for sentries or men guarding vital points, and cooked their rations as best they could on our few charcoal braziers. Tea, bully beef, bread and 'marg', plum and apple jam, and large biscuits of astonishing toughness formed our staple menu in the trenches; officers could occasionally supplement this (on their mess accounts) with sardines and pineapple chunks, which we grew to loathe. We tried to let the men rest in the daytime as far as possible (though sleeping wasn't easy), for so much had to be done at night; but a vital daytime task was the care, cleaning and inspection of all weapons, especially important in the case of the Lewis gun, liable to stoppages if the magazine drums were damaged or dirty.

In addition to the endless work of maintaining, draining and revetting trenches, wiring parties were out every night. Forward companies were responsible for repairing and strengthening the defensive wire on their front, including that protecting listening posts and saps. Careful planning was necessary, for all wiring of course had to be done in the dark, in silence and as fast as possible, since wiring parties were extremely vulnerable where our and the enemy lines were only 150 to 300 yards apart. If the enemy heard or suspected something, he would send up flares and blast our line with machine gun fire or shelling. Unlike the Germans, we didn't, to my knowledge, go in for 'tactical wiring'. They were very skilful in laying out tactical wire designed to shepherd attacking troops into apparent gaps covered by machine guns; in the confusion of the attack men made for such gaps, and were slaughtered.

We tried to liven up our existence in the trenches, sometimes in odd ways. A friend and fellow platoon commander rudely known as the Turd, of a melancholy and solemn disposition, had a disconcerting way with revolvers, and frequently let fly with his own. I have a sketch of him holding a revolver in each hand and firing both into the trench at his feet. Most trenches were infested with rats, we accounted for a great many and became useful revolver shots with constant practice.

One day I had an idea of pulling his leg when he had settled down to his morning duty. There were lots of German rifles lying about between the lines and any quantity of ammunition. Equipped with both, I stood some thirty yards off. The Turd was given adequate time to get his trousers down and to settle comfortably. Aiming at the sandbagged cover to his lair, I opened rapid fire, bringing down showers of earth and small stones. He came out shaken, very dishevelled, his hair full of sand. Hiding my rifle I would ask him what on earth he was up to, drawing enemy fire every time he went to the loo. This charade was kept up for a week. The men played up delightedly, doing their best to look grave and normal. Such childish pranks did something to relieve the grim monotony.

About this time the new Mills bomb was issued. It was described as absolutely safe. It was nothing of the sort as numerous tragic accidents were to prove. We all became enthusiastic about offensive bombing. Our large Irishmen were particularly good at this form of play. They really loved it. They were better and more aggressive than the Germans and could throw bombs further than the opposition with a greater accuracy. Both sides took to this grim sport in a big way but we always seemed to have the upper hand. Nonetheless, I remember seeing Monty Gore-Langton knocked down thrice one morning by exploding bombs when by unlucky chance he had almost fallen into the arms of a German bombing party.

As I have said, nearly all our NCOs and guardsmen were reservists at this time, old soldiers recalled to the colours when war broke out. They came from every county in Ireland; a few, of Irish parentage, had been recruited in English cities where their parents had established themselves. To command such men, an Irish background was enormously helpful, though it was not essential; in 1915 I suppose that a third or more of our officers had homes in Ireland and lived there, and most of the others had close Irish connections. But there were some like my close friend Stephen Christy, or 'Kowski', Lieut. Rodakowski of Polish extraction, with no very tangible Irish links; this was also the case with Johnny Kipling, who had joined the regiment despite his shockingly bad eyesight because of his father's friendship with F. M. Lord Roberts, colonel of the Irish Guards.

Those of us who had been brought up in the Irish countryside did have a natural advantage, an understanding and sympathy and fondness for the people who lived about us, known to us from childhood. It would indeed have been strange had this not been so. In times of stress this business of 'belonging' was particularly valuable. Alex is a good example, for in his case this was borne out again and again. He had like me, in a neighbouring county, ranged far and wide with his rod or gun from early boyhood, coming to know the country people at their own firesides. Admiration and affection was mutual. Alex of course was exceptional in many ways, but not entirely so in this respect. He was never shy, and all he did he did exceedingly well. He could, even as a commanding officer, get up onto a table and dance an Irish jig without appearing in any way ridiculous, because the performance was both faultless and spontaneous.

In general, the system of 'territorial' recruitment, drawing men from a regimental area, has everything to commend it, particularly perhaps in the case of Irish and Scottish regiments where some vestige of a clan spirit still survives and where, I dare suggest, men are possibly more responsive to an appeal to the heart than to the head. Strong personal, sympathetic leadership is desirable everywhere, but it is essential in the handling of Scottish and Irish soldiers, who must be led, not driven. Alex was a past master in the art of leadership – unbounded courage, an engaging personality and a natural self-confidence were allied to a first-rate military mind.

At a humbler level, one's talents for leadership as a young officer were exposed, or developed, by frequent patrolling in No Man's Land. The forward companies sent patrols out every night, consisting usually of an officer and eight other ranks, to listen for and report on enemy activities, wiring parties etc. They usually stayed out for a couple of hours. Absolute silence was essential so no one with a cold or a cough was ever taken. They were only to fight if cornered by an enemy patrol.

My country upbringing proved invaluable. One knew instinctively how to move and when. How to walk or if necessary crawl silently. What ground favoured concealed or silent movement. How to stand or lie stock still if caught in the glare of lights, constantly sent up by the enemy or by our own side. Occasionally one was bound to be caught thus, and then any movement was fatal. Like the innocent birds and beasts I had so constantly pursued and harried through Irish bogs and heather, it was now my turn to be harried and everything was to be gained by following their pattern of behaviour. The townsman was at a great disadvantage and many an officer was lost, and members of his patrol with him, through lack of imagination. There were strict commonsense rules that all interested in survival could follow. Obvious ones were: never leave or rejoin our lines at the same place or time. Never follow the same route. Always ensure that our own troops knew exactly when and where re-entry to our lines was to be made. Failure to follow these sensible instructions could result in a friendly patrol being shot at close quarters by its own side with the Germans joining in.

A frequent task at night was, like my first patrol, to bomb the enemy out of occupied craters which we then took over, sometimes incorporating them in our own trench system or turning them into listening posts. There were also occasional minor raids or fighting patrols, an officer and perhaps a dozen other ranks, to act as a 'snatch squad' in modern parlance and seize one or two prisoners, for the identification of enemy units. The objective was strictly limited – surprise and speed in execution were essential to success. This meant getting into the enemy trench, which in turn meant cutting a way through the defensive wire without being heard or spotted. It was a nerve-wracking job to lie on one's belly working away with wire cutters in the dark, a few yards from the enemy line: fortunately the Germans seldom pulled their wire taut, so when one finally severed a strand of barbed wire, there wasn't a telltale 'ping'. The subsequent rush into the trench to grab a prisoner was child's play in comparison. The patrol then had to get back through the narrow gap that had been cut – not easy in the excitement – and back across No Man's Land as fast as possible before the inevitable and swift enemy reaction of heavy shelling of our front line and of machine gun fire sweeping over wire and parapets.

Infrequently there was a major trench raid, an aggressive punch designed to inflict maximum loss and damage in a very short time. A raiding party usually consisted of two officers and up to twenty-five other ranks, carefully selected and specially equipped; the target was often a specific enemy position or pillbox which was a particular threat to our line or responsible for an unacceptable drain of casualties. Here again getting through the enemy wire was the problem. A later 'solution' was an infernal device called a Bangalore torpedo, which you were supposed to push under the wire and then detonate. I once had to use one. It was heavy, and awkward to lug across the crater-pitted surface between the lines, and perfectly useless at cutting wire when it blew up. I don't think the battalion ever bothered with them again.

Chapter Three

1915: Loos

During the summer of 1915 we had seen a good deal of the Prince of Wales, for he paid frequent visits to see Lord Desmond Fitzgerald, our adjutant, who it was said had been asked by the King to befriend him. We all liked HRH enormously, he had a charming personality, always friendly and unassuming. Had Desmond survived the war I feel that history could have been very different. We might have been spared the sadness of the abdication.

In August our commanding officer Jack Trefusis left us, to be killed some months later as commander of a brigade. He was succeeded by Gerry Madden who was soon to be mortally wounded when a shell scored a direct hit on Battalion Headquarters. Our brigade commander Lord Cavan left us about this time to take command of the Guards Division that had just been brought into being; he had been and always remained a most popular and successful commander. Our old 4th Guards Brigade now became the 1st Guards Brigade, while other Guards units and those newly raised at home (of which our 2nd Battalion was one) formed the 2nd and 3rd Guards Brigades of the new division. Towards the end of August we were relieved and moved into rest billets around Béthune. Preparations were already in hand for offensive action on what was intended to be an overwhelming scale. The object was for the British to break the enemy lines near Loos whilst the French attacked in the Champagne country. The master plan aimed at a breakthrough leading to a 'battle of manoeuvre' in the plain of the Scheldt.

The battalion left the Béthune area and marched to Thiembronne. Halted for a night on our way, we met and dined with our newly formed 2nd Battalion which had arrived in France two days earlier. Our men had already christened our sister battalion 'the Irish Landsturm'. That splendid pair Alex and Eric Greer came with it as company commanders. It was a convivial and memorable evening.

Training for the coming offensive began in earnest and we knew what lay ahead. Many were given two days home leave, Stephen and I among them. My uncle, Colonel Alexander Stuart who was then on the staff at GHQ, sent a car to take us to Boulogne to join the leave boat. We got to Victoria very late at night owing to various delays and a rough sea. We made our way on foot to the Carlton Hotel at the junction of the Haymarket and Pall Mall, now vanished like so many good things. Never forgotten has been that first brief leave from France. The joy of a boiling bath, good food and above all the heavenly feel of cool linen sheets after months in trenches with hard ground for a bed and my haversack for a pillow.

Our forty-eight hours were crowded but soon flown, and we were on our way back to France. Reaching railhead we had great difficulty finding out where the battalion was, since it was already on the move towards the battlefront. In the end we caught up, for owing to mass movements of troops progress was slow. That march to the front was not only long but very exhausting for troops because of the frequent checks, halts and starts, due to gross congestion. Being less heavily laden than our men, many of us tried to help those in distress by carrying their packs or rifles. At last we reached our destination, Vermelles, in the early hours, and the weary men could be fed and sink to rest. We were to stay there for days being shelled before going forward to occupy ground and trenches taken from the enemy by our assault troops. On the 21st September we were inspected by Lord Kitchener. Lord Cavan, now commanding our division, attended and wished us God speed on the eve of 'the greatest battle in the world's history'. This did nothing to cheer us up. Clearly we were expected to win. We would of course do our best at whatever the cost. Such was the quite unjustified optimism in high places at that time. It was no substitute for sound intelligence and this turned out to be very scanty. Preparatory 'softening up' of enemy positions by bombardment had been totally inadequate, his strongholds virtually undamaged. Enemy wire uncut. As usual, the British infantryman paid for this with his life. It was all he had to give. He gave it willingly, but in material terms it was not enough.

Three days earlier all commanding officers of the Guards Division had been ordered to carry out a reconnaissance of the country between Cuinchy and Loos. What they saw, as Rudyard Kipling wrote in *The Irish Guards in the Great War*, was 'a jagged, scarred and mutilated sweep of mining villages, factories, quarries, slag dumps, pit heads, chalk pits and railway embankments'. What they could not see or imagine was that all were 'connected above ground and below by every means that ingenuity and labour could devise to the uses of war. The ground was trenched and tunnelled with cemented works of terrifying permanency that linked together fortified redoubts, observation posts, concealed batteries, rallying points and impregnable shelters for waiting reserves. . . . Triple lines of barbed wire protected a system of triple trenches, concrete-faced, holding dugouts twenty feet deep, with lifts for machine guns which could appear and disappear. . . . Observation posts were capped with steel cupolas'.

Our brigade, veterans of previous battles, was not required to take part in the initial assault. The 2nd and 3rd Guards Brigades, newly formed, were 'blooded' and pressed into the attack. Our brigade followed in support, ordered to occupy and hold all ground taken from the Germans. We were shelled, mostly shrapnel bursting overhead, all the way to the front line but luckily had few casualties though Drill Sergeant Cory marching close to me was one.

This was the first major battle in which the troops of the Territorial Army took part on a great scale. They were all volunteers, had been trained in haste and despatched to France. They had no experience of war, but this splendid material was squandered, it seemed to me then; I feel it after sixty years – the pain of it.

The sight that met my eyes as we reached the scene of the initial assault of the previous day was horrifying. Long lines of kilted dead, mown down by enemy machine guns firing in enfilade (from a flank) where one bullet could do the work of two. A sad and sickening sight; this had been my first view of mass casualties and it made a deep impression. The utter waste of those silent dead, who had they lived would have made natural leaders as officers or NCOs so sorely needed in the three years of war that still lay ahead, stirred the heart.

We and our fellow battalions of Grenadiers and Coldstream occupied the ground and trench systems newly captured. It was to be our home for ten days or more without relief. We had to work like beavers, for trenches had to be redug to face the right way, digging and wiring madly to make the battered earth and collapsed trenches into defensive positions capable of holding and breaking enemy counter-attacks.

Indeed we had no time to think of anything else. Not even to worry about our own casualties. They were exceptionally heavy because the Germans knew our range exactly since our new positions had been theirs. We were subjected to an almost continuous bombardment by enemy guns of varying calibres, and from mortars. My own platoon lost over half its strength in those ten days, thirty-five men out of sixty. One of the most disagreeable weapons used against us, though not the most lethal, was a heavy mortar that fired a large projectile high into the sky. As it started to fall it would turn over and over in the air. It looked very large, black and menacing. On impact it went off with a tremendous bang. The men called them 'flying pigs'. They were certainly most destructive of trenches and constantly blew wide gaps in ours. Anyone around got buried. I was twice buried by 'flying pigs' landing on or just outside our parapet but was dug out undamaged though slightly dazed, deafened and covered in earth. Very occasionally one would land in a trench and anyone unlucky enough to be close by would be killed by blast if not by fragmented metal. However we managed successfully to beat off minor counter-attacks and bombing raids, but no one got much sleep.

The other two Guards brigades who had taken part in the initial attack suffered sad losses. The fighting, especially around the Hohenzollern Redoubt, had been grim and casualties heavy. Amongst our officers killed was little Johnny Kipling, last seen with his men rushing a German machine gun post established at the entrance to a tunnel in a tall slag heap. His body was never recovered, nor were any of his men ever seen again. On the 10th October as dawn was breaking and our hour of 'standing to' about to end we suffered a grievous loss. Monty Gore-Langton, our company commander, was shot through the head and died without regaining consciousness, with many of us standing by him helpless and in sorrow, for he was clearly beyond human aid. It was a silly, unnecessary death. He and our bombing officer Barny O'Brien had unwisely taken it in turns to examine enemy lines, looking over our parapet again and again as dawn was breaking. This practice was firmly discouraged by Monty himself, for it was an open invitation to enemy snipers who had lain out all night hoping for just such a shot at dawn. Well, one got a sitting shot and in taking it deprived us of a gallant commander, later described by Lord Cavan as 'the bravest man in the Guards Division'. No praise could possibly be greater. Monty's death was a particular blow to me because he had trained and tested me under battle conditions and out of that had come a mutual liking and respect. Our padre, Father Gwynne, was fatally wounded next day, as was Gerry Madden, our CO who lingered for a fortnight. Desmond Fitzgerald took over command though slightly wounded. Of Father Gwynne Kipling wrote 'He feared nothing, despised no one, betrayed no confidence nor used it to his own advantage; upheld authority, softened asperities, and cheered and comforted every man within his reach'. It was ironic that he should have been at Battalion HQ when it received a direct hit, since he spent most of his time – like Father Knapp of the 2nd Battalion – in the front line with the forward troops. No praise is too high for the devoted work of the regiment's padres.

We were saddened by these losses in two succeeding days, but life had to go on. We continued to suffer bombardment. It caused further losses and great damage to our trenches. Damage that had to be instantly repaired. It was, to me at any rate, a welcome diversion when the enemy after some heavy shelling made a bombing attack on the 2nd Grenadiers and we were able to give active help to these comrades. When it started I had been busy taking pot shots with my revolver at some partridges which were running about in bewildered fashion outside our wire. They were difficult moving targets and being fond of partridges I was glad to miss them. Life went on for most of us until at last on the night of the 14th October we were relieved and moved back to what was left of Vermelles. Our losses in the 2nd Battalion in one short day had been eight officers and over 300 other ranks. Total British losses in this battle for Loos were estimated to be 50,000 men and 2000 officers. The gain a vulnerable salient 7000 yards long and 3000 yards in depth, some of which could not be occupied. No bargain would you say? There had been no break-through, nor in all the circumstances had there been the least chance of one, the defences being wellnigh impregnable. Courage and sacrifice were not enough.

The British army was starved of ammunition for its guns (too few and too light, anyhow) in 1914 and 1915, and in the early part of 1916, though by the Somme battles in the middle of that year the position had much improved. By 1917 our barrages were heartening, even spectacular. However the ghastly loss of fine men in those earlier years due to the shortage of shells was not only deplorable but criminal. Enemy wire was never properly cut for attacking troops, nor were his trench systems seriously damaged or machine gun nests destroyed – partly because the too few shells we did fire were predominantly shrapnel, not high explosive. It is hard to forgive and impossible to forget the price paid in British lives for such shameless neglect and lack of foresight.

My great friend Stephen Christy who had got hung up at the Base joined us at the end of the month with a draft of fifty men. It was good to have him with us. Desmond had to leave to have his wound attended to in hospital and Alex was sent from the 2nd Battalion to take over temporarily as our commander. It was not long before we were back in the line and too close for health to the infamous Hohenzollern Redoubt, bristling with enemy machine gun nests, mortars and snipers posts.

On joining the battalion I had had the good fortune to be given as my personal orderly Jim Cleary. He was about thirty and cared for me as a hen for her new-born chick. He shadowed me and made life as comfortable and easy as circumstances allowed. He was brave to the point of recklessness. I was told that early in 1914 when he was approaching his time for discharge he deliberately went absent. He was posted as a deserter which was his intention. Then he loitered in Birdcage Walk and haunted the guard room at Wellington Barracks until the sergeant of the guard locked him up. Just what he wanted; he was brought before authority and forfeited his former service. What could be better? He could start all over again. He loved the comradeship and was devoted to his regiment. We were to have many adventures in the next two years, one of them during this spell in the line.

Accompanied by Jim Cleary, I went on an unofficial prowl in No Man's Land. Just before dawn we dropped into what appeared to be an unoccupied trench and set about checking up. Suddenly we came upon two figures unnaturally still. We approached silently in the dim misty pre-dawn light. Reaching them we found both dead, one a very large German, the other a smaller Englishman. Each had bayonetted the other with tremendous thrusts, they were transfixed, pinned to the narrow trench walls by each other's bayonets. The Tommy had not only thrust his bayonet home but had fired his rifle as he did so with horrible effect. We left the ghostly trench sick at heart. Probably they are still there facing one another, reconciled at last, the trench crumbled and collapsed over and about them, grasses and scarlet poppies waving above.

On the last day of October Michael McCalmont arrived to take over from Alex; he had been in command of an Ulster battalion. In November we moved to the Laventie sector, a damp and swampy bit that lived up to its evil reputation. We were less molested by the enemy than hitherto so were spared heavy casualties, but the discomfort of waterlogged trenches and wet clothing far outweighed trial by bombardment, or so we thought. The wet added greatly to our work. We laboured ceaselessly round the clock. Drainage was a ghastly problem. Already waterlogged, the ground was incapable of absorbing more water. Trench pumps tried to discharge it into the morass outside without success.

If the trench walls were not very well revetted, they would collapse into the mud beneath our feet. To permit any movement at all, the bottom of every trench had to be floored with duckboards. They were wet and greasy, and to slide off meant plunging into water and mud to the thighs – the muck under the duckboards was never less than three feet deep. The reduction in the depth of the trench entailed the building up of the parapet with sandbags – filled of course with mud. We were never dry below the waist, and seldom above: at this time gumboots were only issued by the RE for special tasks such as wiring, so we floundered round in our boots and puttees. A ground-sheet over the shoulders kept off some of the rain and leather jerkins helped to keep us warm, but nothing kept out the mud in which we were plastered from our soft caps (steel helmets were not issued until 1916) to our sodden boots. Later, gumboots became available for men in flooded trenches, and most of the officers took to wearing long 'Norwegian' boots from Cording's; they laced up the front and were splendidly watertight.

There was no way of drying oneself or one's clothes in the trenches, sometimes not even at the billets in 'rest', so men had to plod back to the line in the same wet uniform and boots in which they had left it. But our quartermaster usually managed to rig up some contraption for drying things when we came back. We were lucky in having in Lieut. Hickie a quite outstanding and experienced quartermaster, courageous, efficient and above all resourceful. He had been a Gordon Highlander and had served in India with that fine regiment, and was very experienced. He survived the war; the others of us who did must be for ever in his debt.

We would be met on our arrival at the billets by orderlies with steaming dixies of tea, followed up by hot food such as a good stew which his team of cooks had ready, whatever the conditions. The men's rations were supplemented by fresh meat, fruit and vegetables bought locally – indeed out of the line we fed very well, quite apart from the occasional hamper or food parcel that arrived from home, and was always shared round. In the line, if it was humanly possible to get supplies forward to the trenches, the QM never failed us despite the constant heavy shelling of approach routes and the consequent casualties to the carrying parties and to the horse-drawn transport.

Our forty-eight hours out of the line was never quite what it sounded. The business of being relieved took time, even if the relieving unit was punctual, which it sometimes was not, thanks to straying guides or particularly heavy shelling on the way up. It was often a long, or at least a slow, march back to the billets allotted to us. After hot food the first requirement was sleep. The men in the trenches could get some snatches of sleep from time to time, but if the officer was doing his job he was lucky to get an hour or two's sleep in the forty-eight hours he was in the line. I often fell asleep on the march back to billets, as must have been the case with the men – a procession of robots, their mechanism running down.

After sleep, weapon inspection and, as important, foot inspection. 'Trench foot' was a horrible affliction turning the feet into rotting pulp, but we had very little of it, thanks to a mixture of mustard and lard invented the previous winter by our MO. Indeed apart from suffering killed and wounded, the battalion remained remarkably healthy despite the wet and the mud. In two and a half years on the Western Front, I never even caught a cold, and that was in no way exceptional.

Trying to get clean and dry took up a lot of time; there were fatigues to be done, and occasionally we even did some drill when conditions were suitable. All too soon, and long before forty-eight hours was up, we had to get ready for the journey of several hours back to the trenches.

Back in the line, I did a lot of patrolling, for which there was scope, for in this sector the two front lines were some distance apart; Stephen also enjoyed it, on one occasion rather optimistically flinging into the German trenches an invitation for them to surrender.

Remembering the circular displays of swords and muskets on the walls at Sandhurst, I had decided that a similar display of German bayonets would look well at Marble Hill, so some at least of my solo patrols had an ulterior motive. On one of them, I came across a waterlogged concrete pill box occupied by the Germans. Their bayonets were unattainable, but I took the German name board from it (their identification problems were clearly the same as ours) and went back to our trenches to collect a party to capture it. We found it abandoned, presumably it was too wet, and a later attempt by Stephen and me with some REs was frustrated by bright moonlight. The enemy were back in occupation, but very much on the alert.

The year ended in billets at Laventie. There for a short respite we left our grossest discomforts and quagmire behind us. Our Christmas dinners were held at La Gorgue and attended by Lord Cavan, affectionately known as Fatty, who had been promoted to command the newly formed XIVth Army Corps and had come to say goodbye and a lot of flattering words about our conduct. He handed over command of the Guards Division to Major-General 'Gaga' Fielding. Our new commander's regimental nickname proved no more than mildly scandalous. He was a kind and adequate divisional commander under whose direction I recall no unusual disasters.

Thus 1915 drew to its unlamented close, with its heroism, its losses, all its waste, discomfort and squalor; and bright hopes of victory in the field brought to naught.

If it could be claimed that anything good emerged from the horrors and hazards of trench life, it would be the true comradeship that embraced everyone. We were all in it together, were dependent on one another, facing similar perils. We shared a common humanity and recognized this profoundly though it was never put into words. A generous feeling of understanding, appreciation and respect developed naturally. This had nothing to do with discipline as generally understood, which rightly and necessarily remained as rigorous as ever. That discipline was part of our fabric, and so was easily maintained in active service conditions. Only once, soon after arriving at the front, did I see anything that savoured of brutal – and hence faulty – discipline. Though I was young, junior and inexperienced, I was deeply shocked by (and reacted swiftly to) the sight of a man seated on the ground, his arms stretched wide and lashed to the wheels of a limber. This degrading method of correction was known as Field Punishment No. 1, and admittedly was only used very occasionally.

Yet it seemed to me repulsive and primitive, too humiliating an experience to be forced upon a brave if erring man who might well, within days, have sacrificed his life. Other protesters with greater influence must have shared my disgust, for the practice was soon afterwards abandoned in our Guards Brigade, and in due course I believe throughout the army.

The true discipline of self-respect and mutual respect held us together. No one could serve with men like these without admiring them; no officer with the disagreeable task of censoring men's letters home could fail to be touched by their fortitude and their extraordinary generosity to wife or mother out of their shameful pay of 1s. a day. Discipline of the brittle sort was decreasingly important, it was strengthened and then replaced by a bond of sympathy and understanding that nothing could break.

Chapter Four

1916: Ypres and the Somme

The New Year found us floundering in mud amidst rotten parapets and waterlogged trenches needing continuous repair. We were relieved unexpectedly and moved to billets in St Floris, thence to Merville for active training and Lewis-gunnery. Ten days later we returned to crater fighting, patrolling and very active bombing. Casualties, though not heavy, came daily. Blake was killed during the night by a stray bullet whilst laying out wire on his company front. He was one of three senior officers of the Royal Irish Constabulary who had been seconded for the duration of the war to serve in the Army. Only one survived it. My nineteenth birthday was spent in noisy, damp conditions. Trench pumps failed completely to clear the water that made life a misery. One of the mine shafts flooded without warning and drowned two men in a listening post. Dangers that had to be guarded against in winter included the sudden flooding of deeper dugouts, drowning men asleep in them, and the possibility of asphyxiation from fumes from slow-burning braziers. These were installed in limited numbers in an effort to warm men who had been on watch for hours. Both hazards were greater when the line had been captured from the enemy. Germans seemed to go in for deep dug-outs with steep steps leading down from the trench. These had almost no ventilation. How many lost their lives from such hazards is not recorded. I once had a narrow escape; waking suddenly I got two companions out, clambering up the dug-out steps as water cascaded downwards. In minutes all was under water up to trench level. It was important to remain alert, even when asleep, which may sound impossible but was not really so, for some of us developed a sixth sense.

Occasionally when out of the line for some days we had distractions such as visits from VIPs. During the first days of February Prince Albert (later King George VI) visited us and breakfasted at battalion headquarters. A week later came Lord Kitchener, then Minister for War, and colonel of the regiment. He elected to inspect our brigade on a ghastly wet day that soaked us to the skin. So continued a troglodytic existence, as much a battle against the elements as against the enemy. Forty-eight hours in the line and forty-eight hours out.

During the previous winter I had acquired a concertina and played it with more enthusiasm than skill. My music suited an undiscriminating audience. Even the Germans failed to greet it with a shower of machine gun bullets. Those not sold on Bach or Mendelssohn may have liked our popular songs; thirty years later this happened when *Lili Marlene* became a favourite with both sides. Occasionally on clearing the trenches at 'relief', Company pipers played us back to rest billets. When pipers were not available, my concertina rendered *Tramp, tramp, tramp the boys are marching*, a battle song of the American civil war which went down well with my platoon, as they marched wearily from the trenches at dead of night to rest billets in some neighbouring town or village. *Brian Boru* was a favourite with the men, if not with the sleeping inhabitants. As the music paused there came a great shout, a Celtic battle cry of great antiquity. This savage tune is attributed to the King himself as he drove invading Danes into the sea at the battle of Clontarf. Local citizens were more accustomed to nightly disturbance by random shells falling amidst ruined buildings and on to cratered roads.

In mid-February we moved towards Steenvoorde in a hurricane of wind and rain, to a flooded camp near Poperinghe. Thence continued a twice weekly pilgrimage to the front line. The Ypres salient was a death trap; Kipling called it 'a gunnery school for German artillery'. The enemy surrounded Ypres on three sides and held the high ground dominating that doomed city. Through the fourth side passed all our supplies, rations, reinforcements of men, materials and ammunition. The Germans appreciated the enormous advantage they enjoyed, and pounded all approaches day and night. The British suffered untold casualties over the years from enemy fire, not only in the front trenches but among those whose duty it was to keep us supplied. Some argued that our precarious hold on Ypres should be abandoned; that the appalling cost in lives and material of clinging to it for reasons of prestige was quite unjustified. Cling we did with true British obstinacy until the end of the war.

In Poperinghe we got to know the Reverend 'Tubby' Clayton, who ran a hostel amidst the ruins where all soldiers off duty were welcomed. This establishment was known as 'Toc H' and became famous. There was also a photographer in Poperinghe – no doubt greed had overcome fear, for he enjoyed a lucrative trade with troops. Stephen and I had ourselves photographed wearing gas masks and looking like prehistoric monsters. Our parents were not amused.

At the end of February in bitter cold and snow the battalion moved to a rest camp at Calais for a week of intensive training. There it was to suffer a devastating loss. I had been late in turning in, engaged in writing letters in our mess tent. Only two others, Michael McCalmont the commanding officer and Desmond Fitzgerald, now our second in command, were still about. When Desmond had left the commanding officer asked me to find Desmond's servant and order him not to call his officer until the battalion had moved out of camp. I did as I was bid – but a battalion marching off is noisy. Of course Desmond awoke, and in the company of the padre went to see the training. This was spread over a big area. In my case, with Claude Chichester and others, we were being instructed in a deep depression among sand dunes in how to handle a German machine gun – load, fire, dismantle and reassemble. Desmond and the padre happened to visit a party under Tim Nugent engaged in bomb throwing. Father Lane Fox asked the instructor whether he might throw one, was told why not, and handed a Mills. The bomb he threw burst prematurely at head height, and everyone was wounded, Tim seriously, Desmond mortally. News reached us in dramatic fashion. A sergeant threw himself over the edge of the depression and slid down it shouting 'Lord Desmond is killed', repeating it again and again. Naturally we lost interest in German machine guns and unbelieving grabbed the sergeant and told him to pull himself together. Convinced at last, we rushed to the spot where the accident had happened. We could only help with casualties. Everyone had been hit but only Desmond fatally. The padre lost an eye and some fingers. From these injuries it was clear that the bomb not only exploded prematurely but almost as soon as it left the thrower's hand. Great sadness descended on us all, for every officer and man in our battalion loved and admired Desmond, with reason. He was an outstanding officer, brave, courteous, sensitive, efficient and a charming personality. It is not possible for me to write without emotion though over sixty years have passed. He was buried on the 5th March in the public cemetery at Calais, the whole battalion in deep sorrow with heads bowed lining the route to his grave. Only a few nights before his death he had looked into my tent and invited me, in the kindest way, to stop making the night hideous by practising on my cornet. After his death I never had the heart to play it again. In my view Desmond's death was a disaster not only for the regiment and the army and a tragedy for his family, but also dire for his country. He could not have failed to wield great influence on events. It may be true that 'no man is indispensable' but there are a few whose death is an unbearable disaster.

Desmond had a rare magnetic quality that drew us to him instinctively. He was by nature brave, courteous and gentle. He was patient too with those of us who were then very young, inexperienced and immature. Could I do better than to quote what are said to have been King David's last words?

> 'He who rules in justice, who rules in the fear of God, is like
> the light of the morning at sunrise, a morning that is
> cloudless after rain and makes the grass sparkle from the
> earth.'

This is the kind of leadership I associate with Desmond, a quality of leadership so rare, so potent and as sorely needed today as in the past. Tragically his leadership was to be lost to us and to his country through his early death. There are great men who achieve much but tread upon the susceptibilities of others, ruthless men whose footsteps leave scorch marks upon the ground, powerful men under whose shade nothing ever grows. Desmond was none of these. He was like 'the rain that makes the grass sparkle from the earth', one who allowed and encouraged others to grow. In so far as it was physically possible in our continuous struggle with the enemy, he provided conditions under which we very young and rather thoughtless ones might come to mature manhood and learn to believe in ourselves.

Leadership is a mysterious thing. It can be expressed in a dynamic manner, in a certain mysterious charm, or in a wholly elusive quality of life which springs out of a man's inner relationship with the divine source of all life, power and influence. Desmond's quality of lead-

ership was of this last kind. Added to his natural charm and
consideration for all but himself, it made our love and admiration for
the man absolute. No wonder we loved him and still do, and with
great reason mourn his loss.

We were back in the Ypres salient by the 6th March at Wormhoudt.
The French had become as mad about bombing as we were and
parties of French officers arrived to see our bombing competitions.
We managed not to kill any. Relieved on the 16th and billeted near
Vlamertinghe for St Patrick's Day, we were marched into camp by a
naval party to *Life on the Ocean Wave*. On the 23rd March our brigade
took over a new sector of the front. That night we were joined by
three naval officers and twenty-five petty officers who were to spend
four days with us. When out of the line we were still close to it, housed
in dug-outs bordering the canal bank at Ypres; my company was in
cellars under the city ramparts. Here my soldier-servant, Paddy Bell,
made a magnificent Irish Guards Star, four feet across, of glass and
powdered brick from a convent garden. This curiosity is mentioned
in Kipling's history of the regiment without giving Paddy Bell's name.

When we weren't in the trenches at Ypres, Stephen and I spent
hours trying to shoot pigeons in the ruins of the Cloth Hall. The birds
were difficult shots for revolvers as at every explosion they would
desert the rafters and soar upwards, for the roof had long gone. After
a while they would settle for a moment above us, then at the next
explosion take off afresh. The poor birds led a disturbed life. So of
course did we. Life in the line in front of Ypres was always disturbed.
Troops carrying out reliefs were constantly shelled and suffered a lot
of casualties. So did transport behind the lines engaged nightly in
bringing forward supplies. The Germans went in for indiscriminate
shelling of communications, causing much damage and loss. For
example RSM Kirk and others returning from home leave were
caught by shelling and killed in the street in Ypres.

One night at the end of March the enemy bombarded trenches
held at the time by the 2nd Grenadiers with our battalion in support.
'It went up from end to end, and the King's company was wiped out
almost to a man' Kipling wrote. This had been a prelude to an attack
which never materialized. We took over from the Grenadiers and
were bombed and shot up from the moment we moved in. The
Germans were behaving in a most aggressive manner, and we did our

best to return the compliment. At this time I always seemed to relieve or be relieved by a Grenadier company commanded by 'Wall' Grigg, later, after a distinguished political career, Lord Altrincham. One night with our relief under way I passed a robust figure in the dark front-line trench. Having handed over to Grigg I asked him who his new 'young officer' was who looked exactly like Winston Churchill – or had I been seeing things? It was Winston, doing a short attachment before taking over command of a battalion of the Royal Scots Fusiliers. At Wieltje we took over a line that had been reduced by shelling and bombing to a string of bombing posts, like grouse butts. It took some time and casualties before, working all and every night, we managed to produce a tolerable trench line. I was sent on a week's bombing course and returned from it miraculously unscathed. By now I was in command of my company, predecessors having become casualties or sent home sick. Our brigade was relieved in late May and moved to a back area, to the pleasant village of Longuenesse near St Omer.

The shadow of preparations for the Somme fell upon us. In active training we dug trenches and in full battle order assaulted them. We were pretty heavily accoutred, even though the men's big packs and great coats were left behind at B Echelon when we went into action. In addition to rifle, bayonet and ammunition, haversack with rations, water bottle and entrenching tool, gas mask and ground-sheet, the men were also loaded up with extra Mills bombs and often (and very necessary in a captured trench) a full size shovel. Officers in the Irish Guards carried blackthorn sticks – in 1914 they had gone to France with their swords. It was not until 1917 that officers were ordered to dress like their men and carry rifles in the attack, to make them less conspicuous targets for snipers. It was a good idea in theory, but an officer's activities in the assault and subsequent consolidation inevitably marked him out, and enemy snipers were not slow to recognize him.

By now we had been issued with steel helmets, which perhaps gave some protection against spent bullets or shrapnel, or small fragments from a shell bursting some distance away. I wore a tin hat as little as possible in the line, though I had to carry it about with me for show. Incidentally after the war some of us on training exercises wore an admirable cardboard imitation tin hat made by Walter Barnard of Jermyn Street. They looked just right and were exceedingly light.

Unfortunately when they were soaked by rain, the rim got corrugated and floppy, which gave the game away; our senior officers were not amused.

Early in June we were back at Poperinghe and in the line again by mid-month. Before Poperinghe was too heavily and regularly shelled to be habitable as a 'rest' area, the Guards Division ran a cinema and a big canteen in a hall there, which was a boon to men coming out of the line; in decent weather there were also football and athletics competitions. We never ran to a divisional or brigade concert party, but the 3rd Coldstream had a splendid all-ranks troupe known as the Lilywhites which gave a lot of pleasure to us all. It was organized by Drum Major Shrimpton; he survived the war, to run a garage near Belgrave Square, where naturally most of us in the Household Brigade bought our cars.

It must, I suppose, have been in the late spring or early summer in 1916 that news reached us of the Easter Rising in Dublin; I am uncertain for the good reason that it made no impact on the men of the battalion. All company officers got to know their men very well – sharing as we did the same dangers and discomforts it would have been surprising had this not been so. One took part in countless discussions and could not help overhearing the men discussing things amongst themselves, but I can recollect no talk about the Rising or its implications. Perhaps the problems, all day and every day, of staying alive made news from home unreal and irrelevant. If there were differing views among guardsmen on the future of Ireland, they were as unimportant on active service as the fact that the battalion contained Protestants amidst its massive majority of Catholics.

About this time Stephen's company and my own were in the front line together. One day I joined him in a sniper's post where he had an extraordinary escape. An enemy sniper put a bullet through the narrow slit in the steel shield. It grazed his right ear and made it bleed profusely. Having patched him up, I congratulated him on his escape and considered him secure for the rest of the war, for no one could possibly have been nearer death. Alas, my congratulations were ill-timed.

Enemy snipers were extremely active, inflicting many casualties. Just as we excelled in bombing, the Germans were more successful as snipers. Perhaps it was a matter of temperament, for one supposes that our equipment was just as good. But our approach to this most unsporting form of aggression was amateurish. Few were like Julian Grenfell who is said to have recorded kills in his game book, three Pomeranians following on the bag for his last day's partridge shooting in Oxfordshire. A friend of my family, Geoffrey Gathorne Hardy, himself a keen and excellent rifle shot, was inspired with support from my uncle Colonel Stuart to set up a small school near St Omer for the training of selected men as snipers, many of them stalkers from the Highlands. How successful this venture proved I never discovered, but something like it was badly needed if we hoped to compete in a solitary, cruel, cold-blooded sport. Not to my taste.

The struggle for Verdun had been going on for months, the Germans suffering enormous casualties in their relentless assaults. The pressure on the French never slacked so they too, in a gallant and stubborn defence, had paid a terrible price in men and material. This 'gateway to the heart of France' was a prime objective of the Germans at that stage. It was vital that they should be denied entry, whatever the cost. French losses had become so serious that France's allies tried to ease the pressure by taking offensive action on a major scale elsewhere. And so the build up for the battle of the Somme began.

We all realized what lay ahead, but were not as yet directly concerned. Poking about in a disused trench I came upon a small locked store and broke in. There were a few boxes of what turned out to be parachute flares, beautifully made like small shells. No one had seen them before or knew what they were. The opinion was that they were German or French. Naturally I was intrigued and set about resolving the mystery. I built a strange Heath Robinson mortar-like weapon out of wood from broken ammunition boxes held together by old signal wire. The breech block was a problem. Next thing was to fire the beastly thing. No one would come near to witness this experiment. Having bored a hole in the breech block and inserted a nail to act as a striker, I gave it a bang with a hammer. The recoil blew the breech block smartly to the back of the trench. I had anticipated this and stood a little to one side before firing. At last I knew what I had got hold of as the little rocket shot into the sky, then floated down on its paracute. In due course a much superior Mark II of my rocket launcher was produced, and solemnly taken and handed over with other trench stores by Grenadier or Coldstream battalions when they relieved us.

We relieved the 2nd Grenadiers on the night of the 11th July. Much of that afternoon I had spent with Stephen in his small dug-out on the bank of the canal north of Ypres. He was clearly unwell. I tried to persuade him to report sick. When he refused I thought him gallant, but unreasonably obstinate. I have often wondered whether he had some premonition of what was coming and was preparing to face it. Eventually I had to leave him to lead my own company into the line. In the night the enemy shelled all approaches and the communication and support trenches as usual, hoping to inflict casualties on relieving troops. They seldom failed. About midnight a shell exploded on the edge of the trench along which Stephen's company was moving, and a shell splinter penetrated his steel helmet killing him instantly.

It was not until the following morning that I heard in a sympathetic note from his company commander, who knew how close we were. Having recovered from the initial shock I must have gone quite crazy. Against all the rules I grabbed the nearest Lewis gun and two loaded drums (magazines) and standing on the fire-step, head and shoulders in full view, I sprayed bullets at every gap in the German line opposite me. A demand for further ammunition was rightly ignored by my subordinates. Though full of sympathy they decided not to encourage a potential suicide. It was a reaction, blind rage, for very few of us felt any personal hostility to the individual German. We were all in it together. Whether we liked it or not, it was our lot and duty to serve to the best of our abilities. Of personal rancour there was none. The night had cost us Stephen and three other ranks killed, and seventeen men wounded. It was not a happy life. I missed Stephen terribly, always have and always will. In 1931 my elder son was christened Stephen after him.

Ten days later a very senior captain was posted from England to take over my company. This did not please me. On two previous occasions I had done a stint of twenty-eight days in command, entitling me to the rank of temporary captain and, much more important, to additional pay, and had then stepped down when a senior officer was put in command. Twice either the Germans or sickness had removed them. This time my relief reported to me after I had dispatched my company to the line under my second in command. After I had put him in the picture regarding the company

and the front, we set out in darkness to join them, I leading, he and
our orderlies following. Still well short of the front line, the enemy
started machine-gun 'harassing' fire. Bullets came disagreeably
close. I pointed this out aloud to our little party and walked on. In due
course I repeated the suggestion that it might be wise to halt for a bit.
No reply. Looking round, I could see no one following. Going back I
found my relief on the ground with a bullet in his arm. So that was
that. As he had been officially reported as having joined, this was to be
the third time I had been done down to no purpose. Some brother
officers made the libellous suggestion that I had lured him towards
the front and had shot him or arranged for him to be shot by men of
my company so that I might continue to command them. From then
on authority gave up and I was left in undisputed command.

In the last days of July the battalion was relieved and moved to an
area south of Poperinghe which itself had been heavily shelled and
completely evacuated for a time. Our losses in four months routine
trench work had been four officers and thirty other ranks killed, five
officers and 153 other ranks wounded. This steady drain was not
exceptional. It was the experience of all units engaged in holding the
line. These losses were insignificant compared to the toll to come.
Withdrawn from the line, we moved Sommeward, with an interlude
when the regimental band came out from England; on the 9th August
the King visited our division, and officers of the battalion were
presented to him in an orchard.

The Battle of the Somme was by now six weeks old, a savage
struggle with casualties high on both sides, but particularly on ours,
being the attackers. It was thought that our division might be
required to link up with the French armies and that it would be a good
thing in anticipation of this to pay them a liaison visit. Some one in
authority had decided that I could speak French, so I was detailed to
spend a week in the French front lines. It was an experience. They
were very kind and persuaded me to drink copiously of vin ordinaire,
which they downed at every meal. The French troops in that part of
the line behaved in a way quite strange to me. Units relieved one
another above ground, sometimes in daylight. There were no sanitary
arrangements so that everyone was forced to squat in shell holes
outside the trench system. All this would have been quite suicidal
further north. It was an extraordinary change for me coming from a
much livelier front. Even the Germans were peaceable in the

extreme, and apart from an odd token shelling did no visible damage, they allowed the French to live unmolested. Perhaps there was some understanding here between the opposing forces? Returning at the end of my strange week with our allies, I related my experiences, but did not recommend modelling ourselves on the French pattern.

About this time an order was made to the effect that any officer who had served continuously in the trenches for a year should be sent home for a two-month rest. I qualified having done eighteen months, but was fit and happy where I was and said so. My parents were much upset by my refusal to go home, and pressed me hard. In the end I agreed to a compromise. This was that if I were offered a staff appointment in France I would accept it, provided I got back to the battalion at the end of the two month period.

At GHQ I was brought before General Charteris, at that time head of intelligence. He handed me a French book from which I read out a passage and translated it. It was a very elementary test which took about fifteen minutes. I was then provided with a car and ordered to report to Headquarters IXth Corps as artillery intelligence officer. I was slightly dazed, for my knowledge of gunnery was nil; hitherto I had always been on the receiving end. On arrival I was welcomed by the chief of staff and told I was to meet the corps commander in the evening. Meanwhile, furnished with a sergeant, a small clerical staff, miscellaneous equipment, maps and a hut, I was told to get on with it. It was an interesting job concerned with counter-battery work. Accurate plotting of German artillery positions was the most important part. Despite my ignorance of artillery I was given every facility and a completely free hand. Every morning reports reached me from a variety of sources. Reports came in from infantry battalions, brigades and divisions holding the corps front. More reports reached me daily from artillery units and from sound ranging sections. One of these with its delicate recording instruments was on Kemmel hill, one of the few dominating features on the front in our hands. Reports came from the Royal Flying Corps and from kite balloon sections. All gave bearings from their own positions to points behind enemy lines from which gun flashes had been spotted or enemy movements seen. I set up three large-scale maps, and plotted and recorded relevant information daily. When several sources had reported enemy activity at a common point I alerted all sources. I could and did ask the Royal Flying Corps to carry out reconnaissances and to photograph suspect areas. Appreciating the danger to pilots and aircraft, I only called for sorties when verification of a target was thought to be vital. At first I found interpretation of aerial photographs difficult but did better with practice.

Information was recorded under three headings: enemy artillery positions known, tested and verified; positions suspected, awaiting confirmation; finally positions known but temporarily abandoned which had to be kept under close observation in case of re-occupation. Our most difficult task was locating enemy batteries that were well hidden and never fired a shot. A proportion of our own artillery units adopted the same tactic for the same reason – that they remain undivulged. Then it was decided that we knew the precise location of a sufficient number of enemy gun positions to justify a counter-battery shoot. This resulted in a great concentration of fire being brought down onto comparatively few known targets. With luck this could mean their total destruction. One such shoot took place towards the end of my time and was thought to have been a success – certainly much ammunition had been expended.

Probably the most vulnerable of my sources were the kite balloon sections, sitting ducks up there in the sky and frequently shot down by German aircraft. If warned of attack in time, which seldom happened, they were hauled down with admirable speed, but many were lost. I visited those responsible for reporting to corps headquarters to show that we valued what their reports told us and to thank them. These visits were appreciated. When I visited a kite balloon section, I felt honour bound to go up and see my frontage from a great height; it was very fresh and peaceful up there. Whilst enjoying the view, I kept a sharp eye out for enemy aircraft, and was glad in due course to return to the ground. I remembered how we had watched an observation balloon being shot down in flames earlier in the year, a dramatic spectacle witnessed by our entire battalion during a march back to rest. Of its two occupants one escaped by parachute, the other hesitated, then jumped to his death. A Grenadier friend and staff captain rode up to me to say that the dead man had been Basil Hallam, a music hall star of the day. I had seen him on stage at the Empire when I was last on leave. His famous song and dance as 'Gilbert, the Filbert' the pride of Piccadilly, was always well received by an uncritical audience. Sadly the introduction of conscription in May had caught up with him and put paid to his career and to his life.

This job called for some imagination, attention to detail, accurate recording of essential matters, and common sense. When the time came for me to return to the battalion, the corps commander did his best to persuade me to stay on. I had enjoyed it, had learnt a lot, and was sad at leaving. Still, I had looked forward to returning to old friends and was back with the regiment two months to the day.

The battalion was then out of the line and billeted in Hornoy. It had been through a rough time on the Somme along with all units engaged in that bloody battle of attrition. The two engagements in which it had taken part were those of the 15th and 25th September and losses were heavy. In two days it had lost seven officers killed and eleven wounded with some 580 other rank casualties. It was a high price for our limited successes, but the battalion had done splendidly on both occasions and was to receive the highest praise. Dicky Tisdall who had accompanied me to France in 1915 had been killed, so had Jack Greer who had been in my company, and we missed them sadly.

I have always held that the Somme accounted for all that was left of the old British Regular Army, which had until then, with the enthusiastic volunteers of 1914 and 1915, managed to survive previous encounters. It was noticeably so in our case and their loss seemed a disaster to me. Every effort was still made to cling to the Irish connection, but the heavy casualties in the field force inevitably meant the acceptance of good men from other quarters. The men of 1917 in the Irish Guards were steadfast, loyal and brave, and bore their hardships gallantly, and as cheerfully as those who had gone before. But good as they were, I felt that the newer generation of NCOs did to some extent – and not surprisingly – lack something of the quality of the old.

Units of the 'New Armies' had gone into action at the very beginning of the Battle of the Somme on July 1st. Their losses were appalling, whole units, even formations, being consumed in the course of a day. Total British casualties on the Somme have been put at nearly 420,000 in the four and a half months it lasted. It is claimed that German casualties were very high, and no doubt our artillery pounding the enemy by day and by night for weeks on end was effective. It had become a war of attrition. Killing on a grand scale, in any way, and at all times, had now become the policy of both antagonists. Perhaps the great ones who then controlled our destinies had finally despaired of breaking the deadlock of trench warfare. The opposing armies were dug in to the ground from the North Sea to the frontiers of Switzerland.

Defences on the German side were formidable, well sited and in great depth. Their positioning of tactical wire and enfilading machine guns was masterly, inflicting terrible loss of life. Our attacks had done little more than dent these defences, never sufficiently deeply to allow a breakthrough that could lead to open warfare and to battles of manoeuvre. The overall position was one of ghastly stalemate. In these circumstances the slaughter of opponents seemed to be the only hope of winning. By reducing the available man power, physical prosecution of the war might collapse. The political will to fight on might falter. Such was the broad, sad, discouraging picture of general frustration.

A dinner for officers of both our battalions was held at the Hotel London in Hornoy on the 7th November. Three days later we were off to familiar camping ground near Carnoy, in winter a sea of mud, and into a dreadful camp near Montauban. Back in the line on the 13th, north of Lesboeufs and subjected to continuous indiscriminate shelling that in forty-eight hours killed four and wounded fourteen in my company. Three men disappeared, they were found by exhumation parties three or four years later and identified by rags of guardsman's uniform or by a button. The really horrible sight, alas a common one, was that of dead men of either side hanging pitifully on uncut barbed wire. So horrible that we, and doubtless the Germans too, tried when possible to bring them in under cover of darkness for burial. It was a filthy bit of line without communication trenches. A waste without landmarks.

The 2nd Grenadiers relieved us at midnight on the 16th December and we returned to ice cold Nissen huts at Montauban, I don't think I have ever been so cold at night as in that foul and filthy camp set in a quagmire. It was nearly impossible to sleep however tired, and I spent hours hunched up in my sleeping bag hoping to warm my feet by rubbing them together. For all of us, the conditions called for a form of endurance not much less than that required in the trenches. In the last days of November we were visited by corps, divisional and brigade commanders. They made kind remarks, sympathized with our discomforts, and shaking as much mud as they could off well polished boots departed for the comparative warmth and comfort of their various headquarters. Who could blame them?

On the 3rd December we moved to a camp known as Maltz Horn. It was slightly less unpleasant than the camp we had just left. Meanwhile the great ones had decided that the Army should by degrees take over a new stretch of the French line from Le Transloy to a point opposite Roye. Our share of this was a thousand yards of trench at Sailly-Sallisel till then held by the 160th Regiment of the French *Corps de Fer*. Installed on 6th December we found the 156th French infantry on our right with the Coldstream on our left. The enemy were reasonably well behaved, though when suspecting reliefs he dropped barrages on approaches and support lines. We were relieved on the night of 9th December by the 2nd Grenadiers who had been delayed by having to dig floundering men out of deep mud. It could take as much as eight hours to cover four or five miles in a continuous nightmare of mud, darkness, loss of touch and sudden engulfment of heavily loaded men. Alex arrived to take over command of the battalion at this point, replacing Michael McCalmont who had been given a brigade, and I was ordered to take command of a new company, No. 4, on dear K's (Lord Kingston's) departure to hospital because of illness and an earlier wound.

The year drew to its close with regular spells in the front line the last of which was from the 25th to 27th, so the men missed their Christmas dinners. For me it had been a particularly sad year, since I had lost many friends and my greatest friend among them. Stephen's younger and only brother Basil, an ensign in the Coldstream, had perished on the Somme, their parents left to mourn two splendid boys within three months. The wiping out of a family, the extinction of bright hopes. Such is the sickening futility of war, leaving scars that can never be healed. We who may fuss over trivialities would do well to think about those whose hurt is infinitely deep and incurable. To these losses I had to add that of my uncle, Colonel Alexander Stuart, a splendid officer who had just been given command of a brigade. He was killed by a stray bullet behind the support lines. Fate in its capricious way removed one who was set for an outstanding career. Had he survived the war, his star in the ascendant, his wise guidance would have been invaluable to me. He and so many others were often in my thoughts and in my prayers. So we passed from one traumatic year to yet another, hoping that we might meet new challenges courageously and even overcome them.

The redeeming factor in our squalid existence proved to be the staunchness in adversity of our men. Long since gone was the colour and pageantry of battle – banners flying, knights in armour charging one another, shields emblazoned with their arms, the sun flashing on swords, axes and pikes. For the combatants of 1916 there was no glamour whatever, little to buoy up the spirit or to inspire. All that the average guardsman could look forward to with honour was to be carried off the field still living. Men died, were mutilated or wounded in vast numbers, by an enemy unseen and unseeing. Battle was impersonal and mechanical, remote from the individual. Yet in the last resort it was the uncomplaining, sustained courage, good humour and fortitude of our guardsmen that remained. Their leaders, particularly we junior ones in hourly contact with such splendid men, had every reason to be proud, respectful and humbled by their example. And nothing could have been finer than the conduct at all times, of the non-combatants – medical officers, priests and stretcher bearers. They were simply magnificent, and any rewards that came their way had been earned a hundred times. Unarmed and engaged in errands of mercy, they worked without regard for their own safety. Many were killed and all, in time, were wounded.

Chapter Five

1917: Messines and Passchendaele

Despite high hope, tireless effort, and appalling losses, our front had only advanced some eight to ten miles in the two years since in late 1914 both sides had settled down to static trench warfare.

Bitter frosts ushered in the New Year and continued for many weeks. Our brigade, in reserve near Carnoy on the first day of February, went into the line in the same ex-French sector near Sailly-Sallisel, but this time close to St Pierre Vaast Wood. That wood was the stuff of which nightmares are made, with many disagreeable reminders of past conflict. The most bizarre was a large mine crater filled with the bodies of French colonial troops, their white skulls in many cases still adorned with jaunty red caps.

The hard frozen ground made digging impossible. In consequence the enemy, whose problem matched our own, remained relatively quiet. When snow fell it gave away movement on either side. There was some shelling, but light and intermittent; we suffered few casualties.

The iron-bound ground faced us with a problem of hygiene that had never before arisen in our experience. The solution – since there was no other and nature had to take its course – was to adopt the French method, and scatter our largesse as widely and as inconspicuously as possible. One day our brigadier arrived to visit his units. He found them hale and hearty, even welcoming. He was disturbed to see about him some unaccustomed litter. Medical officers of the three regiments were ordered to attend him. His proposal was that a chemical dye be found which, mixed with men's tea, would betray the origin of these nuisances. White for Grenadiers, red for the Coldstream, blue for the Irish – the colours of the plumes worn in our bearskin caps in peace time. His plan was certainly original, but to his chagrin his advisers were unable to recommend it.

In the third week of February the frost broke, the brigade commander's concern for hygiene faded, as ground so recently hard as rock turned into quagmire. To quote Kipling, 'Trenches caved in bodily; dumps sank where they were being piled; duckboards went under by furlongs at a time; tanks were immobilized five feet deep and the very bellies of field-guns gouged into the mud'. Kipling mentions tanks, but he must have been referring to another part of the front. We certainly never had any of the too few tanks in support of the battalion's attacks. Indeed I never saw a tank during my service on the western front, although nine were allotted to the Guards Division for an attack in September 1916.

Things were beginning to move. The Germans decided to withdraw from certain positions, to straighten out salients, shorten their line and gradually to move back into new defences covering what came to be known as the Hindenburg Line.

On or about 17th March (St Patrick's Day), orders were given for a general advance by our troops in co-operation with the French. To conform our brigade detailed the senior commanding officer – in our case Lt Col Gillie Follet, Coldstream – to command the advance guard. Each battalion furnished two companies to come under his command. Our two companies were my own and Rodakowski's, both in my charge. Off we went and met with little opposition other than shelling and long-range machine-gun harassing fire. It was wonderful to get away from devastated ground into virtually untouched country. Our advance was cautious and slow, too slow I thought at the time, but we had been warned about booby traps, mines and mined dug-outs, and attention to these necessary warnings slowed things up somewhat. Our probing advance went according to plan with minimal casualties.

A sad loss was that of Major Young (one of the three officers seconded from the Royal Irish Constabulary) who had come forward to see how things were going with us. We were engaged in consolidating an old enemy position known as Bayreuth. I was sad to miss him, but lucky, for he was hit by a shell that fell on my company headquarters. At the time I was forward coping with a minor crisis. My fellow company commander had passed out completely. Arrived at his headquarters I found him unconscious, and spent half an hour aided by his CSM in a vain attempt to revive him. We slapped his face, poured water on him, pummelled him, and even stuck pins in him to wake him up. All to no purpose. Perhaps we did all the wrong things but we knew no better. Our treatment failed completely to stir the sleeping beauty. Having told his senior subaltern to take over and to let me know when Kowski came to, I returned to my ruined headquarters, to learn of Young's mortal wounding and of the death of Sergeant Travers, one of my best NCOs of whom I was particularly fond. By the next morning Kowski was himself again. I think he was quite exhausted physically and mentally, for we had had lots to do and practically no sleep since we had set out on our advance.

I had a similar experience in 1940 in a renewed contest with the Germans when, for the same reason, one of my company commanders passed out temporarily under pressure. Disconcerting, and a bore at times of crisis when all are stretched to the utmost. Such breakdowns are mercifully very rare.

When we were out of the line we were engaged energetically in training for 'open warfare' – too optimistically as it proved, since the enemy's meticulously prepared new Hindenburg Line was even stronger than his old positions. Back in the line, we moved forward slowly to the next ex-enemy trench system, known as Gotha, where we were held up by a tremendous concentration of high explosive – evidently the Germans were still putting the finishing touches to their new positions. When the shelling eased, long-range machine gun fire made further progress a slow business. Towards the end of March we were shifted from this sector to Combles, and then back to Le Transloy.

One day a signal arrived from Headquarters 1st Army demanding to know if I could be spared for a day? If so, a car would be sent to collect me. To my surprise my father was one of a small, pretty high-powered mission just arrived from home to which General Horne was host. It was an emotional moment, for I had not seen my father since 1914; there had been no time, of course, to go home to Ireland on my forty-eight hour leave in 1915. The mission was required to investigate the conditions under which our troops lived and fought and to report on their morale, always high, despite many trials, and also on the man-power position, linked to the introduction of conscription. The ranks of volunteers, most of whom had already perished, just had to be replenished. Forty years later during a tour of inspection of Army cadet units in the north of Scotland and a guest at

Lord Horne's home, I found my father's signature in the visitors' book, dated 1917.

In mid-April the battalion moved into a camp at Bronfay, abandoning for a short time active confrontation with the enemy. We began intensive training. By the 1st May we had moved to Etricourt where training continued but in more agreeable surroundings. There were wild flowers to be gathered, and an orchard in blossom to show that the world still lived naturally. Men spoke affectionately of Etricourt 'where shell holes were so few that you could count them'. On 20th May we marched to Corbie on the Somme, there to continue our training. There was talk of an assault on the Messines Ridge which had commanded for too long much of the flat, shell-bitten Ypres salient. It overlooked the shattered town of Ypres and the British positions round it, and was a major factor in making the salient tenable only at a vast cost in lives and material. If there was to be a break-out from the trap of the salient, we had a shrewd suspicion that the Guards Division would be involved – which put an edge on our training. This continued in early June near St Omer, where the land was so heavily cropped that the only training ground available was the Forest of Clairmarais where we learnt the art of wood fighting.

Here we gave a dinner to honour a friendly field ambulance to whom on various occasions we had owed much. It was a merry evening; the story was told that in the small hours our guests went home on their own stretchers. Other amusement took the form of indifferent polo in a field near my company mess, with improvised sticks made by our pioneer sergeants, the mounts being our company chargers. It was always a joy, out of the line, to be re-united with my groom and my faithful Cork, even though nature had not built him to be a polo pony. Jimmy Coates and Charles Hambro were welcome polo enthusiasts from the Coldstream, the latter to blossom after the war into being a leading figure in the city.

Meantime I had been awarded the Military Cross. In October 1915 I had been told unofficially that Monty Gore-Langton had recommended me for an award shortly before his death. His successor, Guy Yerburgh, later a close friend, confirmed this. But the shell that soon after landed on battalion headquarters, killing the CO and the Padre, also destroyed all the documents there, so no more was heard of that recommendation.

Messines was to be the scene of the greatest British mining effort of the war. Both sides had indulged in this form of attack since 1915, and it required very special skills and courage. Shafts would be sunk in our own front line from which tunnels were dug forward to a point below the enemy wire and trenches, the end of the tunnel packed with explosive and then set off. The trouble was that the enemy were also tunnelling, so the work had to be carried out in silence, with constant vigilance for the sounds of enemy activity. Counter-mining was the art of tunnelling *beneath* the enemy's tunnel, to blow it up at what was judged the appropriate moment. There were occasions when the opposed tunnellers met and fought underground. I remember from time to time being ordered to evacuate our forward line, or part of it, when it was thought an enemy mine was about to be touched off; RE officers, gallant men, would go down our mine shafts with listening devices to locate the proximity of the German tunnel. In the event we were lucky, and I don't think we ever suffered from this form of beastliness, though I recollect that we rather disapproved of being ordered out of our trenches, even temporarily and for our own good.

On the 7th June nineteen mines at Messines went up together – the explosion was clearly heard in London – and attacking troops of the 2nd Anzac and IX and X Corps went into the assault. And very successfully, for the whole German line on that front was forced back for a distance varying from one to two miles.

About mid-June we began to move towards the salient and bivouacked in woods south-east of Proven on the Poperinghe road. On the 25th we moved from Proven into the fringe of the battle area, and here came under the fire of a long-range German gun that caused us no casualties, merely cut up the fields about us.

Air activity was stepped up tremendously. Both sides were hard at work trying to put out each other's 'eyes'. One casualty was an observation balloon of ours shot down in flames close to our camps. Bombing of back areas was continuous and caused many casualties. I was shown the damage done to a camp, where a tent full of sleeping men had been hit – all that was left was a shallow circular crater. The beneficiaries of this activity in the air were our artillery units who with good observation and, at last, a plentiful supply of ammunition did tremendous destruction on enemy positions in the Ypres Salient.

On the 1st July we were back in the line in the Boesinghe sector of the Ypres Salient relieving the 2nd Coldstream near the Yser Canal.

It was a point of junction of allied forces, where we linked with Belgian and later with French troops on our left. We suffered much shelling and lost an officer (Shears) killed and some others that first night. We kept the enemy in tension by constant raids, which led to the Germans sending up their SOS signals with unusual frequency, often followed by barrages causing damage and constant casualties. On the night of the 5th July for example, quite a few gas shells fell on a working party of my company and knocked out nineteen men, three of whom died on the spot or a day or two later, and one of my subalterns (Bagenal) was gassed. As for myself, going round my line constantly in darkness, the gas was a crashing bore. I could see nothing with my mask on, so took it off when making a dash between posts, then put on the suffocating thing when at the halt, recovered my breath, and repeated the process. It was a beastly bit of line, in no sense continuous, just a series of posts that we did our best to join up whilst subjected to constant bombardment round the clock.

In 1915 we had not taken the threat of gas so seriously, in spite of the appalling suffering caused by the first gas attacks. Gas sentries were posted in the trenches and outside all headquarters with primitive alarms – they blew a whistle or waved a rattle or banged on an empty shell-case dangling from a string. Needless to say there were some false alarms. By 1917, when a bombardment often contained a mixture of gas shells, employing phosgene and, later, mustard gas, and high explosive shells, we had learned to be wary. But at Ypres no precautions could prevent casualties.

Alex had gone home to attend a course at Aldershot and I was due for a short leave. I handed over my company to Jack Eyre, my senior subaltern, until I should return. Though I was very fond of him he was at that moment mildly out of favour. Why? Because at lunch Jack had taken a swipe at a wasp, had hit it, and the infuriated insect had taken it out on his commander and stung me under one eye. In imagination my eye was already swollen shut, scarlet and horrible. What sort of reception could I expect in this condition from the pretty girls I was so shortly to meet? In the event the wasp sting caused none of the problems imagined at the moment of impact. The incident was soon forgotten and dear Jack forgiven long before I left the line that evening. I was never to see him again. On my return a week or ten days later I learnt what had happened.

On the 14th the enemy raided my company's line. The raid was preceded by an hour's 'box' barrage of guns, trench mortars and machine guns concentrating on the frontage of the two platoons. A shrapnel-barrage fell on the supports at the same time. A 'box' barrage, it should be explained, was a heavy concentrated curtain of fire brought down on the front, flanks and rear of the area to be assaulted. It was designed to isolate, and to cut off reinforcement by supporting troops attempting a rescue operation. It was generally highly effective and the hapless platoons, thus cut off, could be certain that an attack was to follow. It appeared that there were two enemy parties involved in the assault. One crossing the canal was broken by our fire. A second was momentarily successful in storming over our parapet between two firing bays. By now our trench, half blown in, was full of scattered groups groping in the pitch dark, unable to distinguish British from Germans. Most unhappily poor Jack, attempting to sort things out, ran into a party of the enemy. No one knew what happened next. His steel helmet and revolver, all chambers fired, was found near the wreck of a firing bay. It was learned later that he had been captured, mortally wounded, and had died that evening. His loss saddened me greatly. He was a particularly good and brave officer and one of whom I was very fond.

On my return I had found the battalion out of the line in the training area at Herzeele, in readiness for the battle known as Third Ypres, which was eventually to end in the mud of Passchendaele. Representation of the ground to be attacked on the day of battle, with its trenches and farms, was marked out, and studied by company commanders and others. The weather was perfect, but as soon as we moved to Proven and once more into the battle area on the 25th July, heavy and continuous rain began to fall. As on the Somme, this was destined to cripple our attacks.

The battalion had been roused at 2 a.m. on the 25th by gas alarms. We were required to provide over 500 men for working parties to get material up to the front line. Whilst so employed ten men were killed by shelling and one of my company officers (Maxwell) and seven others were wounded. Next day we moved forward under casual shelling and on the 27th established ourselves in support near Bleuet Farm. On 28th we went forward in the evening to relieve the 3rd Coldstream in the outpost line, from Douteuse House to where it joined the French forces. No. 2 company under Rodakowski crossed the canal (about 70 feet wide, mostly soft mud into which a man sank without trace) on improvised bridges of slabs of wood nailed across rabbit wire and canvas, and lay up in an old German front line. I had two platoons forward and two back. We were all shelled equally throughout the night with gas and lachrymal shells plus barrages on all lines of support. Nothing could be done to strengthen the newly occupied trenches, as there was no wire on the spot; engineer parties, trying to bring it up, were pinned till daylight by a ceaseless shelling of their approach routes. Our barrages were tremendously heavy from 3.50 on the morning of 31st July prior to our attack. It was a splendid, encouraging sight. German casualties must have been heavy, and the intensity of our shelling demoralizing to survivors.

As for ourselves, we were shelled all day but suffered relatively few casualties. That evening I decided to move my two forward platoons, who were getting more than their share of the enemy's attention, back about 200 yards to trenches in which I had placed my supporting platoons. This movement had just been completed when on my way to join them through an orchard I was flung into the air by a shell bursting close under my behind. At that stage I had no idea what had happened since I had heard nothing, nor was I in pain, merely surprised and angry sitting on ground that I'd met with a bump. Cursing the Germans and trying to get up, I could not do so. This led to more bad language. Then it started to rain again. Finally I noticed blood and realized that I had been hit. My two orderlies following a little behind me were both hit by fragments from this shell, one seriously. Well, that was that, some men came forward to care for us, and two, with my arms round their necks, got me in the dark to our battalion aid post. Soon after being given the usual tetanus injection I was bundled into a field ambulance and driven in pouring rain and pitch darkness over shelled and cratered roads to the casualty clearing station at Proven. I will not easily forget the sight of row upon row of wounded lying patiently on stretchers, casualties of that morning's affray. Those that could not be got under cover had ground sheets spread over them against the rain. It was not long before I was operated on for the removal of the shell splinter that had floored me. Before being 'put under' I was told of the death of our 2nd Battalion's padre, the most splendid and gallant Father Knapp. I could well have done without this information at that particular time. The mask was slapped over my face and I was no more until the following morning when I came to feeling strange, being sick, with the sound of torrential rain beating down on a corrugated iron roof above my head. Later I was told that Eric Greer, commanding the 2nd Battalion, had also been killed instantly on the 31st by a shrapnel shell bursting over his advanced headquarters. This was a sad blow for the regiment, as he was a quite outstanding officer. In due course, I was sent by ambulance train to a base hospital and kept there for some days, perhaps a week. During this time the heavy rain never ceased, and my thoughts turned constantly to my comrades still battling with enemy and elements alike.

Before going to France two years earlier, I had extracted a promise from Lady Carnarvon that if I became a casualty, she would accommodate me in her hospital in Bryanston Square. The chances of my holding her to this undertaking were high, for few of my age group survived undamaged for long. I had kept her waiting for a long time but was now on my way. Our cross-Channel trip by hospital ship was calm and uneventful. On landing we were put aboard an ambulance train and were soon on our way to London. At Victoria Station I was more than surprised when two men entered my section of the train calling me by name. Collected without further ado, I was carried to a waiting ambulance that took off for Bryanston Square. It was a lovely summer evening and a great many people had gathered at Victoria to greet and cheer the wounded as ambulance trains arrived to discharge their loads. Though unable to move I was disgustingly fit.

The hospital was small and quite delightful, very efficient and well equipped. There were four wards with five beds in each. Lady Carnarvon was a good and very active matron, helped in her work by kind, efficient nurses. Everyone went to great lengths to care for us. There was no nonsense about visiting hours and lovely creatures came to cheer us and hasten our recovery. One in particular, and perhaps the loveliest, became and has ever remained a life-long friend. Our days passed in great comfort and we were thoroughly spoilt. My wound had been a deep one but did no permanent damage. It took time to heal because it was not allowed to do so quickly for medical reasons. In order to control things a plug was inserted deep into the wound and it really did hurt when this had to be extracted about once a week, and a new plug inserted.

I had plenty of time to contemplate life, and to think of friends battling in the line, and of the trials and difficulties facing them, particularly in vile weather. Those long casualty lists published daily in the papers were a nightmare. They seemed to grow longer every day and it was with dread that we scanned them. Letters began to reach me from the front, brave letters, giving news of their doings. One could 'read between the lines' much of what went unsaid. Two have survived both wars. One amusing letter began 'I'm so glad you were wounded' but it was kindly meant, and went on to say that a respite had been earned after a long and lucky run. It also claimed that the whole of the Ypres Salient had been lit up by flames in the burning of a great mass of papers, orders, messages, records, etc. found in my kit prior to its being sent home after me. Happily quite a lot survived, including a detailed map I had drawn of our positions in the 'Brickstacks' sector a little over two years earlier, and my field service pocket book also, with entries up to the moment of my wounding. Twenty years later my field service pocket book (vintage 1940) was returned to me by the Admiralty. It had fallen out of my pocket into one of the destroyer's boats which took us off in June, 1940 from Dunkirk.

Quite a lot of photographs of 1915–1917 also survived the burning. So did a water colour sketch of me done by Tom Butler Stoney (killed three months later) who was a clever amateur artist. It was entitled 'The War Lord, July 1st 1917'. Though I had become a very active and enthusiastic soldier in the previous twelve months, the title was a little 'offside'. I had had a splendid company, four good platoon commanders and a lot of excellent NCOs and was justly proud of them. It was a happy and successful company in all it undertook, in and out of the line. We never behaved in a tyrannical way, except perhaps in our dealings with the enemy. It was our job to hot them up and we always did our best to give as good as we got, with an occasional bonus now and then for good measure.

Other letters arrived from France that told of continuing foul weather. I knew well from experience the added load that such conditions brought in their train, and was distressed that there had been so little improvement, for it was August and still summer. Kipling records conditions thus: 'Rain falling without a break for the next four days drowned out the sad fight. At that stage our Armies, as had happened so often in the Somme, were immobilized. The clay ground was cullendered and punched by shells into chains of pools and ponds. All valleys and hollows turned into bogs, where, if men wandered from the regular tracks across them, they drowned or were mired to death. If they stayed on the planking the enemy's guns swept them away.' Lying comfortably in my bed, warm, dry, well fed, and cosseted, I felt sad and useless and thought constantly of those battling away who could enjoy none of these things.

Throughout August and September the battalion went in and out of the line as usual, accepting such casualties as came their way, for instance two of our companies were caught during relief, 1000 yards behind the front line, by an enemy barrage and lost twenty-seven men killed in half an hour. In October it took part in an attack on the 7th, again in foul weather, the advance floundering through deep mud but reaching its final objective. It had cost us dearly. Pat Ogilvy, Roda-kowski and Alfonse Wells (one of my splendid platoon commanders) were among the five officers and forty-seven other ranks killed, eight officers and 158 other ranks wounded and ten missing, doubtless drowned in the swamp of mud and water. Later Pat's mother, Lady Airlie, told me what had happened as related to her. Pat had established his company headquarters in a captured German pill box when a heavy shell struck it – all inside had perished in the blast. The loss of three such dear and gallant friends in one day was a horrible blow.

That year in France bad weather continued without respite. Eventually rain and the quite appalling conditions on the battlefield brought operations to a halt. Not before terrible casualties had been suffered, ghastly suffering endured, and unimaginable conditions overcome by our front line troops, as ever steadfast, brave and enduring.

In due course, my wound nearly healed, I was sent to a convales-cent hospital in Suffolk run by a friend of Lady Carnarvon's. It was a large and very pleasant place, and there were few restrictions. Before long I got myself before an Army Medical Board and was pronounced fit enough to return to duty with our reserve battalion.

I was promptly put in charge of young officers' training and given a free hand. This was fun, gave me plenty of scope, lots to do and I enjoyed it. Perhaps some of my pupils found the going hard, for no one was spared, their comfortable existence soon ended, yet there were no rebellions. I had all sorts to deal with, the indolent, the idle, the keen, even the adventurous. It was a grand job and had a sound practical purpose to it. This was to fit all these young officers – a few considerably older than I was – to command platoons in action, with luck to stay alive, and more important, help save the lives of their men. Oliver Baldwin was one of my trainees. I liked him because he amused me, was intelligent and unorthodox, facts which explained his unpopularity with our seniors, who failed to be impressed by unorthodoxy, especially in the young and inexperienced. All would soon find themselves in the front line. The more each knew about what lay in store and how to cope, the better for the men they were destined to lead. The class was put to hard physical work in digging trenches at night, and made to assault and defend them and to carry out patrols in darkness. Many pleasant evenings in London were forfeited, but in a good cause, for it was likely that quite a few lives would be saved. I impressed on them that heroics were 'out' except in the rarest circumstances. They were trained to lead their men in action and should be satisfied with that by no means simple duty. Any fool could die if he had a mind to, the Germans would be delighted to assist. Of what use was a dead officer to those he was supposed to lead, often at a time of great confusion when his leadership was all important? Most of them got the message.

The work of stimulating and training those put in my charge was important because it became ever more necessary to provide a constant flow of well trained junior officers to replace mounting casualties in our two battalions in France. The outlook at the end of 1917 was not a cheerful one, now that so many German divisions, released from Russia by its collapse in revolution, were pouring westward.

Chapter Six

1918: Last Lap

My job of training junior officers went forward steadily. Our commanding officer, Tom Vesey, of whom I was very fond, had been severely wounded in 1914, had gone out again but the physical conditions in the line proved too much for him. At Warley he was then in an aggressive mood. The 'officers call' was blown with great frequency when all would gather about him, some to be condemned for sins of omission or of commission, their iniquities laid bare and suitable warnings given; occasionally officers, nearly always the same ones, would be put under arrest. It often fell to my lot to find such offenders absent from the battalion and bring them in. Their offences were often trivial, the offenders mostly friends of mine. Soon the novelty of this unsought exercise wore off, for it was a great waste of my time.

The pleasanter things in life did not pass me by, time was found to attend agreeable parties in London and to make new friends. As it was most unlikely that I should long enjoy the comfort of life in England, but would soon return to the hazards of war, the CO let me loose whenever possible. Thus from late 1917, my wound healed, and again mobile, I was encouraged to accept weekend invitations to places within reach of London. Cliveden in Buckinghamshire for instance, where the Astors, kind and hospitable as ever, sought to make their guests welcome, whether humble or distinguished. I had not stayed there since the war began. Outwardly little seemed to have changed, though the pheasants may have vanished, for I did not see them. On a pre-war visit, Waldorf Astor had shown me his splendid collection of pheasants, Golden, Silver, Amherst, and other varieties.

At this time I paid my first visit to Hatfield, the splendid home in Hertfordshire of the Cecils since the days of Good Queen Bess.

Taken there by Mabell Ogilvy who was Lady Salisbury's niece, I was duly impressed. Who would not be by that superb Jacobean house with so much history attached to it?

I never met Lady Gwendolen Cecil, a memorable personality and a tremendous character 'whose habit of life was eccentric, irregular and unpredictable'. For example, before she had a car she drove about the countryside on charitable errands in her pony trap, her dog running behind. Her dog barked ceaselessly, to stop this Lady Gwendolen evolved a plan based on the concept now called the conditioned reflex. Knowing the dog to be frightened of gunfire, she argued that if every time it barked it heard a gunshot it would associate the two events and stop barking. The pony cart set forth, the dog barked, Lady Gwendolen fired a revolver. The pony ran away and the dog barked more than ever. 'Such episodes (claims her nephew) filled her day-to-day life with unexpected adventures and misadventures'. She was a source of constant entertainment to her family. Whilst she devoted herself to many public causes, 'her compassionate heart, easily inflamed, forgot all else in a desire to relieve suffering or to get wrong righted'.

On my twenty-first birthday I gave a dinner party at Claridges for thirty relatives, brother officers and friends. An air raid took place in celebration of the event – a rarity in that war; no one was upset or inconvenienced by it. When the party broke up at midnight, not a taxi was to be found, though finally everyone got home safely in over-loaded vehicles with odd guests sitting on the roofs.

On the 7th March a telegram arrived from the Lord Chamberlain requiring me to be at Buckingham Palace two days later to be presented by the King with the Military Cross I had been awarded a year earlier. The award had given pleasure to my parents, and I valued it because the recommendation had been made by Alex whose standard was of the highest. I had seen so many acts of real gallantry performed during my years in France, mostly unrecorded, that any sense of personal achievement was utterly out of place.

A fortnight later came the great German offensive in France, it had not been wholly unexpected, but its violence and initial success had not been anticipated or allowed for. It was to be the Germans' last effort to win the war, and they put all they had into it. The offensive began at dawn on the 21st March, our 1st Battalion was in the neighbourhood of Arras. Kipling records 'the evacuation of the town, during the next two days, was a nightmare of flying masonry, clouds of dust, the roar of falling brickwork, mobs of drifting civilians, their belongings pushed before or hauled after them, and no power to order them where to go'. This scene was to be repeated for me in 1940 at Tournai, where the shambles and lack of direction of the civilian population was even worse owing to a total breakdown of civilian morale, and to lively action by German dive bombers.

The German attacks, launched mainly against the British Fifth Army through dawn mist, swept forward apace. Foremost positions were over-run, and the German tide swept in from one to three miles deep and was racing onward. The following morning (22nd) was also foggy and the German infantry, no longer attacking in massed waves, infiltrated our lines unseen in relatively small numbers, and were quickly reinforced. It was a disastrous defeat, even the Channel ports were thought to be threatened. The Germans flooded forward, recapturing all the ground taken from them at appalling cost on the Somme and elsewhere. For those who had survived these past bloody encounters it was quite heartbreaking and I for one, could not believe it. Our 1st and 2nd Battalions, (the latter led by Alex), became heavily involved in plugging gaps, fighting like tigers with their comrades in the Guards Division to stabilize the situation. The fighting was desperate and losses severe. The 4th Guards Brigade, after fierce fighting on the Arras front, had been despatched to the flat country round Vierhouck, and there spent itself in the desperate fighting round La Couronne and Vieux-Berquive which gave time to bar the enemy's way to Hazebrouck but wiped out our 2nd Battalion. At last the German advance ran out of steam and was brought to a halt.

It was likely that I should soon rejoin my battalion in France, and in anticipation of this, my commanding officer packed me off to Ireland to see something of my parents. A telegram found me at Marble Hill; 'Please report Regimental Headquarters Irish Guards Buckingham Gate at 10.30 a.m. Thursday 18th inst. to join BEF train leaves Waterloo station 11.35 acknowledge prompt'. It was a brief compelling summons and the 18th April saw me on my way. On my last evening at home Mabell Ogilvy and her mother Lady Airlie dined with me at Claridges and we went on to see J. M. Barrie's play *Mary Rose*. It was a very happy evening unspoilt by premonition of tragedy so soon to overwhelm, in varying degree, all three of us. I was to join Alex commanding our 2nd Battalion and looked forward to serving him again, for none commanded greater respect or inspired greater confidence than he.

Billeted in farms round Hondeghem, north of Hazebrouck, we strengthened the defence systems in that area, and were fully prepared to deal with the Germans should they appear. They did not, but we were subjected to a certain amount of shelling and Charles Moore was one casualty, hit by shrapnel. The battle for the line of the Lys had by 20th April come to a standstill with the enemy held in check, well pounded by our artillery. We thought that the Germans in the south might be preparing fresh assaults, so our brigade was despatched to Barly with orders to move into the GHQ line and hold it against attack. A lot of time had of necessity to be given to the training of young NCOs to replace recent casualties, for there were still battles to be fought; we did miss those grand experienced NCOs lost at Loos, the Somme, at Messines and in the years of trench warfare, whose example and help in the training of newcomers would have been invaluable.

In mid July it was decided that the supply of NCOs and men was now insufficient to keep two battalions up to strength and replace whatever battle casualties might still be suffered. So it was decreed that our very depleted battalion should with other elements of our brigade be turned into a training unit for newly commissioned officers before they joined their units. With this object we moved to Criel-Plage, near Dieppe, where we set up camp. We did not know or even suspect that it was to be the end of the war for many of us. Indeed we were still at Criel when the war came to an end and the armistice was signed. Meanwhile, we trained vigorously for offensive action with good and varied ground at our disposal and attacked each other and anything in sight. My enthusiasm for patrol work revived and my company was practised in it at night, as in much else. We all became very fit as a result of these antics, and won the brigade sports comfortably, indeed every single event, despite our depleted strength, Alex, Brookes and I contributing to that happy result. The Guards Division had again been in battle in the great attacks that were now rolling the Germans back, and means had to be found to make good the losses arising from these actions, so the whole of the 4th Guards Brigade was drawn upon to make good the wastage. It produced a draft of 600 men that claimed to be one of the finest that had ever been furnished, 'trained to the last ounce, and taught to the limits of teaching'.

Somewhere I thought I had heard of chasing partridges on horseback. As there were a lot about, I had a polo stick made, mounted my charger Cork which had been one of Charles Moore's hunters, and set out to see what might be accomplished. I soon put up a covey, and away they went straight as a die with Cork in hot pursuit and into them in no time. Off they flew again, the pursuit continuing, they lit down in tall grasses and this time would not get up but ran about and were difficult to see or hit whilst on horseback and I failed to score. It was essential that the pursuit be rapid, full tilt over any obstacles, so as to give the birds as little time as possible to recover. It was great fun, but exhausting for man, horse and birds. A brother officer to whom I had remarked that Cork was superb, went like a rocket, and never moved away when I had dismounted to pick up a bird, drew a grossly libellous sketch showing me in action, poor Cork dejected, head down, tongue out, knees bent through fatigue. I only succeeded in getting one other officer to accompany me on these forays, this was Barry Close, soon to be transferred to our 1st Battalion and killed in action at the end of September. He had only one chance to come out with me, and it ended in something of a disaster, but with shouts of laughter. We flushed a covey and were in hot pursuit when Barry came a cropper, his girths had not been properly tightened so his saddle ended up under his mount's belly leaving Barry sprawled on the ground.

One of our company commanders had behaved unwisely, so much so that Alex decided to deprive him of his temporary rank and command. I was ordered to take him on and though reluctant I agreed, indeed I had no option. I had always liked this unhappy creature who though erratic was intelligent and amusing. Now he was very depressed, embarrassingly contrite and wholly co-operative.

This was by no means the first time I had been cast in the quadruple roles of Nanny, Father-Confessor, Councillor and Guide. Indeed I had at various times been ordered to care for lame ducks. They were nearly all eccentrics, bashful soldiers too intelligent to find any joy in battle, and though I liked them they caused me anxious moments in my efforts to steer them safely through the troubles that at times beset us. Happily whilst in my care all survived, and one or two gave useful service later in the more relaxed, elegant and less exacting field of diplomacy. Earlier in the war I had twice protested unavailingly to my commanding officer who had posted elderly subalterns to my company who must have been all of thirty years of age. At twenty I pointed out that one was old enough to be my father, the other my grandfather. No notice was paid to my protests, and both survived with me, but were sadly killed later.

On the 14th October our little world at Criel was shattered by the news that Alex was to take over command of the 10th Army School, and four days later he left us. The finest commanding officer imaginable, in action and out of it, he was deeply missed by the men and by the officers of the battalion.

My own private world was shattered just before the war's end when I was given the heartbreaking news of Mabell Ogilvy's sudden death in London following an operation. Never one to spare herself, her resistance had been weakened by her sustained and gross overwork on behalf of the British Red Cross. A fall from an Army Remount horse that she was exercising resulted in damage that had called for surgical treatment. Thus ended tragically a precious life of charm, great promise and of unselfish labour for others. A brave and charming letter came from her mother Lady Airlie that brought some consolation, but a desperate sense of loss remained, which for me was overwhelming. Though I had known her for little more than a year I had found her enchanting, a little mysterious, almost fey, and irresistibly attractive. She was very much in the world, yet somehow not of it, a vital, lovely, generous personality, wise beyond her years. I was desperately unhappy for a long time and moved by a sense of personal loss wrote a brief memorial poem, my first and last; short, simple, direct and written from the heart, it said all there was to be said. As to why such tragedies occur, we may never understand, perhaps we are not meant to, and must be content to echo the Crusader's cry – Deus Vult – God wills it. There is no other explanation, but it is a hard one to accept, harder still to understand when the young, lovely and innocent are snatched from us.

The war ended on 11th November whilst we were at Criel, and no one could quite believe it. Whatever may have gone on in London and in Paris that day, there was little rejoicing on our part. I remember, when news of the armistice came through, standing at the entrance of our mess tent in a mood far removed from rejoicing, remembering only too vividly the lost ones whose sacrifices now seemed in vain, and whose absence in the years ahead would be sorely missed in ruined homes and in the country at large. As in all wars in which the British engage, the bravest and the best were always sacrificed from the outset, and the war just ended was no exception. We were to pay most bitterly for this terrible waste for decades, are still paying and will do so for generations.

Three days after the armistice the battalion and the rest of the 4th Guards Brigade rolled stately out of Criel, clean, polished and splendid to behold. Our train wandered round northern France, halting for hours in a battered world just realizing that the weight of the past four years had lifted. At one place we found that the 4th Grenadiers who had got ahead of us were held up because the rail in front was reported mined. We suggested politely that they might hurry on to test the truth of the rumour, but they declined. It proved no more than a rumour, and we all reached a ruined Cambrai within forty-eight hours, and on to Maubeuge where we joined up once more with the Guards Division. Thence we marched with the 2nd Guards Brigade to Vieux Reny through a welcoming countryside. On the 20th November we reached Charleroi where we were met by the town band, all in bowler hats, and where we stayed for three days mobbed by the deliriously excited inhabitants. We took the opportunity to carry out some drill, which excited them even more.

On the 24th November we moved to Presles where we had comfortable billets, officers being housed in the chateau. It was extraordinary to be in a building with doors and windows and an intact roof. I alone had a 12 bore shotgun and a modest supply of cartridges, and with one or two others scoured the woods about the chateau picking up some pheasants for the pot. As our march continued and opportunities arose, a few of us went in search of game. One day a boar shoot was laid on by our brigade, and many including the brigade commander turned up for it armed with service rifles. Beaters were ordered to drive the boars towards us and a splendidly be-whiskered *garde de chasse* was dug out to show us where to stand and to advise on how the beat should be conducted. This done, he was placed in line on the extreme left. Following a great deal of shouting from the beaters out came a very large, fierce looking boar, contemptuously he trotted slowly along our line. Everyone had a shot and everyone missed, except the ancient keeper from whose stand came a loud explosion. He had let off his blunderbuss charged with shot, nails and whatever, and floored the boar, wiping all our eyes. He had been hunting this particular beast for years, he told us, and described his victim as 'le gros solitaire'. We had other boar hunts, some not well organized, since everyone went about with loaded rifles and was quite ready to let them off. On one such occasion, bored by a long wait, I led our medical officer into the woods and ran into a small herd of wild pig which rushed past us in the direction of the guns. Realizing what was likely to happen, and quickly, I made the MO lie behind a fallen tree – only just in time, for there followed a fusilade of shots in our direction.

Our long marches through the country of the Ardennes were rather trying and billeting was a problem in the sordid little hamlets and poor farmsteads at which we halted each night. At one I and others shared the concrete floor of a byre with a number of ill-kempt cows. As we progressed towards the German frontier the inhabitants appeared less welcoming. Perhaps they had down the years come to terms with the Germans, and did not relish the need to adjust to the whims of newcomers.

On the 22nd December we crossed into Germany at Port Brucken, and days later, our march at an end, we entrained for Cologne. Arrived at the outskirts of the city, the battalion was quartered in Pioneer Barracks fitted with electric light, drying rooms and baths. The occupation had begun, and from its beginning men noticed how keenly curious the inhabitants were to discover what we had in our minds. It seemed that we, the victors, were in the dock; the vanquished our inquisitors, cautious, cunning, arrogant, treacherous, biding their time.

My officers and those of another company were given quarters in a modest house. It was unattractive, dingy and rather noisy with traffic passing on the road outside. My dissatisfaction led me to seek other accommodation, suddenly I had a brain wave, what about the zoo? The tall railings that encircled it faced me and it was shut to the public, it was Verboten to enter and many notices said so. That arrogant word encouraged me to break in. With the assistance of my soldier servant I did so and advanced upon the curator's comfortable home, who with his wife greeted me with astonishment. I said that I wished to billet myself in their house and this was agreed to. I was shown to a large bedroom and a sitting room, the windows overlooking green lawns with flamingoes strutting about on them. I demanded keys to the nearest gate, they were handed over without question. One key was for my personal use, I said, the other for troops whose duty it was to guard me, who could be expected to appear at any moment, by day or night. I daresay my hosts were happy to oblige me, for in their eyes I must have seemed a good insurance against molestation. I was delighted with my find, kept it secret, and established myself in a comfortable house where peace was absolute, and there remained until I left Cologne to take up other duties. As days passed my hosts became kinder and more solicitous, I increasingly ashamed of my mistrust of their race. But had not Froissart written centuries before 'never trust a German knight'? Had not Edmund Spenser advised caution in dealings with strangers:

> Trust not the treason of those smiling looks
> Until ye have their guileful brains well tried
> For they are like unto the golden hooks
> That from the foolish fish
> Their baits do hide.

I was unprepared to act 'the foolish fish' or to rise to the golden hooks of kindness and solicitude, so I courteously rejected their advances; but when I left we parted friends.

On Christmas Day I thought it would be an interesting experience to attend the big service in Cologne Cathedral, and was not disappointed. The Cathedral was packed and I was given a rather special seat, I don't know why. The service was impressive, the congregation vast and devout, many British service men attended, a lot of Germans still in uniform, and a great mass of civilians, the women in black, mourning their dead. It was the first peaceful Christmas after four traumatic years of war in which a whole continent had been ravished and millions killed in battle. To what purpose? You might well ask. Here we were, representatives of many nationalities, joined together for a little time in thanksgiving to God for the advent of peace, celebrating and commemorating the birthday of the Prince of Peace and of love, who through our ignorance, greed and arrogance we had so shamefully and wantonly betrayed. Well might we seek His grace and forgiveness, seek His help in the mending of our ways.

Chapter Seven

Unaccustomed Peace

A few days after our arrival in Cologne as part of the army of occupation, I was offered a staff appointment as ADC to General Godley, commanding XXII Corps. The war was over, the occupation might well go on for years and the battalion remain in Germany for a long time – not an alluring prospect. A staff appointment offered the chance of an earlier return to England and a more interesting life than groping about in a then rather grubby German city, its people hostile and resentful. I reminded myself that I was not joining the 'gilded staff', which we had so abused, until after the last shot of a ghastly war had been fired.

Any account of the 1914–18 war would be incomplete without mention of the unreasoning gulf that existed between the front line soldier and the staff. Throughout the war front line soldiers had a mild, some a vigorous, contempt for staff officers of all grades. It was unreasonable and quite unfair but understandable. They had beds to lie on, dry boots and clothes to wear, and lived comfortable lives far removed from reality, from the danger, discomfort and real hardships of the fighting troops. They were regarded as parasites, if as nothing worse. When things went wrong through faulty orders, or the failure of essential supplies to arrive resulted in casualties – all was blamed on a breakdown at staff level. These charges were sometimes justified, but more often not.

I accepted the appointment and on New Year's Day of 1919 was on my way to take it up. I had had a farewell dinner with the battalion, and then rode down to the station on my faithful charger, Cork. It was sad to think that it might be the last time I should ride him, for he had always carried me well, and I hoped we had enjoyed each other's company. In parting, I gave him a lot of sugar lumps and other titbits.

I spent five months as General Godley's ADC, first at Mons and then at Düren. I had an assistant, George Eltham, a subaltern in the

Life Guards, who was great fun though not the most efficient of staff officers. He was the eldest son of the Marquis of Cambridge, and hence a cousin of the Prince of Wales, who used to come to our headquarters quite often to see him. HRH had a knack of picking days when the general was away to make his visits, driving himself in his Rolls; perhaps he found the general rather daunting – certainly in his absence we had some merry lunch parties.

I was plunged almost at once into making the arrangements for a ball at the Concert Noble in Brussels. It was a glittering affair. The flowers were superb, all brought from Paris – banks of roses everywhere and masses of other flowers arranged with great skill and taste. I collected my general to dine with Countess Van den Steen, a plump amusing little woman who gave us an exquisite meal, and later took him to the Concert Noble, then went to collect special guests, among them the Marquise Imperiali who with her husband and my general received the guests. George and I stood by patiently as people streamed past, it was all too much for my companion who in low tones treated me to a pretty unflattering running commentary on those being received. At last we were let off the leash and found attractive companions with whom we danced the night away. We had three bands, that of the 1st Life Guards, a large American jazz band and another for dancing. Supper arrangements were admirable, the food scrumptious, and a torch-light procession brought the evening to a close about four o'clock. We had entertained seven hundred people and the ball had been a great success. Unlike the Duchess of Richmond's ball on the eve of Waterloo, to which it was compared, ours took place after the fighting was over.

The following day was my twenty-second birthday, and my general suggested that I should breakfast with him about ten o'clock, before returning to Mons. George was ordered to rendezvous with our second car. Time to go – no George. After half an hour's wait for his missing ADC our master started to fume; though I made a lot of excuses for the missing link, the general accepted none of them, but insisted on going in person to George's hotel. I was sent upstairs to rout him out and found him still fast asleep. I told him that George had never been called, an unlikely tale, but could not help laughing, for the sight of George's guilty sleepy face rose vividly before me. The general was very angry indeed, abandoned the sleeping one, and drove back to Mons in gloomy silence. George returned about three and emerged as usual quite unmoved from the general's room following a lively dressing down. My companion had a disconcerting habit of taking flight whenever the general's bell rang in the ADCs' room, leaving me to beard our master, while he found it necessary to make a dash for the loo and lock himself in. It was a harmless ploy, this bogus indisposition, and amused me for a time. There was no difficulty in finding work for him when he returned to his desk.

General Godley was very hospitable, and at his headquarters I met many interesting people. I remember in particular, when we were at Mons, several occasions when the Prince and Princesse du Cröy – his sister – were our guests. She had been an active worker for the allies in occupied Belgium, and recounted her experiences in working for refugees and fugitives, and the system for passing on information gleaned by Belgians spying for us behind the enemy lines. Much of this dangerous work was carried out by women who were marvellously courageous. The Princesse herself had fed and sheltered and then passed on to Nurse Cavell in Brussels many of our men who had been wounded or cut off in and about the Forêt de Mormal in the first months of the war. When Nurse Cavell was seized by the Germans, the Princesse's links with that martyred woman were uncovered. She was herself arrested and sentenced to three and a half years' solitary confinement, so she had spent the rest of the war imprisoned in Germany.

My general had to undertake a great deal of travelling in the course of visiting his formations and allied troops: I had to organize these trips and accompany him on them.

Two were of special interest, to Verdun and to the US Army. The latter had been arranged by General Pershing who himself welcomed us. The staff system and the organization of ports and bases was explained, and we saw the very effective methods employed for training troops in battle conditions. Our visit included a battlefield tour of the American sector, in particular the St Mihiel Salient, the scene of ferocious fighting in the spring of 1918. At Verdun a French officer who had been in action there gave us a fascinating account of that grim battle; he led us through miles of underground tunnelling to the summit of Fort de Souville, a mass of tangled wire and craters, which overlooked Verdun battlefield and the neighbouring forts of Tavanne, Douaumont and St Michel.

In marked contrast were several visits to Paris, where peace-making was in full swing. At lunches or at parties one saw plenty of the delegates – the Prime Minister with Mrs Lloyd George and Megan; Mr Massey, the New Zealand premier; Bonar Law; Austen Chamberlain, regarded as a sober-sides but dancing furiously; Orpen, busy painting the nabobs like Clemenceau; and many others that I knew. At one dance I was delighted when Alex suddenly appeared, passing through Paris on his way to Poland; I would have tried to go with him had I been free to do so.

In contrast to all this festivity was a long, slow train journey from Mons to Paris through what was probably the most devastated area of France. We passed through La Bassée, totally destroyed, and then along the La Bassée Canal, with Cuinchy and Givenchy on our right, bringing back memories of my first days in the trenches four years earlier. The old road we used for reliefs from St Preol, and tracks through the marshes, were still clearly visible. All buildings along the canal had of course been smashed flat, and all bridges destroyed; large parties of German prisoners of war were at work on the banks. Béthune was just as badly burnt out and smashed up.

I had been too clever by half in thinking that a staff job would get me back to England quicker than regimental soldiering, for in March the battalion went home from Cologne, while I was still in France. I had had a leave, of course, soon after I was appointed, primarily to dump my combat kit and collect new uniform. I spent two days in Hampshire with Stephen Christy's parents, and made a hurried trip to Ireland to see my own; in London I saw Lady Airlie who felt the loss of Mabell keenly, as did I. The death of dear friends was uppermost in one's mind then, coupled with surprise at one's own survival. That, no doubt, was a factor in the mind of some troops at Dover and Folkestone, clamouring for immediate demobilization and creating a lot of trouble; it was taken very seriously by the authorities who were well aware of the difficulty of maintaining discipline in a largely civilian army.

In March General Godley moved to IV Corps Headquarters at Düren, between Aachen and Cologne, his ADC in tow. My French had proved adequate in the preceding few months, but my German was certainly not up to dealing with a German housekeeper, or engaging a local cook. Though the shops appeared to be full, all food had to be left for the local population, and orders were very strict about this. Very proper, but I could not see victorious Germans behaving thus. In April we received a secret order giving warning of a reported plan, alleged to have been concocted in unoccupied Germany, to kill, one night, all French and British officers in the occupied area. I thought it highly unlikely that anything of the sort – if true – would be attempted, for the retribution would have been savage on the part of the French. Unlike us, they were realists, hated the Germans like poison and might well have relished the excuse such an outrage would have provided to kill off a lot more of them.

In fact, almost the converse occurred on May Day, when there were noisy meetings in the streets, with no interference from us: a number of Germans strongly disapproved, saying that such behaviour would never have been tolerated by their own authorities. One day I drove to Cologne and called on the curator of the zoo in whose house I had installed myself after our march into Germany, and had a warm welcome from him and his wife. All the animals I had got to know were still going strong, though feeding them must have been a problem.

I had been angling to get back to the battalion, so I was delighted when my general had a letter from regimental headquarters asking him to let me return. My replacement was Bruce Ogilvy, a son of Lady Airlie; I inducted him, said farewell to General Godley and spent a month's leave in Donegal before returning to duty on 1st July.

Duty was not very onerous, since it was straightforward and not exacting; mounting guard at Buckingham Palace and St James's took up much of my time, for that duty was shared with only one other, and was linked with the officers' leave roster – a very important document to us. One or two captains would carry out all guard duties while our companions were on leave. On their return off we would go – subject of course to leave being cancelled at a moment's notice in an emergency, and to instant recall if anything went amiss in one's company. It was a golden age of shoots, parties, dinners and balls for any young unattached officer in the Brigade, and most of us enjoyed it thoroughly.

We wore blinkers against the changes in the world around us. We were young, the war had been won, we had survived it, and that was enough. But not quite, for there was a deep hurt, and secret moments when the memory of fallen comrades closed in and brought me to the edge of tears, and sometimes beyond.

While I was enjoying this elegant, frivolous life, the rightness of which in thoughtful moments I questioned, I was aware of a general swell of discontent. Hordes of men had been demobilized and released from the services, many scandalously treated, with prospects of finding work a mirage. Large-scale resettlement was a fearful problem, but it was not being tackled vigorously enough. No doubt every one was weary, but so with greater reason were the men returning to 'the land fit for heroes to live in' which politicians had promised them; many felt cheated and betrayed. There was nothing new in this shameless treatment of combatants once their essential usefulness was over, it had been so for centuries after every war, but this time it was on a gigantic scale.

There were strikes, in one of which I was bottled up with my company in Billingsgate goods station with a mass of rotting fish to be guarded against possible looting! We had been ordered to 'show a low profile' as modern jargon has it – a useful let-out for politicians enabling them to have it both ways, and to find a scapegoat if things go wrong. All soldiers detest duty 'in aid of the civil power'. Orders are always of the vaguest, perhaps deliberately, leaving ample room for misunderstandings.

The New Year of 1920 found me in Ireland taking long walks every day in pursuit of snipe and woodcock in wintry weather. In February I had another few days' leave there, and found the country in a very disturbed state; shooting was prohibited, and there were frequent arms raids on police barracks and private houses – though there was no trouble at Marble Hill. The news continued to be discouraging, with the declaration in Ireland of a general strike, and hunger strikers locked up without trial in Mountjoy prison, while the government vacillated between threats and surrender to disorder. There was an international crisis too when the French marched into Germany, seizing several towns including Frankfurt. They were infuriated by Britain and America, which brought pressure to bear on them to withdraw, but loud in praise of the Belgians who sent troops to their support.

I had a busy March that year, for I was sent on a long course at the Machine Gun School. We had been late, as usual, in recognizing the value of the machine gun which the Germans had used with such devastating effect against us – it probably caused more allied casualties than all the other weapons, singly or in combination, in the German armoury. Belatedly we had formed a Machine Gun Corps which, highly trained in the proper handling of that weapon, had served with distinction in the last two years of the war. As a respite from machine gunnery, I led our regimental team in the Army Cross-Country Championships. I was very stiff and tired on parade next day, St Patrick's Day, for the presentation of shamrock by Queen Alexandra, 'so frail and so charming that I should have liked to embrace her, lèse majesté notwithstanding', my diary recalls.

My father suggested that I give serious thought to my career, whether to make it in the Army or in diplomacy which he thought might be more stimulating and rewarding. I dutifully thought about it, but I was happy with my lot and took no action. I do now much regret my failure to take advantage of a plan whereby I might have gone to Oxford on secondment from the Army. Had my uncle, Colonel Stuart, survived the war, he would have advised me to abandon frivolity in search of reality, fresh experience and achievement, perhaps in Africa or India. I was unambitious and continued to enjoy the good life. That included shooting parties in Yorkshire and in different parts of Scotland, a high point of the latter being my first visit to Airlie. Lady Airlie was always a delight to be with, ever kind, thoughtful and stimulating.

In 1921 the battalion moved to Aldershot, where Alex joined us as a major, and second-in-command, after a well deserved long leave at the conclusion of his Latvian campaign. He had commanded a considerable mixed force of Germans and Letts fighting to keep the Bolshevik army out of the Baltic provinces, in bitter weather, poorly supplied and ill-supported. They had suffered and inflicted many casualties, Alex himself being wounded. His charm and energy and resourceful leadership had welded men of differing loyalties into a reliable fighting force, and in the process he had won the admiration and affection of Germans and Letts alike. This was borne out by one of his 'Baltic barons', the German landowners who had been Russian subjects in Latvia. As quoted in Nigel Nicolson's *Alex*, he told the *New York Times* correspondent in Riga 'We wanted to march on Riga, and perhaps we ought to have done it in our own interests, because those damned Letts had seized our estates and it was not likely that the British or the French would do much for us to get them back, as the Germans would have done. But in that case we should have had to knock Alexander on the head, and we liked him far too much, so we stayed quiet in our trenches. . . .'

At Aldershot, one damp evening, Alex asked me to come for a walk, during which we surveyed rows of mist-enshrouded dustbins spaced at precise intervals along barrack walls. He said how depressing and soul-destroying he found the scene, and wondered how he could face an endless period of inactive peacetime soldiering. The Army was very near to losing one of its outstanding commanders. A year later, commanding us in active service conditions, he was in his element.

Another friend who was to rise to high rank was 'Boy' Browning, later commander of our airborne forces at Arnhem. 'Boy' hailed me one day as I walked through the Grenadier camp, said he had made up his mind to become a hurdler, and would I watch him jump? I did and was impressed. Would my battalion allow our athletics trainer to coach him? I saw no reason why not, and soon arranged it. This determined officer was to become with a brother officer, Lord Burleigh, one of the country's foremost athletes. For sheer determination to succeed in whatever he chose to do I had never met his equal.

Our civilian athletics coach, Harry Andrews, was very experienced, enthusiastic and successful, for our battalion won the brigade sports year after year. He often told stories against himself, some true, some fictional. One was how in his early days as a coach he had fallen for a pretty girl about to compete in a bicycle race. The pretty one was hopeless and had no chance of winning, but her looks persuaded him that something must be done; under cover of night he visited the bicycle store and loosened the chains on all bicycles bar one. The race started. To everyone's astonishment the hopeless one, riding at her normal speed, won comfortably, while her bewildered adversaries pedalled like mad to little effect. He claimed no reward for this misdeed, for such pranks gave him satisfaction. Though a civilian and a most unmilitary character we later took him to Turkey, disguised him as a sergeant (unpaid by the Army), for so dressed he could enjoy the hospitality of the sergeants' mess.

On St Patrick's Day, 1921, the battalion paraded at Aldershot for the first time since the war in full dress. It was a colourful sight, tailors had spent weeks fitting everyone out, the NCOs instructing their men in the cleaning, fitting and wearing of equipment – white belts, pouches and shoulder straps. Many came from London to admire us and feasted in our officers' mess.

In June Field Marshal Lord Plumer asked me to become his ADC; he was then Governor and Commander-in-Chief in Malta, and thought I could help in organizing the ceremonies connected with the forthcoming grant of self-government to the island, when the Prince of Wales was to represent the King. I had met the field marshal in Germany and had a great respect for him as a commander with an active interest in the welfare of his troops, and so I was very pleased to accept, and took up my duties in September.

Apart from an ADC's normal work, and the very enjoyable social life in that fascinating island, I was kept busy by a succession of visits by VIPs for the celebrations, culminating in the Prince's arrival in HMS *Renown* – he was on his way to India. Fortunately everything went without a hitch, and the two houses of the new legislature got down to business.

At that time the Mediterranean Fleet, based on Malta, was a very powerful force, and made an immensely impressive sight, whether in the Grand Harbour or engaged in fleet exercises. The Army presence was relatively small, and accordingly I made many friends in the senior service; at one point I was spending almost as much time afloat as on shore. This was all good fun, but it wasn't soldiering; and when I heard a rumour that my battalion was being sent abroad with Alex in command, I asked Lord Plumer if I might apply to return to the regiment. He was very kind and understanding.

I left Malta in March 1922, but not before my sister Mary had arrived on a visit; she looked very pretty and created quite a sensation. The journey home was via Rome, where I spent a splendid few days, and Paris, where I stayed for longer than I had planned. It was such a lovely day that when my train was about to leave the Gare du Nord, on an impulse I flung my baggage on the platform and jumped after it. I spent a happy day wandering around the city and took a brisk walk in the Bois, where ahead of me I saw a strange figure in an Irish saffron kilt. This intrigued me and I soon overtook the man, it turned out to be Lord Ashbourne, a friend of my father's who having married a Frenchwoman was now living in Paris. He was agreeably eccentric, according to my father he made a point of speaking Irish in France and French in England and Ireland. His father (first Lord Ashbourne) had succeeded my grandfather as Lord Chancellor of Ireland in 1883.

In London by the 20th and to Ireland to see my parents, only just in time, for all leave to Ireland was soon stopped. Early in April I rejoined the 1st Battalion at Windsor, and three weeks later was on my way to Turkey.

Chapter Eight

Constantinople

On 22nd April 1922, the King accompanied by the Duke of York drove from London to inspect us at Windsor, to wish us God speed. This was his thoughtful practice when units of his household troops were dispatched to battle or to service overseas. His visit was followed by one from Field Marshal Lord French, now colonel of the regiment, then the battalion embarked from Southampton on the SS *Derbyshire*, a ghastly tub that was to be our unwelcome home for a fortnight. We were below strength – some 600 in number – but buoyant in spirit, and a youthful, happy lot, curiously free of home ties, for married officers had been left behind. Alex had just been promoted to command, so with a young commanding officer, loved, trusted and admired, we left England in a confident spirit. Hugo Gough was our second in command, Sidney Fitzgerald adjutant, I commanding a company. Our destination was Constantinople.

A dangerous and tricky situation had developed in the Near East between Greece, Turkey and the Allied Powers. During the war, King Constantine of Greece had dismissed his pro-allied prime minister, Venizelos, and sided with the Central Powers. Venizelos formed a rival government in Salonika with allied support, forced the abdication of the king and declared war. By the time Turkey surrendered in October 1918 and an allied occupation force was established in Constantinople under British command, Greek troops had recovered most of European Turkey and in 1919 seized Smyrna on the coast of Asia Minor, a city with a population of a million, half of whom were Greek. The peace treaty of Sèvres between the allies and Turkey confirmed Greece's possession of these areas and of Gallipoli, and put the Dardanelles under international control. It was accepted by the Sultan but repudiated by a new Turkish national assembly at Ankara, headed by Mustapha Kemal.

Meanwhile the Greeks in a plebiscite rejected Venizelos and

recalled King Constantine, thus forfeiting allied support, and launched their army from Smyrna against the Turks in Anatolia. At first
all went well, and in June 1921 the king went to Smyrna in readiness
for a triumphant entry into Ankara. In August the Greek army was
decisively counter-attacked by Mustapha Kemal, and the long retreat
began. Their lines of communication, through country they had
ravaged in their initial advance, were constantly threatened; to feed
the army was almost impossible, to supply it with munitions was
utterly so. However, the Greek army was able to halt and hold a line
about 150 miles from Ankara, but with no prospect of resuming the
advance. The victorious Turks were in no mood to accept the terms
of the Treaty of Sèvres. A confrontation was inevitable between the
allies (in effect the British) and the Turks, both at the Dardanelles
and in Constantinople. To add to the dangers, the allies were
undecided in their attitude to Greece.

The *Derbyshire* bucketed through bad weather to take us to this
complicated situation. Our men were sleeping in hammocks, the
food was revolting, but they endured the discomfort with stoical good
humour. I was reminded, as so often in war, of the statement
attributed to Napoleon that, given British troops and French officers,
he could conquer the world. The staunchness of the British soldier is
superb, at his best when things are at their worst. Such men deserve
inspired leadership, and in Alex they had it.

Passing Gibraltar and entering the Mediterranean, spirits revived,
cheered by the re-appearance of the sun, calm seas and schools of
porpoises. We docked at Alexandria, and I lost no time in visiting
Cairo with three companions; we stayed at Shepheards, and like all
good 'sahibs' of those days dined tidily in dinner jackets and later
joined a gay party in festive mood. Early next day we raced our camels
round the Pyramids, climbed to the top of one, set out for Memphis,
visited the Cairo Museum, the Citadel and two mosques before
returning late to Alexandria. On the following day the Royal Munster
Fusiliers passed through on their way home for disbandment. The
disappearance of those splendid Irish regiments that had given long
and distinguished service in all parts of the world in many hard-
fought campaigns was sad, but politically inevitable.

To relieve the tedium of the *Derbyshire*, a bathing party was
organized. It set out, with Alex as coxswain, in a ship's boat rowed by
guardsmen, oarsmanship not of a high order. The ship's company of

HMS *Caradoc*, lying nearby, lined the rail to cheer our erratic progress.

After leaving Alexandria and entering the Dardanelles off Cape Helles, we passed the ill-fated 'Lancashire landing' and saw two ships, a merchantman and a French light cruiser, sunk but in part still visible above water. Anchored off Chanak, on the Asiatic shore of the Straits, for medical clearance, we noticed forts on both sides greatly damaged by our naval bombardments, broken off too soon because of faulty or non-existent information, a fact which was later confirmed to me. Constantinople came in view at 5.30 on 12th May and we berthed alongside the quay, hard by Galata Bridge spanning the Golden Horn.

The Commander-in-Chief, Allied Forces, General 'Tim' Harington – whom I had known for some years – came aboard to welcome us. Disembarked, we marched through Constantinople with fixed bayonets, Alex and the colours at our head, my company in the lead. A mass of people thronged the streets in silence, their curiosity aroused.

Tash Kishla barracks stood high on the outskirts of the city overlooking the Bosphorus. The barrack rooms were very large with many windows. Sanitary arrangements left much to be desired, but were soon improved. Officers slept in Nissen huts – like ovens in the summer, refrigerators in winter. The officers' mess had a long verandah overlooking the Bosphorus. We enjoyed quite a splendid view of that waterway, of Scutari – shades of Florence Nightingale – and of the Asiatic shore beyond with the scrub-covered hills of Asia Minor as a background. The outlook was superb at night, with fire-flies gleaming in the darkness and a stage moon reflected in the waters below us. There were several warships there including two French battleships, one of these with six funnels the troops promptly named 'the packet of Woodbines'.

We were warned of the risk of drinking a fierce local absinthe, for it had a treacherous delayed action, our men called it 'Doosico'. One morning a number of them who had returned to barracks the night before 'clean and properly dressed' were found to be drunk after drinking their breakfast tea. They were dealt with, but not too harshly, for they had by demonstration done everyone a service.

Our transport had been augmented by some fifty Kalmucks, little men of Mongolian appearance from the Russian steppes, who got on famously with the much larger Irishmen despite language problems. They were in the charge of Col Paul Rodzianko, late Colonel in the Imperial Guards Cavalry and a distinguished horseman, now an unofficial sergeant in the Irish Guards. He fed in the officers' mess, for we all admired him and enjoyed his company.

I joined a very small select party to visit the Seraglio, the ancient palace of the sultans beyond the Golden Horn. It was a fascinating place renowned for its antiquity and bloody history. The Seraglio had been the scene of the massacre of the Janissaries, soldiers of the old Turkish foot-guards, formed originally of renegade prisoners and from tributes of Christian children. They bridged the centuries from 1330 to 1826, but when they were thought to have become too powerful and their loyalty suspect, their elimination was sudden, brutal and treacherous. A swift current sweeps round the Seraglio point on which the palace stands, for the waters of the Black Sea pour down the comparatively narrow defile of the Bosphorus westwards into the Sea of Marmora. So simple and convenient a way of disposing of unpopular politicians, unlucky generals, and others who fell foul of authority could not be neglected. Nor was it, so many, innocent and guilty alike, doubtless of both sexes, found their way into weighted sacks, thrown into the sea off the Seraglio point to be carried swiftly and silently into the depths of the Marmora. It was most unusual for us to have been allowed into the Seraglio at any time, especially during a religious feast. The sultan's personal approval had to be obtained, and it was one of his ministers who showed us round.

I asked him about our failure to force 'The Narrows'. He told me that had we continued to bombard these forts for one more day, the fleet – accepting a risk from unswept mines – could have got into the Sea of Marmora since the Turkish forts had exhausted their ammunition. In Malta some months earlier I had heard about these operations from Sir John de Robeck himself who as naval Commander-in-Chief had been given the task of forcing his way through to Constantinople in order to drive Turkey out of the war. Had naval action succeeded, the thousands of lives lost on Gallipoli would have been saved. The Admiralty dared not risk further loss of capital ships, and intelligence had failed to uncover this Turkish weakness.

Later Alex and I were shown round the Dolma-Bagche Palace by the Grand Vizier and his son, both cultivated and very charming. Like the Seraglio, it was filled with wonderful and priceless things mingled with rubbish. On the 24th May Alex and a number of us witnessed the service in the great mosque of St Sophia on 'the Night of Power'. Taken to the topmost gallery just below the vast dome, we could look from a great height on to the multitude of kneeling figures – they were said to number close on seven thousand. The weird cry of the imam reciting the Koran, the enormous size of the building, the great height, the lights below us, the heat, the smell, the lines of swaying heads and bodies as everyone in this mass touched the floor with his forehead, are unforgettable. Greatly impressed, we left at midnight and were able to scramble about on the great roof of St Sophia. Within a year the Turks had clamped down on all such visits and the sultan himself had gone into exile.

We were recipients of much hospitality, from the Navy, the Commander-in-Chief and from the British, French and Italian Embassies. Less elegant entertainment there was in plenty for those who sought it. For any who sought peace and something of the atmosphere of a small London club, there was the Cercle d'Orient of which some of us became members. The Rose Noire was probably the best of somewhat dubious night clubs, with better food, a cabaret and dancing. It was clean and had a certain charm. The waitresses all claimed to be princesses. It is possible that some of them were, for thousands of Russians had fled their country at the time of revolution five years earlier. As penniless refugees they had flooded westwards from the Crimea and Black Sea ports. The White Russians told horrific stories of their escapes, of hardship, starvation and death, of barges floating silently out of the Black Sea down the Bosphorus laden with refugees all dead of typhus – drifting on to the shore near Scutari. Most taxi drivers claimed to be ex-Tsarist officers and some certainly were.

In June I had the misfortune to sit for over fourteen days on a court to uncover a major pilfering racket. There were forty-two witnesses, all shameless liars, and five different languages to cope with through interpreters. A striking display of ponderous British justice, quite incomprehensible to the Turks, used as they had been for centuries to swift and summary punishment. Needless to say none of the considerable losses of the War Department's stores was ever recovered, for they had already been distributed far and wide throughout the Balkans.

On the King's official birthday, the battalion trooped the colour on the Taxim parade ground. The C-in-C and our ambassador, Sir Horace Rumbold, stood together at the saluting base. The French general was so thrilled by the parade that at its end he embraced Tim Harington to our C-in-C's great embarrassment. On 14th July it was France's turn, and the French forces mounted a ceremonial parade. That night all the French and British warships in the Bosphorus were illuminated.

Life was not all ceremonial parades, however. There were rumblings of discontent in the city. The Turkish inhabitants were glad to be protected from a possible Greek attack, while the large Greek minority were grateful for a shield against the Turkish nationalists, but except when a crisis boiled up, they united in disliking the occupying forces, which was hardly surprising. I was made garrison field officer, and as such I had to visit outlying guards, and the wireless station at Osmanath, between Constantinople and Adrianople. This meant a long ride over rough country, on abominable tracks. The guards here were Russian, at the corps WT station Serbian – it was a very cosmopolitan force, and one never knew quite what to expect.

I did a lot of riding for fun as well as on duty, it was a good way to see the countryside, in particular the Forest of Belgrade which lay between us and the Black Sea. I kept fit by training runs and in football with the men, played on our only level ground which was an Armenian cemetery. In July we moved out of the city for training, to Kutchuk Checkmedge. Our camp stood high above fields of uncut wheat, about ten minutes walk from a sandy beach on the Sea of Marmora. Tim Nugent produced a cricket eleven which endeavoured to play on a pitch of melting tar. Our field training was vigorous, and began to look very necessary.

King Constantine had withdrawn two divisions from the army in Anatolia to reinforce the four Greek divisions in eastern Thrace, and in July threatened to march on Constantinople. General Harington promptly moved some troops to the Chataldja lines, the old (and very strong) Turkish defences on the west or Thracian side of the city, and said that any Greek move across the lines would be treated as an act of war. French colonial troops with a mobile British column in support had orders to oppose any such move by force. It struck me at the time as quite a sensible move on the part of the Greeks, and not unsatisfactory from our point of view because it forced some decisions on the vacillating governments of Britain and France. The Greeks could have seized Constantinople, despite the thirty British warships there, since they had a force ten times the size of the allies', but the ensuing international fracas would have been enormous; wisdom prevailed and the Greeks declared that their troops would not enter the neutral zone without the allies' permission. The flap subsided, though we remained on the alert.

All praised the action taken by the C-in-C who was shortly to face another confrontation, this time with the Turks. I had previously enjoyed several weekends at Maison Krupp at Therapia, his residence, where General Tim was very hospitable. Here I first met Lady Harington. She was a very unusual person, who often appeared irresponsible, even childish, but was very amusing. They were a devoted couple though she must have embarrassed her distinguished husband occasionally. One of her delights was to toboggan downstairs on a large tray. One evening after dinner the guests were invited to follow her example. The French ambassador was pressed to take part and did so with such grace as he could muster. Arrived at the foot of the stairs, his white tie and the Legion of Honour awry, he emerged from the ordeal with credit and dignity, and I wondered at it. (This fondness for tobogganing was no passing whim, for years later when General Tim was governor of Gibraltar she still followed this strange practice. She also became joint master of the Calpe hunt.) Her regard for protocol was minimal, her contempt for pomposity immense. She was mad about horses and rode a great deal, often alone save for a groom in the Forest of Belgrade which was said to harbour brigands. Her general disapproved but she was an independent person, and as a resourceful, fearless Irishwoman felt capable of dealing with any situation. Incapable of hurtful malice, her antics, innocent in the extreme, won her many friends.

In August I arranged with a member of the sultan's entourage to take me and two brother officers to attend the Selamlik (the passage of the sultan to prayer) at the Yildiz Palace. It was an interesting sight, but pathetic if one considered how magnificent a display it must have been before the war and the ruin of the Turkish Empire. No more than 500 troops attended, variously dressed, some poorly. We drove to the palace gates and on dismounting were led into a drawing room, off which was a terrace overlooking the roadway and processional route. The first parties of soldiers in varied uniforms soon appeared;

by one o'clock all troops were in position. Most impressive were the household troops corresponding to our Brigade of Guards; there were two companies of these in dark red uniforms, breeches and jackets with white astrakan headgear and long black boots. The household cavalry – about half a squadron – were magnificent in blue and gold tunics and cherry coloured breeches. The mounted troops were drawn up immediately below our terrace, men and horses looked very well and in good condition. There were small representative bodies, rather ragged, of engineers, artillery and of Anatolian infantry, the latter dirty and ill-equipped, who marched badly, their drill poor, and finally a representative group of the Turkish navy. At one fifteen, the sultan made his way to the mosque in an open carriage, passing alone in front of us.

As he passed the troops shouted thrice what sounded like Hoch, Hoch, Hoch! Again as he entered the gates of the courtyard of the mosque came these three great shouts. I found this thrilling, imagining how tremendous must have been those shouts from the throats of many thousand men that had attended the sultan in the past. Following the sultan's carriage came a company of his foot guards, who when he had passed into the mosque were halted in the courtyard outside. Ten minutes later, attended by a palace official, we were allowed to watch the service. When it was over, the sultan came out, got into his carriage and bowing like a decrepit jack-in-the-box, drove back to the palace. This time the usual compliment was paid, but there were no shouts.

On the 24th August the battalion moved by train to Hadem Keui. Thence after a two-hour march over bad roads and tracks it reached camp pitched on the side of a gentle valley just east of Ak Bunar Fort. We arrived after dark, but the new moon that followed a very beautiful sunset gave us some light to help in the distribution of kits and blankets. The position we occupied was that on which the Turks had finally halted the Bulgars in the Turco-Bulgarian war of 1912. A line of ridges and spurs dominated a plain stretching to the Chataldja hills and Thrace. The ground about us was still littered with shells, many unexploded. Our defensive positions ran north of the French outpost troops and south of Colonel Kelly's mobile column. It was a wonderfully strong natural defensive position, where I could so place my guns as to bring a devastating enfilade and cross-fire to bear on any attacking troops. Some old trenches existed but these I located and bridged so that ammunition limbers and guns could be got forward at a gallop.

Our stay was brief, for on the 7th September we moved out of camp in two groups, the smaller marching to Kutchuk Checkmedge, the larger to Constantinople. Alas, whilst the limbers were being loaded, a pack mule crushed my mandolin beyond repair. Lightly equipped, I enjoyed the march, Alex marching all the way with the leading company which happened to be mine, so I had a delightful companion throughout. The country was very hilly, the roads rough, winding and full of ruts. Just east of the village of Chillinger we recovered two army deserters, who were stupid enough to make off across country; we pursued and recaptured them. Chillinger was a delightful village of twisting cobble-stoned streets, with many archways; fig and pear trees abounded. Our men were tired when we reached our halting place at Chinar Han (a field just east of the Forest of Belgrade and close by the old Roman road) and night had fallen. Blankets were drawn and a meal prepared while the men went off in parties to wash their feet in a neighbouring pool, so did I. That night we slept under the stars – so lovely, distant and brilliant. Morning saw everything soaked by heavy dew and we resumed our march, halting three hours later in a narrow gorge for the men's mid-day meal. We marched past our corps commander on some level ground near 'the sweet waters of Europe' to reach Constantinople before six. The battalion had marched splendidly and Alex told them so, for it had been the longest march they had done (43 miles) since our march into Germany in 1918, a march I had enjoyed and remembered vividly.

Meanwhile things had been going from bad to worse for the Greeks in Asia Minor. Weakened by the withdrawal of two divisions to Thrace, they were overwhelmed by the Turks in August, and on 9th September Mustapha Kemal – whose Anatolian infantry were evidently much better soldiers than the sultan's – entered Smyrna. Appalling scenes of sack and slaughter followed, with the burning of the whole city except for the Turkish quarter. I spoke to a number of friends from HMS *Iron Duke* just returned from Smyrna. All agreed that the great fire was deliberately started by the Turks to cover up their abominable handiwork, that the sights were indescribable, women outraged, dragged from their houses, murdered and flung into the streets and sea. Turks butchered countless numbers of defenceless people, many of whose bodies floated past our ships in harbour. There was no doubt that the fire had been set going first in the Armenian and Greek quarters of the town, and then got completely out of control owing to a strong wind blowing from the wrong quarter.

My sailor friends said how heartbreaking it was being forced to remain inactive, for strict orders had been given not to interfere. The Turks posted strong guards at both ends of the quay, in front lay the sea, behind a holocaust of flaming buildings from which the wretched people fled. As they could not retreat into the flames or move to either flank because of Turkish bayonets, their numbers increased by thousands on the quay. Many were trampled underfoot, many just killed by Turkish soldiers, many pushed into the harbour or deliberately drowned themselves. It was a scene of the utmost horror and barbarity, but good to relate that despite strict orders as to non-intervention many hundreds of these unhappy people were saved and hauled aboard destroyers and the smaller ships. The Navy is not a service that leaves anybody in the lurch whatever the conditions or orders, Nelson's blind eye still pays dividends, and long may it do so.

There was noisy rejoicing in Constantinople, natural enough since any Turk worth his salt must be a Kemalist at heart. I was temporarily in command of the battalion, Alex being away with the C-in-C and others officers ill. Two machine gun sections were ordered to stand by, ready to move by lorry at a moment's notice to stop rioting and looting. All that happened was much breaking of windows in the Grande Rue de Pera. Much more serious than this was the fact that the nationalist forces were now free to move against the area 'protected' by the allies and nominally ruled by the sultan. These were principally the Asiatic shores of the Bosphorus, opposite Constantinople, and of the Dardanelles where there was a token allied force at Chanak. This gave its name to the next flap.

On the 16th September I was called to see Field Marshal Lord Plumer, who was at Therapia with the C-in-C. The field marshal was very charming to his ex-ADC, and sought news of my sister Mary. He told me he had been sent out by the government to report on the situation at first hand in consultation with General Tim. Although his report was not alarmist, it did persuade the government to send substantial reinforcements to Constantinople.

The next day we went quail shooting, starting at six and getting fifteen in two tomato fields. As the thick morning mist cleared we found ourselves facing a line of guns advancing from the opposite direction composed of Turks, Greeks and miscellaneous sportsmen. Knowing that they used dust shot while we used good lead shot, much more lethal, we continued our advance. We shot at any quail that got up between us, some one had to give way and it was not us.

On the 20th September Alex, three company commanders and I crossed to Haidar Pasha, on the Asiatic side of the Bosphorus, thence by drasine to the Maltepe Halt, where we were joined by naval officers and rode round the southern sector of the Dodulu line. Later with two naval officers from HMS *Iron Duke* I reconnoitred our sectors on foot, when it was agreed that I should control all sixteen guns, my own and those from the fleet, and site all posts linking both sectors, organizing their defence as one. Our only immediate ground support was to remain in Constantinople to deal with trouble in the city, whilst I was to have the 1st Sherwood Foresters on my left flank and some French troops on my right. Digging and wiring was to begin on 21st, the navy providing 100 sailors from the flagship to help with this work. Our defensive line was to extend from the Sea of Marmora at Maltepe over the hills northwards through the village of Dodulu, bending in a NW direction to the Bosphorus just short of the entrance to the Black Sea.

Although the British government (in effect Lloyd George) was dead set on a tough policy of confrontation against the Turks in Asia Minor, our allies saw no future in a policy which could lead to war. On 21st September the French government ordered the withdrawal of all French troops from Chanak, the Italians also deserted us. With no help from our allies in preparing, let alone holding, the Dodulu line, it was decided to abandon these defences and to prepare a much shorter line defending Scutari. The feeling was bitter, though not felt for the French commander (General Charpy) who was said to be utterly disapproving of his government's decision and to have said so – 'with tears in his eyes' – to our C-in-C. He had ignored his orders to withdraw for several days, before being forced to put them into effect.

It was feared that Mustapha Kemal, flushed by his easy victory over the Greeks, might try to take Chanak, destroy our small force there, then march to Constantinople. Though outnumbering us 50 to 1 he would get a bloody nose at the outset. Our commander at Chanak appeared confident that had the Turks attacked they could not have broken through, his positions had great natural strength to which had been added four well sited lines in depth, very strongly wired. The Turks patrolled right up to our wire, in two cases they actually established small posts in rear of our most advanced ones. Our men were itching to fight and it spoke well for their discipline that they were prevented from firing on many occasions when presented with irresistible targets; they had even asked, since they might not fire, if they could go for the Turks with entrenching tool handles, for the Turks were constantly provocative. On one occasion Petherick (3rd Hussars) was ordered to gallop his troop to seize a hilltop, and just in time, for a body of about a thousand Turks had been seen swarming up to it. Had they succeeded in establishing their soldiers at the top they would have dominated the Chanak positions. By swift action Petherick arrived two minutes ahead of the leading Turk; ordered off by a Turkish colonel, he flatly refused to move and to his astonishment the Turks withdrew. Had either side begun a fight, the plan had been for our battleships to shell Turkish Army Headquarters, all approaches to Chanak, and to have bombed both heavily from our newly constructed airfield at Kilia, on Gallipoli.

Meanwhile in October there was a conference of allied generals at Mudania, the C-in-C and Generals Charpy and Monbelli (Italy) being transported in HMS *Iron Duke*. General Tim, it appeared later, had been instructed to issue an ultimatum to the Turks; wisely he put it in his pocket and negotiated with General Ismet, representing Mustapha Kemal, a convention which defused the crisis. General Tim's diplomacy led in the following month to the opening of a conference of the allied powers at Lausanne, which eventually led to the Treaty of Lausanne with the Turks, superseding the unacceptable Treaty of Sèvres.

At the time it didn't look so cut and dried, and the Constantinople garrison was reinforced, the Grenadiers and 3rd Coldstream arriving in October, with 800 RAF and some marines. One of the RAF's tasks was the guarding of the Matchka armoury; very large, it held over a million German rifles as well as machine guns and other weapons. I was shown three enormous packing cases of double-barrelled horse pistols, tied in pairs, with the wrapping still on them as they had left the makers, perhaps a century earlier! The 3rd Coldstream had many old friends, notably Francis Gore-Langton, Guy Shaw Stewart, Humphrey de Trafford, Pat Bingham and John Lascelles, not to mention Humphrey's young brother, who it was said had been shot in the jaw at the Gare du Nord by an infuriated French countess. I had some sympathy for their commanding officer in controlling them, but for us they proved most entertaining companions, with never a dull moment in their company.

Turks in Constantinople had become increasingly aggressive, and one night shot a soldier dead, wounded two others and stabbed two military policemen. I was ordered to take the battalion for a route march through the city – a case of showing the flag. Every major unit was ordered to follow suit including 2000 sailors from the fleet. I chose our route Taxim–Grande Rue de Pera–Galata Bridge thence along the Bosphorus to Dolma-Bagche. Our drums and my leading troops received cascades of flowers and confetti thrown from the windows in Pera. A very triumphal march, we were said to be the only troops so honoured. Libellous friends, obviously jealous, said 'It's all those pretty girls and Russian princesses from the Rose Noire, Tocatlion and the Petits Champs'. We were now ordered to wear uniform and to carry arms at all times and it was distressing to be apparently on the verge of another war.

The sultan had been deposed by the nationalists, and in November Mustapha Kemal abolished the sultanate. The sultan was propped up in Constantinople only by the presence of the occupying troops. Fearing assassination, he asked to be sent into exile, and approached General Tim on the matter. The C-in-C however would not undertake to send the sultan of Turkey away under British protection unless the sultan himself wrote a letter asking for such protection on humanitarian grounds signed by his own hand. This document was signed by the sultan on the 16th, the day before his flight. Some days earlier members of the sultan's entourage and household had sought refuge in our barracks, and were embarked at Dolma-Bagche at 1 a.m. on the 16th. Sergeant Murphy, our very large and splendid provost sergeant, had been their guide, friend and very adequate guardian throughout their stay. At their departure he was, despite his formidable size and gorgeous moustaches, subjected to embarrassingly warm embraces that he found overwhelming; it was a sight for the gods. At 8 a.m. on the 17th, in the course of the daily guard-mounting ceremony at Yildiz, two ambulances arrived at the palace, the sultan and a few close retainers piled into one and were driven off. Deposited safely at Dolma-Bagche landing stage, where the C-in-C and acting high commissioner waited to take leave of him, the sultan got into Admiral Brock's barge, which bore him to HMS *Malaya*. Under way, she headed for Malta. Such was the sad and sudden end of a sultanate that had endured for five centuries.

On the 27th November we had the news of Erskine Childers' execution in Dublin three days before, at the hands of an Irish Free State firing squad – a sad end to a remarkable career in the service both of Britain and of Ireland, and to a romantic, brilliant mind. *The Riddle of the Sands*, that wonderful yarn, has overshadowed his other writings. In the savage civil war which broke out after the formation of the Free State in 1921, he had sided with the anti-government forces, which assassinated Michael Collins, the first Irish prime minister, in August 1922; in the aftermath of this deed, Childers' execution was perhaps inevitable, although he himself was not the man to be party to any murder. Irish news was of course much in our minds. I was relieved to hear from my parents at Marble Hill that all was well with them. Nearly all the larger houses in our part of Donegal had been under threat from one side or the other but had not been burnt or too seriously molested, as was the case in mid and south Ireland; one or two in the remotest areas had been occupied for a time, and there had been some looting.

From the point of view of the regiment, the establishment of the Free State meant that we could no longer directly recruit there, as we had continued to do with great success throughout the war. Henceforward our Irish recruiting had to be confined to Northern Ireland, though many men from the south made their way to the UK to enlist in the Irish Guards.

The New Year of 1923 found us still en garde in and round Constantinople, with the Turkish army not far away in Asia Minor and the Greeks operating in Thrace to improve their position while the negotiations dragged on at Lausanne. We continued to show our optimistic faith in the value of a 'military presence', however small or ineffective. I crossed the Bosphorus one day and travelled by train and then a drasine to Gebez, to visit Freddie Lees and his handful of Gordon Highlanders. He was there to watch the movements of the Turkish Army Corps, a couple of miles away. His Highlanders searched all trains passing through, patrolled the area, and sent intelligence reports to HQ nightly. If it had come to a fight, the odds were indeed uneven.

I was asked by Captain Dunbar Nasmyth (who had been awarded the VC for his astonishing feat in taking his submarine through the mines and nets of the Dardanelles into the Sea of Marmora during the Gallipoli campaign) whether I thought it a good idea to celebrate the first occasion since the Crimean War when the Royal Navy and the Brigade of Guards found themselves serving together in the same theatre of operations. We agreed that the opportunity should not be missed. Thus it came about that a splendid dinner took place on board the flagship, HMS *Iron Duke*, attended on our part by the brigade commander, the three battalion commanders and four officers each from Grenadiers, Coldstream and Irish Guards. It was a memorable occasion; in due course we departed not ingloriously over the side at 1.15 a.m. to face a rough trip in the piquet boat and a difficult landing.

The city was tense. There were ample supplies of weapons hidden away for trouble makers. The previous October there had been a big fire in Pera which started in a cinema; the blaze revealed that a quantity of ammunition had been concealed in the roof, which kept on exploding. Our poor club, the Cercle d'Orient, was nearly burnt down, though Alex passed in and out of the flaming buildings without turning a hair. Now, in January, two men of the Coldstream were stabbed, one fatally, in a quite unprovoked attack in the Galata area. Nevertheless, Constantinople was a very popular station with the guardsmen – they were there for a purpose, which is always good for morale, and there was plenty to do when they were off-duty. This was just as true for the officers. There was a great deal of official and unofficial hospitality; sightseeing; visits to the fleet and naval exercises (in one of which we earned good marks by joining in the work of coaling ship, seven hours non-stop work which turned us black as sweeps); a lot of riding; and in my case a number of shooting trips after duck and snipe.

The best marshes were well beyond the allied positions, one got there on a local train, jumping off when it slowed down at a suitable bend. Jumping on again, after a long day's expedition with waterlogged boots, wasn't so easy. On one occasion when I was accompanied by Angus Cunningham-Graham (fleet signal officer) we failed to make it, and had to trudge sixteen kilometres down the line to the nearest outpost, which happened to be French. The Commandant, roused from sleep and in his night shirt and cap, couldn't have been more helpful and found us a meal and a bed in the bug-ridden inn. Next day we had to wait for a train until the afternoon – time well spent in enjoying a banquet with the 3me Battalion d'Infanterie, with many toasts. We gave our kind hosts our bag of snipe and a duck or two. On return I apologized to Alex for being 'absent without leave' and explained why. He roared with laughter and agreed the incident might have helped to improve the then sadly battered state of the Entente Cordiale. The navy C-in-C saw things differently and stopped all shooting leave. Thirty years later I was to see Angus as flag officer (Scotland).

On 2nd June once again we trooped the colour, this time three regiments of foot guards taking part; and a few days later our battalion comfortably won the brigade sports, the best individual performance coming from Alex himself who won the open mile. Later that month I successfully faced an all-day promotion examination board; Alex had already written my confidential report, far too kind and flattering.

In July the Treaty of Lausanne was at last signed, and the allies were officially at peace with Turkey, which secured Smyrna and eastern Thrace from Greece, yielding most of the Aegean islands. An enormous exchange of populations took place, a million Greeks being forced out of Turkey. I saw something of these pitiful refugees, in a deplorable plight. Dr Nansen, the great explorer, who was busy on behalf of the brand-new League of Nations on the repatriation of refugees from Thrace, dined with us one night. He was a very large man with a charming expression and a gentle voice.

There was no longer a need for an allied presence in Constantinople, and we heard unofficially that the battalion would be gone by September. This seemed a good moment to take some overdue leave, and at the end of July, with my cousin John who had joined the regiment the previous year, I boarded the trans-Europe train at San Stefano. When we crossed the Maritza river into Bulgaria, I said farewell to Turkey.

Chapter Nine

Gibraltar

The first part of our journey was enlivened by an ex-cavalry officer who since the end of the war had been engaged in business in the Levant. He had strange tales to tell about his encounters with unprincipled villains, some in high places. In the restaurant car he pointed out a monstrous man who, he said, was the leader of an assassination squad which would undertake to liquidate any individual in Turkey or a Balkan state. His fee depended on the status of the man to be murdered, but it sounded modest; politicians were his usual quarry, and wealthy businessmen reluctant to pay up for 'protection'. It is not every day that one has a successful and respected murderer as a travelling companion.

On reaching Vienna we drove to Sacher's Hotel, equipped with letters of introduction without which the redoubtable Madame Sacher would admit no one to her establishment (on which Noel Coward is said to have based his operetta *Bitter Sweet*). She was said to have been the mistress of the old emperor Franz Joseph, and certainly photographs of him adorned every bedroom, bathroom and loo. For ever smoking a cigar, she was a formidable-looking woman, but of great kindness of heart to her countrymen and women, ruined by the hyper-inflation rampant in Austria and Germany. She fed them and helped them in every possible way; many of them depended entirely on her, and were heavily in her debt.

Inflation was a tragedy for those who were retired or living on a pre-war fixed income; for us it was an embarrassment. I cashed a £5 cheque with Madame Sacher and received one million, five hundred and seventy-five thousand crowns for it; in Budapest, where we went for a few days, the most expensive five-course dinner, with wines to match, after an afternoon of gipsy music on the Margharita Island, cost us in sterling terms five shillings a head. At Leipzig, after we had left Madame Sacher and Vienna to travel to Rotterdam, we breakfasted in the station, dirty, sleepy, unshaven, hungry and two hours late. John, as usual had no money, fortunately I produced 10/- sterling to settle our bill and thought no more about it. Suddenly a little man arrived as we were about to catch our train, from a small black bag he drew out great wads of sealed 1000 and 5000 mark notes. He said it was change due to me, and we were too astonished to argue, as I stuffed these bundles of notes into my pockets. As we boarded our train I gave a bundle, seal unbroken, to the porter who had helped us with our luggage. He nearly fell flat on his face, and I hope had the good sense to rush to the nearest bank to cash and spend the nearly worthless notes before they lost all value. We spent a night in Hanover at the Ernst August (late Bristol) Hotel; it was very comfortable and the food good. There was a very bitter anti-French feeling everywhere, numerous propaganda posters were displayed, French and Belgian nationals were refused services of any kind.

It may be of interest to record that our bill for dinner at Hanover came to three million marks, and our hotel bill to nine million (about 10/- sterling). No wonder the Germans hated the French, who, they claimed, were carrying out their harsh policy in the Ruhr largely because they feared that Germany could recover and turn on them again. Perhaps they were right, but great distress was being caused and bitterly resented.

I felt that something extremely serious was bound to happen in Germany, perhaps in a few years, for the feeling was too bitter not to lead to political extravagance. In view of what we now know, this feeling was only too correct, though my timing was out by years. The build-up to Hitler and the Second World War was soon to get under way, bringing misery and death to many millions, the enslavement of whole populations, and the destruction of the old Europe which had until then survived centuries of conflict.

It was a delight to be back to the green fields and superb trees of the English landscape, even better to be home again in Donegal where I spent three carefree weeks of bathing and sea fishing. The rest of my leave I spent in Scotland, at Tulchan Lodge in Angus and at Camperdown near Dundee. My uncle leased Tulchan, an enchanted place, from the Airlie Estates, for it included an excellent stag forest and he was an experienced stalker. The road from Alyth ended at the Lodge, with a bridle path continuing over the hills to Braemar. It was a glorious retreat, and I loved all that it offered to eye and limb – for the hills at the head of Glencorrie, where we pursued ptarmigan on a couple of occasions, rose to 3500 feet. A welcome visitor to Tulchan was Stephen's charming and gallant uncle Brigadier General E. I. Phipps-Hornby, VC, who as a young horse-gunner officer had won a spectacular VC in South Africa in the company of Field Marshal Earl Robert's only son, similarly decorated, but sadly killed in the action.

Camperdown was a complete contrast – a large and merry house-party gathered for the Forfar and Perth Balls, which had then a certain elegance, and were great fun. The age of the house-party still survived. Guests were made welcome in houses generously staffed, where everything was geared to keeping them happy, interested and amused, no mean task for hosts whose hospitality never seemed to flag. It was great fun for us who were young and irresponsible, and if the writing was on the wall, we never thought to read it.

On my way south I stayed at Admiralty House, Rosyth, with Admiral Tyrwhitt, at that time naval Commander-in-Chief in Scotland, and then I sailed in the P&O *Kaiser-i-Hind* to rejoin my battalion at Gibraltar. A fellow passenger was Lady Munro, wife of General Sir Charles Munro, Governor of Gibraltar, and we soon made friends. Her father, Lord O'Hagan, had been succeeded by my grandfather as Lord Chancellor of Ireland, so we knew something of each other, and I was to enjoy much hospitality from the Munros throughout my time on 'the Rock'. When it was decided to cut our losses and pull out of Gallipoli it was General Munro who had been selected to carry out the most difficult of all tasks in the face of the enemy, that of successful disengagement. He had carried it out brilliantly with the minimum of casualties; his organization had been masterly, and his plans to mislead the Turks had been original and executed with great skill.

My first task on rejoining was to work out a winter training programme for my company, then to engage a retired Professor de Berrit to teach me Spanish. Tim Nugent was due for leave but unable to go, so the leave vacancy to my surprise was offered to me. I accepted, satisfied that my company officers could carry out my training programme without my breathing down their necks. So off I went by 'Grey funnel line' with the VIIIth Destroyer Flotilla going home to recommission. We left in a howling gale and faced mountainous seas all the way up the Spanish and Portuguese coasts. I was given the captain's cabin in HMS *Rigorous*, the flotilla leader, for in foul weather her captain used his sea cabin. The storm was violent enough to break one stay of the bridge and rip its canvas to bits when a big sea came aboard. An effort to go on deck was met by a green wall of water which soaked me and knocked me flat; discouraged, I stripped off and decided to stay in my bunk. It became calmer in the Bay of Biscay and I spent the day on deck, weather-proofed and plied with beef-tea and biscuits. At night I was fascinated by the lights of the twelve ships in the flotilla, all brilliantly lit to the water line. The flotilla split up off Ushant, eight destroyers heading for Chatham and Dover, we and the others for Plymouth. In a storm of rain, wind, and in pitch darkness our dashing captain brought his ship and accompanying destroyers at what looked to me a reckless speed into Plymouth Sound. Standing beside him on his bridge, I was tremendously impressed by his skill and seamanship, so were the commanders of the other ships who signalled congratulations and thanks.

The leave was not as dramatic as the trip home. I spent part of it in London, enjoying the usual round of parties, and part in Mürren and then the south of France. A visit to Avignon and some energetic tennis at Hyères rounded it off, and on 15 January 1924 I was back with the battalion at Gibraltar.

Soldiering on the Rock was not very arduous. Training facilities were limited, though we did what we could in the space available, and of course we maintained our parade ground standards. There was plenty of scope for sport, so it was no problem to keep the battalion fit and in good spirits. A number of us took our exercise in hunting two or three days a week with the famous Calpe Hunt, said to have been founded by the Duke of Wellington soon after the Peninsular War. The master for the past twenty years had been the Marques Pablo Marzales, and one of the pleasures of each hunting day was the hospitality he and the Marquesa gave us at their home, Guadacorte. Their family consisted of one boy and seven girls, of whom two were just grown up; Mercedes and Talia were exceptionally good looking, and always in demand for any dinner or dance in Gibraltar.

Tim Nugent drove me to my first meet of the Calpe Hunt three days after my arrival – the frontier with Spain was of course open in those days, with no restrictions. The Governor and Lady Munro were out, as was Admiral de Robeck who had just arrived in his flagship, HMS *Queen Elizabeth*. All the navy friends I had made in

Malta stood me in good stead in Gibraltar, as they had previously done at Constantinople. The next afternoon the admiral took me in his barge to Algeciras to see Maurice Baring, an old and entertaining friend, and an admirer and close friend of G. K. Chesterton. A contrasting naval occasion was due to Percy Noble, who arrived in HMS *Barham*; my cousin John and I spent two days at sea with him in his great ship during a fleet firing exercise.

Alex, still commanding the battalion, was intermittently suffering from attacks of the malaria that had laid him low in Constantinople. For so consummate an athlete, any ailment was a major annoyance, though it never showed in his demeanour; his command of himself, as of his unit, was absolute. He was fit enough to help us win the open race for regimental teams at the Calpe Hunt point to point, when the ladies' event was dramatically won by Talia, after Mercedes, in the lead, took a nasty fall and was nearly stunned by it.

Tim Nugent and I had some riding of a different kind when, accompanied by Alex, we had a week's leave to go pig-sticking in Morocco; our mounts were lent to us by the French gendarmerie. It rained in torrents and we saw no pig, though I had a good chase after a jackal until he took refuge in a forest of cacti. It went on pouring while we later went snipe-shooting with only slightly better success; and we were glad to borrow dry clothes from our host, Arnold Robertson, the High Commissioner, who was later first British ambassador to Argentina. I had met Arnold and his most attractive American wife on many occasions in London. He explained how the settlement of the Tangier question had been arrived at, for he had taken a leading part. He had the lowest opinion of the Spanish officialdom hitherto responsible for the administration of this territory, now internationalized; maladministration and corruption had been rife. It had been, he said, a cesspool where espionage, intrigue, smuggling and many other abominations had flourished unchecked. We talked of FM Sir Henry Wilson whom he admired and had seen much of as High Commissioner on the Rhine when the Field Marshal had been Chief of the Imperial General Staff. Robertson's view of war was that the only hope of preventing it was to geld all the males in the world, some undertaking I reckoned.

Stormbound at the Legation, I had amused myself and my host's small son by playing games with him and telling stories which I enjoyed as much as he, until he was carried off protesting to bed. The

High Commissioner paid me a graceful compliment when he asked 'How do you know so much about playing with children? It is a delight to watch you.' It was a difficult question to answer; maybe because I really love children who are so uninhibited, wholly natural and easy to amuse, perhaps also a desire to cling to the freshness of youth for as long as possible. Life taken too seriously can be tedious, and in the end, 'you are a long time dead'.

On St Patrick's Day we paraded in a deluge of rain for inspection by the governor who gave us shamrock on behalf of Queen Alexandra. We were all soaked, the number of drums burst by the wet made it impossible to play the national anthem. On return to barracks I ordered my company sergeant major to find, draw or steal enough coal before others did so, to dry out our mens' clothing and equipment. If there was to be a row later I would accept responsibility. He was a resourceful man, found a coal mine, lit fires, dried everything out, no questions were asked, and there was no row. Our dinner party to round off St Patrick's Day was attended by the governor, Admiral Sir John de Robeck, Admirals Fisher and Baird and a dozen others. Sitting beside Admiral de Robeck I enjoyed his lively conversation. Of the Admiralty he said that were he offered the appointment of First Sea Lord in succession to Lord Beatty, he would find it difficult to accept, for his experience of the Admiralty was as limited as his love of it. He told me much more about the Gallipoli campaign where he had been naval chief, engaged in trying to force his way into the Sea of Marmora in the hope of driving the Turks out of the war. The limitations imposed on him by Admiralty interference with his plans had been almost intolerable.

On 30th March ten of us from the battalion dined with the governor and members of his staff at 'the Convent', as Government House in Gibraltar is called. It was a farewell dinner, for we were about to return to England. My last day's hunting with the Calpe was on 1st April – another splendid day, with innumerable wild flowers to delight the eye, the air full of the delicious smells of golden gorse and broom, white and purple. A final lunch at Guadacorte; and by mid-afternoon on the 4th the whole battalion was embarked on the *Glengorm Castle*. The entire Marzales family came to see us off and were promptly 'mobbed' by my brother officers, so I went off rather ungraciously to find other work to do. Noticing this Mercedes broke away and we had a quarter of an hour to ourselves, interrupted by the military secretary demanding my signature for the governor's book. Later I talked to the Marquesa and to Pablo, thanking them for their kindness to us all. Pablo said 'Don't forget, come out soon to shoot', and at six we sailed.

Our ship, lightly laden, rolled appallingly in rough seas and the men suffered badly from sea-sickness. We disembarked at Southampton on 9th April and went by train to Woking, with an hour's march to Inkerman Barracks. It was cold after Spain, and snow fell the next day.

Before long we moved to London and into Knightsbridge barracks deserted temporarily by the Household Cavalry. On bright shining mornings Alex, I and another would run to the Serpentine and plunge into it braving a film of soot that lay on the surface of the water. I rode daily in the 'Row' or in Richmond Park.

I was back at Gibraltar about a year later in the spring of 1925 when I had been invited by Admiral Field to spend a fortnight in his flagship, HMS *Hood*. That magnificent ship was then the largest and most formidable man of war in the world, and the pride of the Royal Navy. I joined her in Pollensa Bay, Majorca, and could admire her elegant lines as I neared her in a piquet boat. The manoeuvres of the opposing fleets, Atlantic and Mediterranean, were tremendously interesting, though not devoid of the comic element which usually attends any martial demonstration on land or sea. Ironically any ship that came within range or sight of *Hood* was decreed to have been sunk, while we on board had the comfort of being invulnerable. Alas, sixteen years later on 24th May 1941 this proved to be an illusion when a shell from the *Bismarck* penetrated the *Hood*'s deck armour, hit a magazine and blew the ship apart with almost total loss of her crew – three days later *Bismarck* herself went to the bottom.

Manoeuvres over, the Atlantic Fleet sailed for home waters, my kind host the admiral putting me ashore at Gibraltar where I spent a couple of days with the Munros before going on to stay with the Marzales family. Since we had left the previous year, they had parted with Guadacorte, sold to the Butes, and gone to live in a much smaller house twenty miles away. It was a delightful retreat, of considerable size, with splendid banks of pink geraniums about the house which was known as 'Tessorio' (the little treasure). The reason for the move had been financial, a legal battle impoverishing all concerned except the lawyers. The whole affair was lunatic, for it was said that more than half the considerable sums in dispute had been dissipated in litigation. Apart from the change of residence all was as before, indulgent hosts, splendid food and drink in abundance. The Marquesa looked regal, the girls beautiful, their little sisters lovely too.

One day we had a picnic, riding to the scene, where friends from Algeciras joined us. The Marquesa drove in a carriage, lunch and servants followed in two others. Table cloths were laid on the ground, spread with an immense array of dishes – all delicious and in great plenty. When all were satisfied, there was no question of packing up what was left to be taken home. The Marquesa ordered servants and grooms to distribute uncut cakes, hams, meats, fruits and bottles of wine to anyone in sight working in the fields. I thought this a splendid custom. Another day Pablo arranged a small shoot, turning himself out in a splendid suit of green, so did his gamekeeper, who carried a shining hunting horn; sadly I had nothing exotic to wear. Our dogs did their best, the hunter blew his horn, I cannot remember the bag but it did not weigh us down.

Days slipped by in a happy atmosphere that was altogether delightful with such dear friends. But after a fortnight of *dolce far niente*, it was time for me to go, for my leave was at an end. I left in a carriage drawn by a team of mules, with the two girls and others intent on seeing me off. It was a long drive to the station, but we got there after problems with the mules; and I duly journeyed back via Madrid and Paris spending two days in each city, to the home counties and duty.

Summer slid by – Ascot, Goodwood and the parties associated with them; visits to Scotland in the autumn as always for shoots and other activities; in the winter parties and dances in London. Gay and elegant as these still were, I had the impression that the pace was slackening. Perhaps the early post-war feeling of exhilaration and relief that the war was over had at length evaporated.

The fabulous parties of the early 1920s, given by hostesses like Lady Cunard and a few others who could afford such extravagances, continued. By many hospitable people however, such display was now held to be in doubtful taste. Mr Beverley Nichols, commenting on the activities of these rich women, said 'they were like great galleons, sailing the social seas with all flags flying and all guns manned, relentlessly pursuing their charted course – and not above indulging in a little piracy'.

With the exception of these flamboyant characters, most people had begun to question the propriety of any form of ostentation. Perhaps sinister rumblings of what lay only months ahead alerted the more vigilant? Perhaps the threat of mounting taxation? More likely an unspoken wish to return to a more normal, less exuberant way of life, to good manners and to a sense of values that had in the immediate past been lowered alarmingly.

At this period I made a number of new friends whose values were still those of the old days. Amongst these was Sir William Berry, later 1st Viscount Camrose; from him and from his family I was to receive great kindness and hospitality for more than two decades. I remember him with admiration and affection as one who enjoyed the company of young people and seemed genuinely interested in their thoughts and aspirations. Above all, I remember him as the most spontaneously generous person I have ever known, for it was his delight and in his nature to be so. Another was Cuthbert Dawnay who had married whilst I was abroad; I was now to see much of him and of his wife, charming and civilized people with wide interests – travel, music, the ballet, pictures. Both were gardening enthusiasts and at their home in Yorkshire the shrubs and collections of rare trees were a delight. Marjorie had been a Loder; her father, keen and knowledgeable, had a notably important garden at Maidwell Hall in Northamptonshire. Her family were owners of Leonards Lee in Sussex, renowned for its unrivalled collection of rhododendrons. A lifelong friendship developed. I learned much from that gentle and sensitive man, who had led his Yorkshiremen gallantly at Gallipoli where he won his Military Cross. These were the sort of people whose values had never been affected by the post-war delirium.

Chapter Ten

From the Irish Guards to the Territorial Army

From the national point of view the most significant event in 1926 was undoubtedly the General Strike, starting on 3rd of May, which fortunately did not affect us one way or the other as soldiers, although some troops were used to maintain food supplies.

Winston Churchill speaking that day in the House of Commons referred to it as 'a concerted, deliberate, organized menace designed to compel Parliament to do something which it otherwise would not do'. The threat was real, immediate and alarming. Publication of newspapers ceased. Wireless broadcasts, made at frequent intervals, kept most people in touch with events, and alerted them to the magnitude of the threat to democratic freedom. The only printed news was provided by a daily issue of *The British Gazette*, a government organ published by His Majesty's Stationery Office, in which on the 6th May there was printed a message and an appeal from the Prime Minister, Stanley Baldwin.

The appeal did not fall on deaf ears. Many thousands of volunteers from all walks of life presented themselves for work in transport, in industry, indeed in all areas where their experience, training or skills might be of value to the community. The response was nationwide and spontaneous. It was this quite remarkable response that heartened the government and brought about the collapse of a strike of such dimensions, which had sought to impose on the majority a monstrous tyranny and to destroy the fabric of society.

The cabinet had had the bright idea of appointing Churchill, its only member with journalistic experience, to edit *The British Gazette*. The proprietors of the *Morning Post* offered the government their plant and offices. All the compositors and most of the machine men were 'out', but all the journalists were 'in', and an abundance of amateur labour was available. Eight days later, the General Strike at an end, *The British Gazette* ceased publication. This unprecedented effort has been described as 'an amazing feat of journalistic enterprise and organization'. In its short life it started with a circulation of 232,000; by 5th May it had reached 836,000, and by the 8th, 1,801,000, by 13th May when publication ceased 2,250,000 copies were distributed. Critics charged the paper with partisanship, but said its editor Winston – who else? – 'I cannot expect to be impartial as between the fire brigade and the fire'.

But for me the important event was being sent to command the Irish Guards company at the Guards depot; it made an interesting change from the normal routine of regimental soldiering. Each regiment of the Brigade of Guards had an established company there to which recruits were ordered to report on enlistment. These men were formed into 'recruit squads' and drilled incessantly until such time as they were considered fit to join their units. They were given some educational instruction, but the emphasis was on physical fitness, drill and turn out. It was quite remarkable to see the rapid progress made within weeks by recruits drawn from many and varied backgrounds. They were built up physically by wholesome and regular food, mentally by instruction and example; and by subjection to a disciplined way of life and thought, they gained a self-respect and confidence that most had previously lacked.

Recruit training was tough, standards were and always had been high, but those who tried to do their best were assisted, encouraged and treated with scrupulous fairness. There was no bullying, nor any excuse for it. The standards set by training and administrative staff selected by regiments to train their recruits were of the highest, if only in the interests of the regiments themselves. For the rare misfit there was, after an initial period of training, an escape route, whereby if judged by his company commander as 'unlikely to become an efficient soldier' he could be discharged from the army. There were always a few men, who would clearly not make the grade, whose inadequacies should have been obvious to recruiting authorities; such men were discharged to find less demanding work outside the army – it was humane and made a lot of sense.

The depot, now at Pirbright, was then at Caterham Barracks in Surrey. In winter it was often enshrouded in fog. A tall brick wall divided it from the local lunatic asylum. The noise made daily by the squad commanders drilling their recruits suggested to some that the other side of the wall was the place to be. Since bedlam reigned was there much to choose? Yet most of us managed to stay on the right side of the divide. During my tour our company won the cricket championship – never before achieved, for cricket is not in Ireland a national sport – and we also won that year's boxing.

The most unusual and eccentric character at the Guards depot during my last six months there was its commandant, a brave and dedicated soldier. He was a religious fanatic, an uncompromising reformer, a latter-day John Knox perhaps, utterly sincere in all he said and tried to do. He might have had a greater measure of acceptance and success had his enthusiasm been tempered by a less rigid outlook and greater humour. Though he must have anticipated a degree of resistance, and even ridicule which spread far beyond the depot's gates, yet he held to his course, braving unflattering comments, indifferent to the many exaggerated stories that circulated freely and far amongst the cynical, the unimpressed, and in the thoughtless tents of the ungodly.

Back with the battalion, I entered on a brief and inglorious career of pugilism. We had entered for the army boxing championship; no one could be found to fight at about my weight, so I felt I should volunteer to fill the gap, though I knew nothing about boxing and there was no time to learn, for even a loser scored a point, a winner only two. Had I known how painful two cracked ribs could be when one coughed or sneezed, I should have been less enthusiastic. Twice I entered the ring unopposed, scoring four points; on the third occasion I faced Arthur Heywood-Lonsdale, a Grenadier friend and a very experienced boxer, who knew the form and had no wish to hurt or to humiliate me, so we exchanged undamaging blows. My Waterloo was at hand and took place, ominously, at Gravesend. I had dismounted King's Guard that morning and was required to furnish a weight certificate, to get it an ounce or two had to be shed. The entire day was spent trying to achieve this in Hamman's Turkish baths in Jermyn Street, being boiled, massaged and starved. Exhausted, I drove back to Chelsea where brother officers saw to it that I was generously nourished with steaks and numerous glasses of Guiness. Then ominously to Gravesend, where I encountered a very tough experienced boxer, a champion of the previous year. Battle joined, it was a lively encounter while it lasted. I remember that uneven contest as a rain of well directed blows, not particularly painful at the time. So ended a short inglorious boxing career; Eddie Donner whose contest followed mine lost on points but raised a cheer when his shorts fell about his ankles. Next day the press report of both encounters treated us generously, we had failed but had I suppose done our best.

That winter I asked Cecil Wigan, a Welsh Guards friend, to shoot snipe and woodcock in Donegal. My parents were as usual at that time of year in Greece, and Marble Hill shut, so we stayed at a small hotel and shot daily. One day far from base rain soaked us and the keeper insisted we sheltered in a cottage, where we met with great kindness. A blazing fire was lit in the 'best room', our outer garments carried off to dry leaving us in our shirt tails. A splendid tea of scones was brought to warm us, for we still looked cold and damp. The lady of the house approached me without warning or embarrassment and pulled my shirt over my head leaving me as my maker thought fit to equip me. The mother of four sturdy children, she suffered from no inhibitions. Blankets were thrown over us and snugly wrapped in them we enjoyed our tea. Cecil had clung to his wet shirt but was delighted by this practical demonstration of good sense. The keeper was embarrassed, but soon got over it when he saw how cheerfully we reacted to this kindly assault on our dignity.

Seeking news on return from leave I was told that 'Dolly' Brooks had left the army and gone to Downside to become a monk. This was news indeed, so I set out to visit him that weekend. Met by Father Talbot on arrival, I was told that 'Dolly' was under a vow of silence to end at noon next day, a Sunday, that the war memorial was then to be unveiled and that I would be welcome to attend the ceremony. I did, was much impressed and at the splendid feast which followed, attended by a number of bishops and other church dignitaries, I met to my surprise a friend of my father's, Sir John O'Connor, a distinguished lawyer; his wife had just died and he had decided to take Holy Orders. In came 'Dolly' offering wine, peaches and other delicacies, fingers to his lips to indicate that his silence could not yet be broken. It soon was, and I spent a happy afternoon in his company before returning to London. Despite the austere life he was now condemned to lead he was, he said, happy and undaunted. In due course he emerged as a priest, growing in stature through devotion and experience to become Abbot, and to live a rewarding life dedicated to others. 'God moves in a mysterious way his wonders to perform' and here was a strange example, for the whole process began in quite a ridiculous fashion. At guard mounting, on the command 'fall in the officers', these braves stepped forward drawing their swords as they did so. 'Dolly's' servant had been idle and failed to secure his sword scabbard to his belt, so that it fell with a rattle onto the asphalt parade ground in Wellington Barracks. This mishap no doubt delighted onlookers peering through the railings in Birdcage Walk, but drove the adjutant round the bend, though the regimental sergeant major kept cool, collected the scabbard, wrapped it in brown paper, and dispatched it to St James's. Disciplinary action followed, which 'Dolly' found humiliating, it was in my view unimaginatively harsh; discouraged, the boy put in his papers and retired from the army. This decision was inspired, for apart from his advancement in the service of his church, he later served in North Africa with our 1st Battalion as its padre and won a Military Cross, going on to serve in Italy so that when the British entered Rome he was to introduce General Alex to the Pope.

I had always been a feminist, because it seemed to me that women – apart from their other attractions – possessed a more practical and sensible outlook on humanity and its activities; they are more likely than men to fight shy of its grosser follies. I had been brought up to hold all women in great regard and to treat them with the respect which is their due, and throughout my life I had been fortunate in meeting and becoming dear friends with women of many different types. Many of course were girls my own age; others were of an older generation. Among the latter pride of place went to Mabell Lady Airlie. Age never wearied her, she was marvellously young at heart and often greeted me with steps of an Irish jig as I crossed her threshold. I suppose there must have been times of depression, for she had suffered grievous personal losses. Her gay courage was immense, her company a delight, perhaps it takes deep suffering to mould such a character and to generate the strength to overcome all with such serenity? To love life and not to hate it for the hurt it had done you, to be ever thoughtful, loyal, patient, kind and to spread love and happiness about you: this and much more was abundantly true of Mabell Airlie as I was to know her.

In 1927 during my annual visit to Camperdown, I met amongst other charmers Rosemary Clerk, a cousin of my hostess Lady

Dorothy Hope Morley. She was of a calm and gentle disposition, and had very large well-spaced blue eyes, so we made friends; large eyes I found enchanting whatever their colour, in child or fawn wondrous, in woman or girl bewitching. I met her again in London in 1928 where we became engaged, and we were married in Scotland in October. The Stirlings lent us their Scottish home, Cauldhame, high on the Sheriffmuir above Dunblane in Perthshire, for the first week of our honeymoon, complete with butler and staff to see to our needs. The rest of my leave we spent in Ireland. Meanwhile the battalion had moved from London to Aldershot, so our first home stood high overlooking Farnham.

During one of our frequent visits to friends in London Rosemary was again presented at court, this time on her marriage. These presentations took place in the evening at Buckingham Palace where each girl, elegantly dressed and with white ostrich plumes in her hair and very long white kid gloves, took it in turn to face their majesties and make a deep curtsey, then pass out of 'the presence' to make way for the next. The procedure was really much the same as for levees which were always held at St James's. Rosemary looked lovely and her curtsey did her credit. Husbands were invited to attend suitably dressed, in my case in full dress – levee order – which I found suffocatingly hot. These presentations were soon to be discontinued and never revived. No doubt they served little purpose in a modern world, but past pageantry with a degree of elegance of any kind may be worth recording.

For example, a state or court ball at Buckingham Palace was a most colourful, impressive and brilliant affair. I had the good fortune to have attended the last of these. It was given in honour of the King and Queen of Italy and I was one of Sir Maurice de Bunsen's small party. He had been British ambassador in Vienna and had attended similar functions in the great capitals of Europe. I asked him how he would compare the splendour of the scene we now witnessed with those at the courts of the Hapsburgs and Romanoffs in the years before the Great War and the ruin of the Austro-Hungarian and Czarist empires. He said that there was no comparison; that nothing he had seen abroad could compare with the elegance, brilliance and beauty that surrounded us that night. Queen Mary looked happy and magnificently regal, sparkling with diamonds; beside her, dwarfed, stood the diminutive figure of the Italian king. The whole affair was conducted with great dignity and ease and with a minimum of formality, so that we all danced happily and enjoyed ourselves greatly.

In 1929 the Irish Guards won the Connaught Cup for the first time, an equestrian event in which all units in the command competed with teams of eight. The competition was an unusual one, a test of brawn, skill and quick thinking. Marks were scored for excellence in turn out of horses and saddlery, and for the execution of orders relayed at the gallop; for the whole affair was timed. Hugo, our senior, shouted orders which at full gallop were inaudible or quite incomprehensible, so imagination, invention and a bogus show of confidence were called for to bluff the umpires to whom we had to relate our orders and offer a tactical solution on the ground. Prior to that there was a short but testing steeplechase course; two of our team fell at one fence, so the rest of us must have given a good account of ourselves. Later that year I won the officers' revolver shooting competition at the London district rifle meeting, and still have a fine whisky decanter to remind me of it. I could now claim to have reached and surpassed the standard of 'marksman' in all infantry weapons – machine gun, Lewis gun, rifle and revolver.

In 1930 the regiment returned to London, this time to the Tower, and we took a house in Chelsea where our daughter Bridget was born. I had once been a keen, even an enthusiastic, soldier, but serious soldiering grew more and more difficult. I had commanded more men as a platoon commander on joining in 1915 than now as commander of a company. Reality vanished, make-believe was the order of the day. Flags and wooden rattles, not weapons, represented machine guns. Tanks were simulated by trucks marked with a large T or by cardboard shapes mounted on bicycles, antitank guns represented by green flags. There was little ammunition for range firing and few blank cartridges for exercises. Two men in canvas clothing carrying 'pole targets' with flapping strips of canvas represented a section, four such a platoon. Imagination was to be stretched to the limit and indeed far beyond. The pleasure of a day on horseback umpiring an exercise could not compensate for the stark unreality of the training: the whole thing was bogus.

The day of the Scrooge and the anti-hero had arrived. Everything – books, the press, the theatre – all conspired to ridicule the services and those who served in them. In addition an economy axe was wielded ruthlessly to the satisfaction if not to the plaudits of a forgetful, complacent, thoughtless people, careless of the future which was to catch up with them in less than a decade. Professionally, like many another who had served in the war, I became increasingly sad and disillusioned. It was a time of deep frustration for any one who thought realistically and was eager to give useful service. With many another I was forced to question the wisdom of remaining in the army with its prospects so bleak, with no glimmer of light ahead. Married, with the prospect of yearly changes of house a strain on finances and the inevitable restrictions on our freedom, I decided in 1931 to retire from the army and joint the regular army reserve of the Irish Guards.

It was a difficult decision and a sad one, but in the circumstances it seemed the most sensible course; it was one soon followed by a number of brother officers and by many in other regiments and corps. Few who had been enthusiastic platoon or company commanders in war could remain indifferent, starved of men, of equipment, or facilities for realistic training. The outlook then could not possibly have been more discouraging, and that situation persisted for years despite the Nazi threat which in under a decade was to explode into war and catch us as always inadequately prepared. As we know now, our inadequacy led us to the very brink of total disaster, to humiliating defeats and to an unnecessarily heavy loss of life. What a shameful price to pay for complacency. Alas, I have been reminded too often in the last twenty years of those attitudes of the thirties, and of their consequences.

After I had left the army, we retired to Marble Hill, accompanied by our small daughter and two faithful retainers, and remained there for six months. The late spring and summer were very pleasant in Donegal, we were never at a loss for things to do, and enjoyed the visits of friends who came to stay. On the approach of winter we moved temporarily to North Berwick where in November our eldest son was born. Rosemary had distant links with Cumberland through the ancient and once powerful family of Dacre, so we turned thither.

In 1932 we leased a house known as Hawksdale Hall, five miles south-west of Carlisle, on the edge of Lakeland, the dower house of a large estate situated in spacious parkland. The house looked small but had ten or twelve rooms excluding kitchen premises, servants hall, bathrooms and so on, and had useful outbuildings. Most of the rooms were small, so that we had to go to London to buy furniture to fit them. We got most of this in an auction room in St James's. The Depression enabled us to get most of what we sought inexpensively, and we were busy for months with redecoration. In the end the little house looked charming, was warm, comfortable and a haven of peace. There was a spacious garden which we improved, with a huge cedar tree; the kitchen garden too was well kept, providing us with all the produce needed, and soon we collected a staff who served us well for years.

The first and most helpful of our many Cumbrian friends were Fergus and Mary Graham of Netherby. He had been a brother officer in the Irish Guards and had been desperately wounded in 1915 – shot in the head and left for dead. Mercifully the delay in collecting him had not proved fatal and he survived to inherit a fine estate and on his father's death his baronetcy. He was godfather to our son, Stephen. He entered parliament in 1946 and served there for many years. In 1958 he was appointed Lord Lieutenant of Cumberland. He was a first cousin of Desmond Fitzgerald, whose sad death in World War I I have described, his mother and the Duchess of Leinster being sisters.

Neighbours were friendly, we seemed to fit in quickly and enjoyed much hospitality. Invitations to shoot were frequent, so we were kept well stocked with game. Fishing too was readily available, for salmon in the river Eden, and for trout in a number of lesser rivers; Caldew flowed barely 200 yards from our entrance gate across the park, with kingfishers haunting its banks. We had been extremely lucky to find such an attractive and secluded house, and settled down there very happily until the outbreak of World War II.

Our little house was within half a mile of Rose Castle, for centuries the seat of the Bishops of Carlisle. The eighteenth-century Rosemary Dacre, after whom Rosemary was called, had been born there, and in due course had married Sir John Clerk of Penicuik. She is shown with her husband in one of Raeburn's finest pictures, now in the Beit collection in Ireland. The story of her birth is a romantic one. The Jacobite army under Prince Charles had seized Carlisle and overrun the countryside. A band of Highlanders led by an officer called Macdonald appeared before Rose Castle, no doubt with a view to plunder, and demanded admittance. The doors opened, Macdonald was implored to spare the castle, above all to avoid disturbing the mother of the new-born baby. Demanding proof of the birth, he was led upstairs to the infant's cot. Satisfied, he took the white cockade from his bonnet and attached it to the cot, saying 'This will be your protection from all marauding Highlanders who may pass this way'. He withdrew his men, and the castle remained undisturbed. He deserved a better fate than that which befell him weeks later, for in the course of the Prince's sad retreat northwards ending at Culloden, he was taken prisoner, imprisoned in Carlisle Castle and finally with many another Jacobite prisoner barbarously put to death.

To revert to the 1930s, a delightful family, the Irwins of Justicetown, lived near us. Colonel Tom was a retired cavalryman, with a very good-looking wife and three splendid daughters. He was Secretary of the Territorial Army Associations of Cumberland and Westmorland, very popular and efficient. In his younger days he must have been 'a dashing blade', for a letter addressed to Captain Irwin, Piccadilly, was instantly delivered to him. Such is fame. There were many others who were kind to us, whose hospitality we enjoyed.

Rosemary's old home, Penicuik, was little more than an hour's drive from us and we went there frequently for family gatherings, shoots and other occasions. On one visit we found a young cousin, 'Jack' Suffolk, who was even then fascinated by loud bangs and the use of explosives. Rosemary's brother John and he spent happy days blowing up old tree stumps and anything else ripe for demolition, happily without accident or injury. Years later this strange attachment to explosive devices was to lead in 1941 to his death by enemy action, when a bomb he was examining blew up. Such was the value of his courageous work in bomb disposal over a long period that he was awarded the highest decoration available to him, the George Cross, his young family left to mourn his loss.

There came a day in 1935 when I had occasion to attend a large luncheon in Carlisle at which two Members of Parliament spoke. What they had to say was uninspiring, what they failed to say even worse. Hitler and his Nazis were already in power in Germany, they grew stronger and more aggressive daily. What were we doing about it? people asked. Nothing much it seemed. Our defences lay in ruins, our naval, military and air forces cut to the bone. Was it not time under threat to make some move to re-arm, to build up and to re-equip our forces? No sir. Such action would be interpreted as alarmist, even provocative. The country was thought unwilling to face disagreeable facts or the cost of re-armament. I was shattered as with Colonel Irwin I left the meeting, disgusted with the inadequacy and apathy of our political masters.

He had been trying for more than a year to persuade me to join the Territorial Army. I had always refused; I had not left the Regular Army, itself in a sad state of disarray, for years starved of funds, of equipment, of armaments, ridiculed in the press, in literature, in the theatre, to join an organization similarly handicapped but even less capable of fighting back. Tommy had chosen his moment well and like the good cavalryman he was, finding me momentarily off balance, he charged. Thus it came about that I agreed to his proposition that I should set an example, accept a commission and prepare others for the day when we might well find ourselves once again in battle.

I was interviewed by the commanding officer of the Border Regiment's TA Battalion; it drew its men from a wild and beautiful area, from the Solway south to the Lancastrian border. The only towns of any size were Workington, Whitehaven, Cockermouth and Silloth, so that many were countrymen, rugged, loyal and of good farming stock. My interview was soon over. I liked Colonel Macdonald who had been a regular soldier and been awarded the DSO for services in the 1914–18 war.

Thereafter things moved speedily. I was commissioned as a major, second in command of the battalion, and ante-dated to 1932. Never having had any previous experience of the Territorial Army, it took me a little time to get my bearings – the outlook was somewhat different from that of the Brigade of Guards, but there were compensations. It was a challenge and there was much to be done, I was happy to be of use, determined to introduce reforms, and to bring a sense of urgency into field training. Such reforms I felt would have to be introduced gradually, the reasons explained and justified. At that time all members of the Territorial Army were voluntary soldiers, and this had to be borne in mind in dealings with them, they had to be led, never coerced. Many Territorial units regarded themselves as men's clubs rather than as establishments training for war, so that training (particularly tactical training) tended to be neglected, and in camp all training had a way of ending at luncheon time. It had been the pattern for years, and worried me somewhat, for I was determined to change that leisurely approach.

The battalion camped in the Isle of Man in 1936, we sailed thither from Heysham, our boat crowded with troops, elements of other units and corps. It was my first experience of a Territorial camp, our outward and return journeys afloat were not without incident. The sea was calm, the sun shone benignly, and I was seated on deck thinking no evil when glancing forward I spotted a man relieving himself over the ship's side. He saw me as I saw him and bolted for cover; full of indignation I drew my sword and gave chase. I spotted him on a companion way leading to the engine room and cornered him there. He preceded me to the deck with my sword point in the small of his back, where, trying not to laugh, I handed him over to authority with instructions to locate his unit and be rid of him.

On our return journey I had an encounter with a man in civilian clothes who had collected a large group of soldiers about him and was preaching the most infamous sedition. He was not drunk. When invited to desist he refused and was extremely offensive. I gave him five minutes to finish his oration, then I appealed to the ship's captain to put him in irons. The captain could not have been less interested, so my sergeant major and another man were enlisted to take him to any cabin in the ship out of earshot, lock him in and throw away the key. There was no sign of him when we disembarked. He deserved rougher treatment than he received.

The following year in camp I was allowed to extend the training day up till teatime and even managed to take the whole battalion out on a night exercise. My commanding officer gave me every encouragement and a free hand with training. The men responded with alacrity, thoroughly enjoying the experience of learning skills which were interesting and worth-while. I realized horses would play no part in future combat, but I made all officers ride, for I knew that it was an activity which would instill confidence and quick thinking. When camp was over, training continued in a more active and serious vein than in the past.

As I was destined to take over command of my Territorial battalion towards the end of 1938, that year was a busy one for me. I was determined to weld it into a happy and efficient unit. There might not be much time left. I approached the Irish Guards with a view to enlisting their help and co-operation. They gave generously of both, and I was able to arrange a number of transfers to fill important gaps in the ranks of warrant officers and experienced senior NCOs. This foresight paid off handsomely.

The abdication of King Edward VIII took place in December 1936. It was a sad event, and stirred the nation deeply. In 1915, throughout the First World War and during its immediate aftermath, when I saw something of HRH, he could not have been more widely admired; great things were expected of him. I have often wondered whether Desmond Fitzgerald, had he survived the war, could have steered his Prince well clear of the irresponsible and baneful people who had latterly gathered round him and came to have such an influence on him, so that eventually things went so far wrong that abdication seemed inevitable. That he was succeeded, though reluctantly, by so dutiful and staunch a brother as the Duke of York was a signal blessing for the nation. This gentle, unassuming man was to lead his country with unfailing courage and distinction in the war that was so soon to engulf us, sustained and encouraged throughout his life by the love and devotion of his splendid Queen.

Chapter Eleven

Once More at War

Command of a battalion is a challenge which can be a joy to those not fearful of the very real and varied responsibilities it entails. It is the last chance for an officer to stamp his personality on those in his charge, for he is in direct daily contact with men and will aim at moulding them into a happy, well disciplined body, with high morale, whose standards can never be too high. As father of his flock, about a thousand strong, the commander's word is law, so it is vital that he should set the highest example personally, and be seen to do so. He must demand the same high standards from his officers, for any claim to leadership on their part demands it. Professional competence is important, but I had known several officers of undoubted competence who failed as leaders because of a lack of human understanding, of common sense, or through a fanatical respect for the rule book. Dealing with men, a sense of humour is invaluable, a sense of natural justice essential; so too is a genuinely sympathetic and realistic approach to all the human problems that men may face and which their leader must resolve where possible. Through intelligent leadership, confidence and trust is built up between leader and led which forms an indissoluble bond, creating a good unit striving for excellence, contemptuous and resentful of the second rate or of any shortcoming within its ranks.

After so many years of blinkered complacency in letting the armed forces run down, the politicians and the public had finally begun to wake up, most reluctantly, to the danger threatening the country. It was little credit to them, for the warning signs had been flashing ever since Mussolini's invasion and conquest of Abyssinia in 1935, followed in months by Hitler's march into the demilitarized zone of the Rhineland. The ideological link of the Axis pact of 1936 between the two dictators led to a physical link in Germany's occupation of Austria in March 1938; in turn in October of that same year, Hitler began his take-over of Czechoslovakia.

I was skiing in Mürren when the Germans marched into the Rhineland, breaking both the Versailles and Locarno treaties. 'If I were a Frenchman I would march tonight', I noted that evening in my diary. Strong and immediate action could have been taken, for the French army was ready poised, and far superior to any force available to oppose it. Protests, demonstrations, empty threats, but no action; Hitler, like Mussolini, was in effect given a free hand by the western democracies. But it took another two years for Britain to take the tiny step of doubling the strength of the Territorial Army; each existing battalion was to be split into two, and by energetic recruiting to be brought up to strength. A little later, in April 1939, the National Service Act was passed, requiring all young men to carry out six months training with the Regular Army, with a choice thereafter of joining the army or serving four years with a Territorial unit.

Much time and thought was given to planning the battalion split, and I got busy sorting out my officers, warrant officers, and senior NCOs. The officer problem was not easily resolved without heart searching, for it was important to be fair as between one officer and another, also to the commander of the new battalion. My battalion would be involved in battle if war came, whereas the sister battalion would remain at home, so it made sense to transfer the more elderly and less robust who would not be so severely tested. I sought potential officers from far afield, and had some clashes with my Territorial Association over this, as over my ideas on how the splitting of units should be carried out. In the end I got my way on both counts, because my plans were obviously sane, whilst the official methods recommended made little sense in my area, and I refused to adopt them.

In the late spring of 1939 I got into touch with my friend and old commanding officer General Alexander, then commander of the 1st Division at Aldershot, the spearhead of the British Army, for I reckoned that if war should come, who better than he to prepare me for it. It was arranged that I should join him and take an active part in the divisional training, and later, when he had moved his division north for beach landing exercises on the Yorkshire coast, I would join him again. The War Office gave its blessing to this plan so all was set for bringing me up to date in the latest training techniques and for improving my knowledge of the composition, equipment and handling of a fighting division.

My planning had been good, probably too good to be realized; *l'homme propose mais Dieu dispose*, though le Bon Dieu had no hand in the matter, but the Devil had, for he and his Nazi disciples were the wreckers. Because of Hitler's action in Czechoslovakia and his threats against Poland the 1st Divisional training exercises and manoeuvres were suddenly cancelled. It was a sad disappointment, for I had been looking forward eagerly to working afresh with Alex, and, as in the past, learning much from him. But it was now clear that short of miraculous intervention we should have to fight the Teutons afresh, so it behoved me to redouble my efforts at battalion level.

In July the first men of the new militia brought into being by the National Service Act started to arrive to swell our ranks. In mid-July the battalion went into camp at Halton near Lancaster where all arrangements to do with the formation of our home service battalion were completed, and embodiment took place. The final days of August ticked away, the situation abroad grew daily more menacing. As the world now knows our Prime Minister Neville Chamberlain tried again and again to come to terms with Adolf Hitler that might prove honourable and lasting. His determination to reach an accommodation with the Fuhrer was pathetic, his patience appeared inexhaustible and led to disgusted and angry accusations of appeasement.

Hitler's patience was always being exhausted and each state of exhaustion led to further outrage and another seizure of territory. Then came the German invasion of Poland and that did it, even the Prime Minister's patience was at an end, so were all hopes of avoiding the deluge; our ultimatum was contemptuously ignored and war was declared on Germany on 3rd September. It seemed that at no time during the previous eighteen months could the drift to war have been prevented – things had previously been allowed to drift too far, and we were now to pay with everything we had for 'the years that the locust had eaten'. Both major political parties were to blame, Winston Churchill alone had given forceful and frequent warnings but had been relegated to the political wilderness accused of warmongering and of disturbing an utterly bogus peace. None could but feel sorry for Mr Chamberlain who had done his best according to his lights, but a man once described as 'a good Lord Mayor of Birmingham in a lean year' was not one to confound the aspirations of the tyranical, greedy and successful monster that Hitler had now become.

I listened to the Prime Minister's broadcast to the nation saying simply that we were now at war with Germany. Though anticipated, it was a slightly emotional moment and I remember going into the drill hall to gather a small group of my men about me to give them the news. They received it in silence, as they did the few words I spoke to them, the gist of them being that I prayed I might be given the courage, strength and wisdom to lead them well through whatever lay ahead. None present had the least idea of what they were likely to be in for, I alone knew something of war, its trials and its stresses.

Next morning I was woken by loud claps of thunder and I remember saying to myself, half asleep, 'You must hand it to the Hun for getting off the mark so speedily'. We had completed our split, had handed over the requisite number of officers, NCOs and men to the new battalion, our arms, ammunition, miscellaneous stores, and cash being divided equally; both units had become independent. On 29th September our 42nd Division concentrated in Northumberland, and I established my headquarters in Barmoor Castle, with companies billeted in neighbouring villages and large farms. The Sitwell family owned Barmoor and remained there during our stay. On my first evening some of us dined with the family, in the drawing room I noticed a photograph of one well known to me from childhood, that of A.E. (Russell), Irish poet, painter and mystic. He had been a great friend of my parents and Mrs Sitwell was a veritable disciple of this strange, untidy man. We had plenty of ground for training and pressed ahead with it, though when we moved to Felton in December, intensive training was handicapped by deep snow which lay for weeks.

It was not until that month that we got our full entitlement of vehicles, and could get rid of the scratch lot of hired cars and lorries we had been using. I don't like being putty in the hands of experts, so I sent myself on a mechanical transport course. I aimed to keep our vehicles in superb condition and to this end they bore the names of Cumbrian hills and lakes or of places associated with the county. It was a sentimental idea which I thought might appeal to my men, drawn from that wild and beautiful area; it worked even better than I had hoped. In this and in other ways I built up the elitist sections with minor privileges but with exacting standards and obligations. Failure to live up to them meant a return to duty as an infantryman. There seemed to me three essentials for the coming battle, good intelligence, good communications, good handling and flow of supplies – this last meant a thoroughly well trained and reliable transport. To give effect to these obvious ideas I selected three officers with care, gave them all support, freedom to select their personnel, and left them to get on with their tasks; none ever disappointed me. I chose Ronald Scott to build up and run my intelligence section which he did speedily and with great skill, consequently I was never in the dark as to what was happening or likely to happen. In this, as in much else I was splendidly served.

Ronald MacNair Scott was among the officers I had persuaded to take commissions and serve with me; he had married a dear friend and was throughout the war a pillar of support, and after it a close and loyal friend. He had all the right ideas. Our brigade commander, who liked his glass of wine, seized up his mental gears, went broody and Cromwellian. Comfortable living, in so far as that was possible, was taboo, everyone was to toughen up and take the war seriously, drink was, if not forbidden, greatly discouraged. All this seemed to me, to Ronald and to others ridiculous nonsense, and our immediate reaction was to order cases of wine from London. It was decided to put our brigadier to the test by inviting him to dine, this was soon arranged to good effect, the puritan weakened and turned cavalier. Our estimate of his ability to hold out was proved right and we heard no more talk of pointless abstinence.

On 15th January the division moved to the south of England, to Swindon, where we mobilized for overseas. The weather was very severe and roads treacherous with hazards after dark, such as fallen telegraph poles smashed under the weight of frozen snow. We practised attacking in co-operation with tanks and demonstrated it for the benefit of three other divisions, the 7th Tank Battalion being our partners; it took place at Tidworth and was very successful.

In February rumour had it that we were to be sent to Norway. Happily it proved groundless, for the fate of British forces then dispatched to that unhappy country was a sad one. They were sent belatedly, inadequately supported, untrained for battle in snow-clad mountains and in insufficient strength to influence events. My old battalion the 1st Irish Guards lost all its senior officers (including my cousin John, then second in command) killed aboard ship in Norwegian waters by enemy bombing. An even worse threat hung over us when all commanding officers were ordered to attend a conference conducted by the then Chief of the Imperial General Staff, General Ironside. We were, he said, likely to be sent to Finland to fight the Russians, at that time allied to Hitler's Germany. It was most improbable, the general told us solemnly, that any of us would survive this lunatic expedition, but that we should be proud to have been selected for sacrifice. This general had in my view important short-comings, the aim of any leader must be to maintain and if possible raise the morale of his troops before committing them to battle. This bulky insensitive creature seemed blissfully unconcerned when he twice made it clear that we should unquestionably leave our bones to whiten in Finnish fields and snows. Luckily for us someone in authority could endure him no longer, packed him off to the House of Lords and made him a field marshal. Sir John Dill was his successor, a distinguished and intellectual soldier and an utterly different character, under whose direction it was possible that things would go better for us.

At this time our masters were hell bent on launching pinprick attacks on the areas of Europe being over-run by the enemy. Always in penny packets, hastily improvised, too weak in numbers, in training, in equipment, and in support, their prospect of success was minimal. We seemed to have forgotten Napoleon's teaching about concentration of force which won him many a battle and an empire. It was quite a different matter to launch commando raids against isolated targets, when surprise and speed almost guaranteed success.

During March we trained in trench warfare, of all things, and the battalion dug trench lines, occupied and defended them against attack by another battalion. The King did us the honour of inspecting the battalion in April before we went to France. Embarkation leave was given at the end of March and on the 16th April, our transport having preceded us, the battalion left Southampton to reach Havre on the 18th. A short train journey brought us to Sablis thence we marched on Bouessay where our transport awaited us. We remained there for some little time and got on famously with its inhabitants.

We soon moved to the Lille area, and engaged in the construction of defences along the Franco-Belgian border, my headquarters at Bondues. We discovered many concrete pill-boxes of the 1914–18 war, some had sunk below ground level, but a few we incorporated in our new defence system. The Duke of Gloucester paid us a visit a few days after our arrival and having been shown round departed satisfied and in cheerful mood. Our gallant Commander-in-Chief Lord Gort soon followed.

The entire British Expeditionary Force had spent the winter and early spring digging quite useless defensive positions along the Belgian frontier. As it turned out, and could have been foreseen, this was a total waste of time, of labour and concrete, of which millions of tons were used, for 'Gort's Girdle' was never put to the test; just as well, for against modern weaponry and assault tactics the line was indefensible. This obsession with defence was defeatist and fatal. A 'Maginot Line' mentality seemed to have taken a firm hold on the thinking of the French General Staff and to a lesser extent of our own. We were soon to be shown dramatically the futility of a reliance on defensive works, however strong.

The area for which the battalion was responsible was at one point right on the Franco-Belgian frontier, marked by the line of a canal. A bridge spanning it was guarded at one end by a Belgian sentry, at our end by one of mine. There were times when I felt like shaking my fist at this *brave Belge* but it would have been bad manners, a waste of time and solved nothing. My reason for this animosity was that, thanks to Belgium's wholly unrealistic neutrality, the defensive positions in which we might have to stand and fight were absolutely useless. The siting was all wrong, dictated not by the ground but by a line on the map marking the frontier. Both we and the French had tried to persuade the Belgians to join in talks with a view to troops of all three nations preparing a defensive line within Belgium that would be strong, well sited, and capable of resistance. The Belgians deluded themselves on the value of neutrality and refused. Their attitude was monstrous, because if attacked they planned to scream for help from the French and from ourselves. In the event their stand on neutrality proved worthless, they did scream for help, which God help us we gave them, to be rewarded for so doing by an early capitulation which placed in the greatest jeopardy their comrades in both French and British armies.

I received a letter from the Mayor of Sablis which read as follows:

Gastines-sur-Eure

Departement   le 25 Avril 1940
  de
LA SARTHE
Canton de Sable
Marie
Gastines-sur-Eure

Mon Colonel,
          Je me permets vous addresser ci-joint, en mon nom
et en celui de mes administres, les felicitations bien méritées
pour la conduite irreprochable dont vos hommes ont fait
preuve pendant leur séjour dans ma commune.

          Cette discipline qui fait honneur à votre haute compe-
tence de conducteur d'hommes, est pour nous français un
réconfort, qui doit nous donner dans l'avenir une juste idée
de la puissance et de la valeur de vos armées, et nous assurer
la Victoire.

          Sur notre Medaille Militaire figure la devise, Valeur et
Discipline, lui aussi s'applique à votre armée, avec des chefs
tel que vous et des subordonnés.

          Veuillez agréer Mon Colonel l'assurance de mon respect
et d'admiration pour votre belle nation.

Le Maire
Sgd. S. Chaffort

Chevalier de la Legion d'Honneur
Medaille Militaire   Croix de Guerre

It was flattering, but I have often wondered what he thought of
British arms later when our armies were out-manoeuvred, outnum-
bered and forced temporarily to abandon the struggle on French soil.
Come to that, how he viewed the capitulation of his own country to
the invaders. For a brave and much decorated combatant of the First
World War, it must all have come as a bitter blow.

The 1st Bn Border Regiment was brought into our brigade at the
end of April to join in the work on which we were engaged, and was
destined to fight alongside our battalion three weeks later. Although

no inter-allied staff talks with the Belgians could take place, the French High Command nevertheless produced a plan based on the sadly optimistic view that, should Belgium be invaded, it was safe to count on the defence holding out for some days on the eastern frontier and on the Albert Canal. Lord Gort, our Commander-in-Chief, agreed on the part to be played by the British Expeditionary Force. This envisaged the British Army moving forward some sixty miles to the river Dyle to take up a position between Wavre and Louvain with the French 1st Army on its right between Namur and Wavre, and the French 7th Army on its left between Louvain and Antwerp. Time as always was an important factor, the British advance was to be made in four phases. In the first the 12th Royal Lancers (armoured cars) were to move to a line some eight miles beyond the Dyle in observation of the approaches from the east whilst our two corps advanced to occupy the British front. The second phase was to be completed by nightfall on the sixth day following the outbreak of hostilities. The third phase, could you believe it, was not to be completed before the tenth day. The fourth and final phase visualized the forward movement of the 3rd Corps, of which our division was a part, to the line of the river Escaut. Such a leisurely approach to our problems was optimistic in the extreme and doomed to early failure. At dawn on the 10th May the Germans invaded both Belgium and Holland. The demoralising wait was at an end, the 'phoney war' was over, and battle joined.

Chapter Twelve

Dunkirk

Dawn had broken peacefully over the sleepy village of Bondues on that fateful 10th of May, herald of a bright calm day of warm sunshine. For others further afield in eastern Belgium, in Holland and in Luxembourg it ushered in a day of death and terror for many thousands of innocent men, women and children caught up in the onslaught. From that day it was to be the lot of millions in many lands to suffer for four years on a scale never before experienced.

Our division, forming part of the 3rd British Corps, was not scheduled to move until the fourth phase in the plan of deployment, due to commence on or after the eleventh day following a German invasion. Events, however, caused our movements to run ahead of schedule. The battalion remained at Bondues, sharpening its wits, and its bayonets as it were, against the day now close at hand when we would have urgent need of both. On 16th May the division was ordered to send one brigade as a special force to form a tank trap on the line Tournai-Lille, to destroy an enemy armoured force that had broken through towards Arras before it could rejoin its main body. A second brigade was detached to accompany the 1st Army Tank Brigade and some artillery to cover the crossings over the river Scarpe. The rest of the division, and this included my battalion, was ordered to move to Tournai, to take up a defensive position astride the river Escaut.

The 16th was a blazing hot day when that morning we marched out of Bondues and crossed the Belgian frontier. There was a never-ending stream of Belgian refugees on the move into France, making use of every form of conveyance. Every vehicle carried as many people as could possibly be crammed on to it. In addition, thousands of young and old were walking, and a great number of young men of military age who had been called up for service added to this disorganized and dispirited throng. These last had received their mobilization papers with orders to report 'somewhere' in France – it is to be doubted whether owing to the rapid march of events, a single one of them was to contribute anything to the defence of his country or to the allied cause. This had been our first sight of a pitiful rabble in flight, few knew whither. After crossing into Belgium we swung off the main road into a copse of tall poplar trees which gave some shade from a scorching sun, for our mid-day meal, and after an hour's halt in these peaceful surroundings were on our way again.

Reaching Tournai we found it deserted, streets strewn with glass from windows smashed by bombing, and a number of fires burning since there was no one left to put them out, all the civil authorities and the town's inhabitants having fled. The battalion was halted and rested after its march whilst I set out with two others on a reconnaissance, before making my dispositions. I seem to remember some shots being discharged in our direction during this reconnaissance, whether by collaborators or by enemy soldiers infiltrating with refugees was anybody's guess, happily they missed us. I ordered two companies to take up positions some two miles beyond the Escaut on the eastern fringes of Tournai, and one company to be responsible for guarding the bridges, holding the fourth in reserve. Battalion headquarters were established in Froyennes.

The situation at this time was that both the 1st and 2nd British Army Corps together with the French 1st Army were already withdrawing to the line of the Escaut. Enemy armoured forces had broken through the French 9th Army to the south and were approaching Péronne, offering an immediate threat to rear GHQ, to communications over the river Somme at Amiens and Abbeville, and to our base areas. Information was scanty, so no one had the least idea then how serious our position actually was, and we went about our tasks in blissful ignorance of what lay ahead.

Having decided my defensive plan and given the companies time to take up the positions allotted to them, I set out to visit them. The forward companies had nothing to report and seemed happy. The company (Blair-Oliphant's) which had been given the task of controlling and guarding the bridges reported some sniping from a house on the eastern edge of the canal. This provided me with an excellent excuse to try my hand as a gunner. As dusk was about to fall I got one of our small anti-tank guns into a thick clump of rhododendron bushes and demanded to be told how to let the thing off. Having aimed the gun at an upstairs window, barricaded and therefore suspect, I acted as instructed and the small shell sailed splendidly into its target followed by two more. There were no further complaints of sniping, so presumably whoever had been the cause of the trouble had been demolished or discouraged. The other thing about this position that I can now remember were two dead geese killed by enemy bombing, one particularly large and fat. Poor birds, they lay on the grass near the rhododendrons. It is strange how such trivial facts linger in our memory.

Returning to Tournai I found that an officer and some twenty Belgian gendarmes, armed and mounted on bicycles, had arrived out of the blue. I cannot now remember what excuse they gave for appearing unannounced, but it failed to impress me. So they were disarmed, protesting, their bicycles stacked out of their reach, and they were locked into a school under guard. We were taking no chances, for we had been warned about infiltrators, fifth columnists and other malefactors who might appear amongst us at any time and in any attire. Trying to look fierce and tapping my revolver, I said to the poor boy posted as sentry 'If any of these men try to escape you are to shoot them without hesitation because if you don't and any get away I will shoot you!' I found it hard not to laugh, for the sentry's eyes were round as moons; born and bred in the peace of the Cumbrian fells, he was no warrior type – at least not then. I had asked Ronnie Scott and our French interpreter (Corporal – later Captain) Paul Loraine to check the credentials of our guests with Brussels. Next morning, after I was satisfied that they were genuine, they were given breakfast, rearmed and released. Before leaving the officer, who bore no grudge, was kind enough to say that had he been placed in my position he would have acted similarly and complimented me on our action.

That night Tournai was heavily bombed and the company I had charged with the duty of guarding the bridges over the Escaut did all that was possible to control the flow of refugees, and prevent them from blocking our lines of communication. It was a difficult task, for there was an endless stream pouring in from Brussels, then in process of evacuation. By the 19th Tournai was blazing, for with no one to cope with the fires they were quite out of control.

Stories were circulating about parachutists dressed as nuns being sent in to do what damage they could, and spread alarm among the fleeing refugees. Additional confusion arose when inmates of a local lunatic asylum were released; abandoning their charges and running for safety, the governor and staff of the asylum had thrown open the gates. The inmates wandered about aimlessly, dressed in white shorts and singlets. If arrested they were incapable of explaining whence they came or who they were, a number we were told had been shot by mistake. We only collected one and unable to learn anything from him sent him to brigade headquarters under escort for such action as was thought proper, since we were much too busy to give the matter further thought.

The house selected for our mess and sleeping quarters stood high on the outskirts of Tournai. Facing it was a fenced paddock, in it a very pretty little chestnut mare and some deer. We released all the animals lest they should be killed or maimed by bombing or by exploding shells. The little mare was removed to safety, for I had visions of carrying her off as a charger, she remained with us until the night we were ordered to abandon Tournai and start our slow retirement to Dunkirk. Needless to say this house had been abandoned, apparently in some haste, by its panic-stricken owners, who like all the inhabitants of Tournai had fled in excellent time. Clearly they had no belief in the ability of the British or the French armies to stem the invading tide. How right they were in the event; but they might just as well have stood by their properties, for their aimless wanderings can have brought no comfort and to many it brought death from the skies, from dive bombers screaming down upon their bewildered and straggling columns. Our excellent home was too conspicuous to escape attention and persistent shelling forced us reluctantly to move elsewhere and headquarters were established at La Marmite, where trenches were dug for a shelter against bombs and shells and for occupation in the event of attack.

The selection of inconspicuous headquarters is important in war, for it is the control centre of a unit or formation and as such a prime target for the enemy, who will always be at pains to locate it, to destroy or at least to put it out of action. Our brigade HQ at this time however had been selected with a contemptuous disregard for these considerations. It was established in the isolated buildings of a large farm painted white, built on the forward slope of a gentle hill facing east — the line of enemy approach. It stood out like a sore thumb. A single dusty road led up to it, and along it would travel despatch riders at speed and at their peril. No doubt most of them were as anxious as the next man to survive, and in the hope of doing so rode fast trailing not 'clouds of glory' but thick white dust in their wake. The dullest, blindest, sleepiest of German artillerymen could not long resist such a target and those cyclists were constantly shot up by German light artillery, so of course were the farm buildings. Strange to relate, casualties were relatively few, perhaps the enemy were only awaiting the arrival of heavier guns to pulverize these buildings at a stroke?

Our brigadier at this time appeared obsessed with the choice of unusually conspicuous sites for brigade conferences. One I remember because it amused and surprised me greatly. Commanding officers met the brigadier at a rendezvous that turned out to be a most conspicuous tower-like building. We quickly got down to business, it was not long before shells came whistling in our direction, some falling short, others behind us. The shelling had stepped up a bit as our conference ended, and I remember standing beside my brigadier, as ever confident of survival and laughing outright. Our commander, like a small boy, seemed fascinated by the sight and sound of explosions. No one was hit, but it might not have been so. It seemed to me a quite unnecessary example of bravado serving no purpose, and setting a very bad example. Had one shell fallen, we would all have become casualties, and our units would have suffered for it.

La Marmite came under heavy shell fire one day which was particularly severe around battalion headquarters, in the course of it one of our ammunition trucks received a direct hit and began to blaze furiously. A good soldier (Private Edmondson), regardless of danger, drove in turn the signals store truck, the mortar truck and the pioneer truck away from the blazing vehicle to a safe distance.

On the 19th the 125 Brigade joined our division and took over part of the very wide front hitherto held by my battalion. The 1st Bn The Border Regiment came in on our left, the 1st Bn East Lancashire on our right. On the 21st the enemy broke into the positions held by the 1st Bn The Border Regiment, but a counter attack at a cost of one officer killed and a few other casualties restored the situation on the river bank. By now it was generally known that the British 1st and 2nd Corps and the French 1st Army were falling back, and that when they had passed through the line of the Escaut our division would form the rearguard of the British Army. Elements of these corps came through Tournai on the 20th after which the bridges were to be blown. The enemy who were not far behind began shelling the Escaut positions in earnest, and on the 22nd attacked along the whole front.

That night our division was ordered to disengage and withdraw. Unwilling to trust higher authority to give me adequate notice of the time when the bridges were to be demolished, I had ordered my two companies holding positions forward of the river line to pack and send back all their transport less two light trucks to a rendezvous west of the river. It was a happy decision, for in the event we got barely an hour's notice for blowing the bridges and for the withdrawal of all troops east of the Escaut. Everything had to be safely on the west bank within that hour. I decided to go forward at once with Ronald to extricate our two companies, to hustle them into a very speedy evacuation of their positions. The bridges over the Escaut were successfully blown on time, and its crossings denied to the enemy.

On our way forward we had had an unusual view from the windows of my car of an enemy fighter being pursued and forced down by one of our Spitfires, for it passed, with a splendid rushing sound and the rattle of machine gun fire, some twenty feet above us before crashing into a neighbouring field.

After darkness had fallen battalions assembled at a brigade rendezvous and a long night march began which for my battalion brought us to Cysoing. Here we were accommodated in part of the original line constructed by the British Expeditionary Force in the winter and early spring. We held our section of this line with three companies forward and one in reserve. Three days were spent in these inadequate defences, during which time enemy movement was seen and there was some light shelling but no attack was made against us.

During the night of the 24th an SOS signal was sent up by a neighbouring battalion when a patrol reported a concentration of enemy in a sunken road on their front; heavy fire was put down on the Germans. It must have been successful, for no attack took place, though we did collect the body of a young German warrant officer killed trying to get through our wire.

We were without news of what was happening beyond our vision – men sat about in the sun and rested, with a few exceptions. One exception was my soldier-servant who with another found a concrete mixer to his liking and set it going with a view of adding to the girth of 'Gort's Girdle'!

The general situation (then quite unknown to us) was desperate. Enemy armoured forces had penetrated the gap between Cambrai and Péronne, had taken Amiens, Abbeville, Boulogne and Calais and had severed the lines of communication by road and by rail across the Somme that had linked the BEF to its bases. The Belgian line on the Lys had broken, and there was real danger of the British Army being cut off from the sea.

One night early in our slow retirement the battalion had rested briefly in a village where Ronald and I billeted ourselves in the chateau whose owners welcomed us and gave us dinner. During the night however they fled without a sound. Before dawn I was woken by a dishevelled staff captain with the unpalatable news that the Germans were already thirty miles behind us – between us and the sea. Half asleep and disbelieving, I cursed him heartily for disturbing me and for spreading bad news, the Germans also for being so inconsiderate, however we were soon under way to test the validity of that report.

On the night of the 26th the battalion, leaving two companies to hold the line for a time, moved to Lessouins and after a few hours there, moved on to Le Bizet, north of Armentieres. That march in darkness to Le Bizet had been a nightmare with French infantry, artillery and transport flooding disorganized onto every road. Routes had been allotted to British and French formations in the hope that this would facilitate movement. French troops however swarmed on to every route causing congestion of fantastic proportions. On one or two occasions our allies were endeavouring to move in both directions on the same road with chaotic results.

Later that morning our two detached companies rejoined us, though their withdrawal had not been easy, for the Germans had succeeded in penetrating part of their line, but it had been accomplished. The march had been a long one and the troops were very tired, in the course of it the leading company had come under enemy fire to which the carrier platoon replied with good effect enabling that company to make good the shelter of a village. The second company had not been so fortunate and had been held up for a short time until their company sergeant major (Mulholland) spotted the point whence enemy fire came and showing dash and initiative engaged the enemy post which promptly ceased firing, and enabled his company to continue on its way. The enterprise displayed by this warrant officer saved casualties, and he was later to be awarded the Distinguished Conduct Medal. At Le Bizet we were joined by some eighty other ranks of the 1st Battalion who had somehow become separated from their own unit, and we hung on to them.

The night of the 28th May saw us on the move again headed for Rousbrugge-Harringhe via Neuve Eglise where we arrived in a very exhausted state soon after eight o'clock, after a gruelling march under appalling road conditions. Tired or not, we started to dig in to prepare modest defences against attack, for during the night firing had been heard from our right rear, which suggested that our line of withdrawal had indeed been cut. This eventually proved to be the case, though the firing got no nearer, and nothing happened during daylight hours. On arrival that morning I spotted a large farm house a short distance from where we were digging in and asked Ronald to tell its occupants that we would use it as my headquarters, also to see what arrangement he could make about breakfast. My emissary returned in due course to say that the family were 'not playing' – that Belgium, having capitulated to the enemy, was now out of the war and that we could do without breakfast. I was in no mood to accept discourtesy or quibbling and asked Ronald to make it very clear that come what might this was war, that their house would be seized and that an adequate breakfast was to be served within the hour, failure to comply would result in their being forcibly ejected. They gave in ungraciously and by early afternoon, the odd shell having burst about them, they had fled leaving their belongings behind them. They were cowardly and ungracious and I could not bring myself to wish them well on their wanderings.

That evening quite lively firing reinforced the fact that our line of withdrawal had been cut, so we prepared ourselves to fight where we stood. About nine o'clock our communication line with brigade went dead. An hour later a motor cyclist got through to us with an order to withdraw to a brigade rendezvous but before doing so to destroy or put out of action all our transport, and to abandon all kit other than that which could be carried on the men. This was a sad business, for we all had great pride in our vehicles which had been so well maintained and which had served us admirably. The depressing order was carried out efficiently and as silently as possible, our bren gun carriers the only vehicles spared. Some hours before I had warned companies that if we were not forced to fight it out where we stood, they would probably get the shortest possible notice of any further retirement, thus all knew what to expect and were ready to comply immediately with any order given. Communication with brigade was never re-established, but happily telephone lines to my companies remained undamaged and my order when given was brief indeed, 'Get out, rendezvous and time'.

Just before dawn on the 29th the brigade assembled and our westward march began as dawn turned to day. At the time I thought the march of so large a body of troops unwise in broad daylight, with clear skies above us likely to invite the unwelcome attention of dive bombers; however in the event we were never molested though enemy fire was sounding from our right rear. The brigade made a detour via Hondschoote and Uxem so managed to get through the ever closing ring. The march had been a successful but disheartening one, for all along our route there were lorries, guns, equipment, and stores of all sorts strewn over the country, abandoned and burning. I could not resist picking up a few of the cast-off weapons still in good condition.

We reached Uxem on the perimeter of Dunkirk about eight o'clock that morning and at once took up a defensive position along the line of the Canal des Chats. Realizing that here at last we would be required to fight it out, I made the tired men dig in properly, explaining that the exploding shells and small arms fire from the rear were just as lethal as those coming from the front; defence works had to make allowance for this and be so constructed as to be capable of all round defence, the 'thin red line' was out of date. We had the 1st East Lancashire Regiment on our right and the 3rd Bn Coldstream Guards on our left. There was some shelling and much aerial activity all that day.

At dawn on the 31st May the Germans treated us to an artillery bombardment, followed by an attack on the canal, on the front of the 1st Division, to which our brigade had now been attached, the other brigades of our division having been withdrawn and embarked some days earlier. This attack was repulsed, all four of my companies were in the front line and one suffered particularly severely from heavy shell and mortar fire. A detachment of seventy men of the South Lancashire Regiment who had got separated from their unit and had joined up with us at Rousbrugge-Harringhe were given to this company to replace its casualties. That night we were ordered to send back all men, such as cooks and so on who could be spared, to the beaches at Dunkirk for evacuation. Unfortunately they were intercepted by enemy armour and made prisoners.

On the 1st June enemy artillery fire increased and one company especially suffered heavily, others less so. Brave work was done by our stretcher bearers; Private Wilson with three other stretcher bearers went out to collect wounded, his three companions were shot, but he carried on alone and succeeded in bringing in eight men, carrying them in his arms unaided. He was later awarded the Military Medal. A distressing loss was that of a brave platoon commander (Brandwood) who with his platoon fighting sturdily was overwhelmed by the attack and taken prisoner. Happily he survived the war to return at its end with a Military Cross, for which I had recommended him for his part in this fight.

Orders were received during the day for the battalion to withdraw after nightfall to the beaches of Dunkirk for immediate evacuation. Accordingly we withdrew that night, covered by the carrier platoon which just short of the town took up a defensive position facing east. Ronald and I returned to the carriers and stayed some two hours with them until midnight at which hour our orders were to destroy them and fall back into the beach-head. It was heart-breaking being ordered to ruin these useful little vehicles in order to deny them to the enemy but there was no other course.

Re-entering Dunkirk in darkness, I went in search of General Alex's headquarters (he was now our divisional commander), but though I discovered what was said to be his headquarters in the cellars of a ruined house there was no one to be found there. Knowing Alex, he will have been actively engaged in speeding up the evacuation of troops, British and French alike, supported by Bertie Ramsay, my friend of long standing, responsible for the naval side of the operation and now a rear admiral. Between the two of them the rescue operations succeeded on a scale which seemed to those at home – fearful of total loss – little short of the miraculous. The battalion had long since vanished into the night and according to orders should have already embarked. Whilst we were looking about, Ronald, my orderly and I were hailed by the boat's crew of a destroyer; we were dragged into the boat and put aboard the ship which just before full light left Dunkirk and headed for Margate.

So ended for the time being our exhausting and far from glorious campaign against a foe who had outmanoeuvred, outnumbered and outmatched us, whose fighting arms and equipment had been superior and decisive, whose tactical handling of armour was masterly, whose air strikes were brutally effective and sustained, whose speed of advance had never been suspected or foreseen by the political or military establishments of either France or of the United Kingdom.

At Dunkirk the French Army were truly our comrades in arms. They resisted with the utmost courage and determination the very heavy German assault on their section of the perimeter, fighting to hold every yard of ground; their gallantry was a major factor in the successful evacuation of so many British and French troops. On the 3rd June the navy made a final effort to save as many of them as possible. A flotilla of fifty craft crossed from Dover that night and managed to take off more than 50,000 of these brave men and their inspiring commander Admiral Abrial.

The sky was clear and blue, the sea calm as we steamed unmolested towards the coast of England. The ship's decks were crowded with rescued troops, most of whom had fallen asleep where they lay. Even Ronald slept or at least he seemed to do so, but for myself sleep was impossible. Arrived at Margate, the destroyer discharged her weary cargo, who were at once swallowed up in a mass of voluntary helpers anxious to be of service in any and every way. It was very heartening to be greeted thus and not by a shower of rotten eggs or over-ripe tomatoes for our lack of success in the field. On landing I at once set about enquiring where my troops were to be found. The short answer to this was that they were not to be found because the plan was to unload the rescue ships as speedily as possible, pile everyone into waiting trains and get shot of them with the utmost despatch. The rescued were being landed at many south coast ports, and none of these were anxious to attract the attention of the Luftwaffe.

No attempt was made to collect units together, all were to be taken by train to concentration areas in the Midlands and the West where things could be sorted out and men gradually reunited with their units. Thus Ronald and I found ourselves hustled into a train that was filled very speedily and was on its way no one knew whither. As luck would have it our particular train was routed to pass close to London. At one stop I spotted a Grenadier friend who was doing some sort of job in the station; slightly shocked at my unkempt appearance he offered to lend me some things of his own, it was a kind thought but he was a big boy, well over six feet tall and portly to boot, I thanked him and said no. He did not know the destination of our train but confirmed that it was likely to be directed to the West or to the Midlands.

The idea of spending some weeks at Blackpool, Pontypridd or a smoky area of the Midlands did not appeal to me, so I determined as our train drew nearer to London to get out of it. Ronald and I did just that and made our way to his father-in-law's house in St James's Place where we were well received by the housekeeper, given a bottle of champagne and a particularly welcome hot bath. From there Ronald rang up his wife who was staying with her parents, the Camroses, at Hackwood, to report his return. He was as amused as I at her reaction to his escape from France, no swooning as in earlier times, just a reminder that the 10.55 still ran from Waterloo and that if we got a move on we should catch it. We did get a move on, and we did catch the train to be met at Basingstoke and driven to Hackwood, clean from our bath, enlivened by champagne. Here we were received with the utmost kindness, our warm-hearted welcome was touching in the extreme especially to me who was not one of the family, and I will never forget it. It was such a happy reunion and such a contrast to what we had had to face barely twelve hours earlier. I cannot remember what happened next, but there was probably more champagne, perhaps luncheon, after which we were led to our rooms to sleep. Twenty-four hours later I came to, having slept blissfully undisturbed.

A day later I reported to the War Office dressed rather oddly, wearing a pair of Lord Camrose's riding breeches and boots, both far too big for me, though I still wore my battle dress jacket; all else had I hoped been consigned to the flames. A senior staff officer who received me kindly did not comment on my strange attire but said that I was to remain on leave for at least a fortnight and would be contacted when required. This was good news, and I set about re-equipping myself, for I had lost a great deal of kit when we had been ordered to jettison and destroy our transport. Encouraged alas by friends who had preceded me to France to make full use of the generous transport we had been given, I had taken all sorts of things to France that had little to do with war. Polo boots, Newmarket boots from Cording, service dress jackets, riding breeches, even a suit of plain clothes for a possible short leave in Paris as in the earlier war. I even had a green canvas tent in which to write my orders and a green canvas 'loo' to match; none used, and none even unpacked, for I had had no need of them.

After four happy days at Hackwood being thoroughly spoilt by dear and generous hosts, two days were spent in London attending to various matters meeting friends, and lunching with my divisional commander and his splendid wife who claimed to be a Bourbon and had some of the characteristics attributed to that often maligned family; then off to the north to rejoin my wife and small family at our Cumbrian home.

Three weeks later the battalion reassembled at Spennymoor near Durham, and soon moved to Northallerton in Yorkshire to re-equip and re-organize. A draft of 250 Seaforth Highlanders joined us there to replace recent casualties and to bring us up to strength. I bade them welcome and gave them a fortnight in which to settle down and to discard their kilts, painful though that must have been. They settled very quickly and happily, and I contemplated forming a pipe band.

Having for a time escaped from the worst the enemy or our allies could do to us, we worked hard to prepare ourselves for the next encounter with the Germans, wherever that might take place, quite possibly on our own shores, in our own fields and peaceful sleepy water-meadows amidst the yellow kingcups and irises. Our losses of arms and equipment in France had been catastrophic and the troops had little but the small arms that each man had carried home with him. A civilian force had been raised in haste for the defence of their homes and localities, they were armed with such weapons as could be found, even with shot guns and with wooden pikes, but the spirit was such that many would have died willingly and defiantly with nothing but these pathetic weapons in their hands.

The feeling of determined togetherness could not possibly be expressed more forcibly than in the stirring, oft quoted words of the great war leader that Churchill had now shown himself to be. In a speech in the House of Commons on 4th June he had said 'if all do their duty, if nothing is neglected and if the best arrangements are made, we shall prove ourselves once again able to defend our island home, to ride out the storm of war, and to outlive the menace of tyranny, if necessary for years, if necessary alone. At any rate that is what we are going to try to do. That is the resolve of His Majesty's Government – every man of them. That is the will of Parliament and the nation. Even though large tracts of Europe and many old and famous states have fallen or may fall into the grip of the Gestapo and all the odious apparatus of Nazi rule, we shall not flag or fail. We shall go on to the end, we shall fight in France, we shall fight on the seas and oceans, we shall fight with growing confidence and growing strength in the air, we shall defend our island, whatever the cost may be, we shall fight on the beaches, we shall fight on the landing grounds, we shall fight in the fields and in the streets, we shall fight in the hills, we shall never surrender'. Has there ever been a clearer 'declaration of intent' or a rallying call more inspired, addressed to a nation in dire peril, demanding of its citizens, with unshaken confidence, universal sacrifice and brave sustained endeavour? Fearful and timorous the spirit, cold indeed and craven the heart that failed to respond.

Chapter Thirteen

East Anglia and Galloway

In Yorkshire our first task was the defence of airfields. Invasion was thought to be a distinct possibility and attacks on airfields, particularly in the south, had been continuous. The German aim was to eliminate all fighter command airfields and to destroy our fighter squadrons prior to invasion. Airfield defence was thus given a high priority, and I spent much time in reconnaissance and in the planning of the defences of airfields, notably those at Catterick and Dishforth. It seemed too peaceful an operation while such strenuous and gallant actions were being fought in the skies above by our fighter squadrons in a battle for survival.

I pushed ahead vigorously with the physical work required to make these defence arrangements effective. Posts were dug and wired on outer and inner perimeters, all designed to cover and support one another with fire. With the co-operation of all RAF station commanders I worked out defence schemes for each airfield so that all serving on it should know precisely what to do if attacked from air or ground. Army and RAF personnel were trained together and exercised in their roles and I do not think that we would have been caught napping but would have given a good account of ourselves had we been put to the test. My work done, I was flattered to be sent a message of appreciation from on high, to be entered in my record of service. That task done, we reverted to our proper role in the division which formed part of GHQ reserve, and exercised ceaselessly as a counter-invasion force.

About this time some awards were announced in recognition of our recent actions in France. They included awards of the Military Cross to Blair Oliphant, to John Musgrave and to Brandwood, the last overwhelmed and taken prisoner; a Distinguished Conduct Medal to CSM Mulholland; and Military Medals to Privates Wilson and Langstaff who as stretcher bearers had done conspicuously well, also to Private Edmonson and to our intrepid French interpreter Paul Loraine, later to serve with distinction in commandos under Lord Lovat. There were mentions in dispatches for Ronald Scott, CSM Storey and for Privates Wilson and Langstaff and for me the DSO, a tribute to everyone in the battalion and much prized on that account. As always there were many whose conduct deserved recognition, for it is ever so in war when pressures are great and much that is not spectacular goes unrecorded. Later in the summer, accompanied by Rosemary, I attended an outdoor investiture at Buckingham Palace to receive the Distinguished Service Order from the King's hand. Vigorous training continued in August and September. We were now largely re-equipped, essential if we were to play our full part in countering invasion.

Inevitably I fell to thinking about the similarities and differences between 1915 and 1940 – apart from the fact that we had just suffered a crushing defeat, which was a new experience. It struck me that senior leadership (which is not the same thing as the quality of military thinking) was infinitely superior to that of the First World War, no doubt because most senior commanders had been well shot over in the earlier contest. They were better trained and had much more imagination. They also saw no merit in incurring unnecessary losses.

My personal experience was that at battalion or brigade level there was not much difference, given that the unit was in good heart and well trained, since in both wars we were concerned at that level with the management and leadership of human beings. Men always react well to sound, firm but sympathetic leadership, and doubtless always have and will. All my men, with the exception of the few who had come to us under the National Service Act, were volunteers, as had been my regular Irish Guardsmen in 1915. One big difference was in the standard of education, which was markedly higher, with it went a general technical ability which meant that new skills could be more readily mastered.

The junior officer was judged by the same standards that had been applied to me – the ability to impose his will on his small command, his men's reaction to his leadership, his commitment to the well-being of his men at all times. There was no room for the idle and the selfish; very very few indeed were found wanting.

Concern for the welfare of the men was very much a battalion or company affair in 1914–18; at a higher level it was by and large conspicuous for its absence, with some notable exceptions like Lord Plumer's 2nd Army. This was one of the reasons for the deep contempt, almost hatred, felt for staff officers of all grades by those engaged in the actual fighting. The attitude to welfare was entirely different in 1939–45, from the commanders and their staffs right down the line. It stemmed not merely from the realization that it was a factor in maintaining high morale but from a decent instinct that those required to risk and often lose their lives against the enemy deserved something better than neglect when they were not in the firing line.

France had been overcome by the Germans, the elderly Marshal Petain having sold his country out. Many theories were advanced as to why French resistance had collapsed so suddenly and completely. I have expressed the view that the French command with few exceptions was obsessed with problems of defence, and psychologically unable to cope or adjust to the extremely rapid march of events which had resulted from the Germans' masterly use of air and armour. It was a sad reflection on pre-war training, with no marks awarded for imagination, improvisation or for determination to resist. This view was confirmed by the experience of a friend, a senior officer sent to represent the British Army at a course run by the French High Command at Versailles shortly before the war. He had found that a defensive strategy held sway, that offensive action, even to counter an enemy attack, was barely discussed. When it was, a counter-attack designed to deal with a serious threat to Paris was to take six days to develop. He said that the French Army had been starved of equipment in order to build the Maginot Line, that most French commanders would have preferred modern equipment, and that some even expressed their apprehension of what might happen if by any chance the Maginot Line was turned and it became necessary to fight the Germans in the open. The French Army, he claimed, was equipped with several battalions of old-fashioned tanks, which looked 'neither bullet proof nor even weather proof'. He thought that 'a fundamental weakness in the psychology of the French commander was the brooding feeling that he would be required to fight with weapons and equipment he knew to be antiquated and quite unfit for modern war, and doctrines and methods with which he did not agree'. Little support was expected from their Air Force, their High Command gave no inkling that the air could assist in battle, beyond observation, reconnaissance, and the bombing of communications. There appeared to be a total lack of co-operation between land and air forces. 'The French put all their faith in the value of artillery support, and the High Command ruled that eight days were required before the necessary ammunition could be concentrated and that therefore no large scale counter-attack could be contemplated before that period had elapsed.'

Germany had astounded the whole world by utterly defeating France and throwing the BEF out of the continent in a whirlwind campaign of only a few weeks' duration. It was a feat of arms which neither the man in the street not the professional soldier had contemplated as being possible.

During the twenty years between the wars military thought in France and Britain should surely have advanced somewhat in line with scientific invention, but it had not. The blame, as in our own country, lay largely with the politicians whose failure to support their armed services with the funds so desperately needed for proper equipment and training brought total disaster to the French and near disaster to British arms. Had it not been for the breathing space vouchsafed to us by the 'phoney war' which gave us a little time to re-arm, however inadequately, disaster might have proved greater, even irretrievable.

We certainly did not lack skilled and intelligent commanders in the field. I remember being asked, in 1940 or early 1941, how it came about that so many senior commanders were Irish. The occasion was a dinner party at Hackwood before it was turned into a hospital, the questioner my host, Lord Camrose. He was thinking of Alanbrooke, Alex, Auchinleck, Cunningham, Monty and others. It was clearly not the time and place for a serious and considered answer, and I thought a mildly frivolous one, which contained the elements of truth, would be in order.

'We Irish' I said, 'from our earliest days have learned by experience that things are rarely what they seem or ought to be. We are used to making speedy readjustments and nothing surprises us. For instance we hurry off to have a bath – out of the tap marked HOT comes a rush of icy water. We are not discouraged. We turn on the COLD, and after the hiss of escaping air and an encouraging gurgle or two we are rewarded by a torrent of boiling water. We are accustomed to door handles and to keys – if there are any – which turn the wrong way. In fact, in our extreme youth we learn to overcome unforeseen difficulties quickly and without fussing.

'What better training for a commander in war? However good and careful his plan, some factor beyond his control will probably send it awry. He must be flexible, adaptable, unflappable and expect the unexpected – he must almost welcome the opportunity to overcome the crisis. We are on the whole in Ireland optimistic creatures, and not averse to a gamble when we know the form. We have a laudable disrespect for "the rule book" except as a guide and prefer to follow a blend of instinct and experience. So in the inevitable confusion once battle has been joined, the Irish commander is well equipped to cope.'

The prospect of a German invasion remained a potential threat, and indeed in September, when we had been moved to Gloucestershire, we were called out on an alarm which proved to be groundless before we had reached the threatened shore, and were deflected to Henley. I always demanded much of my officers, but in return saw to it that where possible they were comfortable; so I asked the Leander Club if they would accommodate the officers' mess. To my surprise and pleasure they agreed at once, and we spent some weeks quartered there, presenting the club with some silver on our departure, in appreciation of their kindness.

Next stop was the east coast, where the battalion spent a bitter winter at Beccles and then at Lowestoft working on and manning the beach defences in that sector. Rosemary joined me there; after renting a furnished house in Beccles, we moved to a hotel on the waterfront at Lowestoft. We had frequent visits from enemy aircraft sweeping in very low from the North Sea to drop sporadic bombs on the harbour, the station and occasionally the town. Rosemary always stood on the hotel terrace to watch these tip and run attacks, which generated an immense volume of firing, with every weapon they had, from all the ships in the harbour. They never seemed to hit anything, not even our own damaged aircraft limping home after an attack on the Germans in France or the Low Countries: there was no attempt at aircraft recognition, and everything that flew was a target.

The New Year of 1941 found the country undaunted and resolute, and the battalion still guarding the beaches. It was a relief in March to be transferred to a mobile role and once again start training for active warfare. In June I felt that the clock had been turned back to the days in World War I when as a company commander I had to wet-nurse misfits of various kinds, for I was ordered to accept as my second in command a senior regular officer who had fallen foul of authority in India. I was instructed to test him, assess his ability and report on him within two months. I protested, since I had every confidence in my existing second in command; I went to the top in the shape of the personnel section of the War Office then at Cheltenham, only to be told that the orders came from the Army Council itself. Rather disheartened, I broke the long journey back to Suffolk by stopping for the night with Rosemary's Uncle Jim, Lord Sherborne, at his lovely home in Gloucestershire with the Windrush, full of trout, flowing through its grounds. I remember the two of us having quite a struggle to get me out of my very well-fitting polo boots, for we could not find a boot jack, but we managed it in the end.

My main worry was solved by my second in command's being sent to the senior officers' school with a view to being given a command in due course. Soon the maligned major from Poona arrived; he was very subdued to start with, and I listened with interest and sympathy to what he had to say. When I got to know him, after he had settled down, I liked him and found him competent; my impression was that he had been badly treated. After a two-month trial, I reported to the War Office as ordered, and was not a little surprised to receive some weeks later a very appreciative letter of thanks from that august body, the Army Council.

In July the Commander-in-Chief Home Forces – General Alan Brooke, (later Field Marshal Viscount Alanbrooke) – came to inspect the battalion. It was always worthwhile to take trouble and to show imagination in the staging of any official occasion, men are put on their mettle, and the visitor is encouraged and, sometimes, impressed. So I persuaded the local cricket club to allow me to hold my parade on the level ground within their enclosure, and to use the pavilion as the saluting stand, with a display of bunting to make it less dreary. The Commander-in-Chief arrived accompanied by a formidable retinue of generals and other senior officers. A thorough inspection was followed by a march past, both went well and after modest refreshment in our mess the Great Ones took their leave. The battalion put on a very good show, and we were told so by our brigade commander.

The outer man having passed muster, it was now the turn of the inner man to be inspected. In August we were invaded by a small party of psychiatrists who spent three days with us checking on some individuals, on specialists and on groups such as our intelligence, signal and transport sections. The War Office had suddenly gone mad about psychiatry as if it were a newly discovered science. We were all rather sceptical as to the value of this. The object of the exercise was of course to uncover square pegs in round holes, and if discovered to slot them into holes of suitable size and shape. We parted from our examiners on excellent terms and I was delighted to see from their report on the unit that they had no complaints or suggestions, that everyone in their opinion was well placed, fit for his work and their recommendation was that no changes were necessary. All this was gratifying to me and henceforward I took a kindlier view of 'trick cyclists' as they were known to the troops.

Early in September 1941, when we were at Shrubland Park near Ipswich, I found myself promoted and appointed to command a sub-district in Scotland. It was a wrench having to hand over a battalion that was in every way a happy and successful one, which I had done what I could to build up, and which never failed me. We had come a long way together since those early days when in 1938 I had taken command. That this was so was in great part due to the energy, loyalty and example of my officers, warrant officers and senior NCOs. Some of these, through the generosity of my old regimental headquarters in London, I had arranged to transfer from the Irish Guards; such men were invaluable with their long training and high standards of drill, dress and discipline. I acknowledge with gratitude the help given me from this source whenever I had sought it.

My farewells were said and on the morning of my departure my officers and some others tied ropes to my car and did me the honour of towing me down the long avenue to the gates of Shrubland Park. It was a touching and generous action which I appreciated and have never forgotten.

I had hoped for forty-eight hours leave before taking up my new appointment, but Scottish Command seemed in indecent haste to claim me, so all hope of a brief respite vanished. My tailor and hatter did what was possible in two hours to turn me out with appropriate badges, a new service dress cap with a scarlet band and so forth. A sleeper from Euston bore me to Glasgow, a car to district headquarters at Bridge of Weir to meet my new commander, Major General Freddie Bisset; he gave me a short briefing, loaned me a staff car and soon I was on my way to Dumfries to launch a new sub-district covering Dumfriesshire and Galloway. It was an area I knew well in pre-war days, for I had been a guest at shooting parties for many years in that lovely corner of Scotland. I had to start from scratch. The immediate need was to choose one of the two places pre-selected as suitable for my headquarters, next to meet people, reconnoitre important areas of the country, decide on priorities, and make a plan.

For my headquarters I chose Newton House, three miles outside Dumfries, and west of the river Nith. My next priority was to meet all commanders, lords lieutenant, home guard commanders, chief constables, town and county clerks and others having responsibility in the area, leaders of civil defence, medical authorities and so on. In emergency it seemed to me essential that we all work in close co-operation. I had never had any time for watertight compartments, for to me they are bound to lead to misunderstanding, confusion and failure. It took me three days to contact these officials, to invite their support, and to glean information helpful in my overall planning.

When only four days after my arrival I was visited by General Sir Andrew Thorne (Commander-in-Chief Scottish Command), I was in a position to put him in the picture, show him the headquarters selected, with my reasons for the choice, and give him an account of the impressions I had formed of the various commanders and civil leaders already met and how I planned to mould them into a single co-operative team. I think his very early visit to me at Dumfries was to see for himself how I proposed to cope with the many problems involved in the build up of an area from its beginnings. He departed well satisfied, for though we met at the commanders' conferences at Scottish Command Headquarters in Edinburgh, he never thought it necessary to pay me a second visit.

'Bulgy' Thorne, as he was affectionately known in the Brigade, was a charming and unusually keen and energetic man who had always driven himself hard and no doubt also those serving under him. I had known him for many years, as a Grenadier major in the First World War and in the peace that followed. I had always liked and admired him greatly as a brave, highly capable officer, likely to go far. I remembered an amusing incident during army manoeuvres in the

1920s when my battalion had been halted by the roadside; a Grenadier battalion suddenly appeared at the double with Lt Colonel 'Bulgy' at its head. As spectators we thought it a splendidly unexpected sight to which some of our men reacted with jests at the expense of any overweight Grenadier who found the going hard. Their commander, always very fit himself, had set them a gruelling pace, and some were wilting under it.

Before parting on the occasion of his early visit to my new headquarters he said 'I hope you will get on well with your generals and handle them firmly'. I undertook to do my best. His reference was to the eight retired generals living in my area, all serving in the Home Guard of which there were six battalions of varying strengths. Whilst my small staff was being selected and posted to Dumfries, I spent every moment I could spare visiting senior commanders, lords lieutenant, police chiefs and civic heads, and was encouraged to feel that I had already won their confidence. As soon as my head-quarters had been set up all these officials were invited to attend my first conference. I was gratified that there were no absen-tees.

Having welcomed them, I set out my plan for the defence of the area and action to be taken where, and by whom, in the event of invasion. Broadly I undertook to place all my resources at the disposal of the civil authority in a pre-invasion emergency situation. If however invasion took place I would expect to take over the control and direction of all civilian organizations such as police, civil defence, hospital services, transport and communications. Having jointly worked out very precise plans to cope with any situation we would test their effectiveness by joint exercises. (This we did successfully at three monthly intervals.) The aim was to ensure that in emergency there would be no confusion through lack of good planning or failure of full co-operation at all levels; the 'fog of war' was at all costs to be avoided. Having dealt with questions, I felt the time had come to make a personal plea for loyalty and full co-operation. The gist of my appeal – addressed to all, but primarily to the generals – was that here was I appointed to rule over them with every intention of doing so, yet realizing my obvious inexperience as compared to theirs. Could I count on their patience, understanding and support? For my part I would welcome suggestions from any quarter likely to make our defence plans more efficient. All promised full support and this first conference ended very happily with drinks all round. In my two years as commander I was never once let down.

I was lucky to have on my staff a first-class brigade major. Francis Sandilands was a highly intelligent and efficient officer. He was certainly the best staff officer of the many I have known; later in the war he rose to lieut. colonel's rank on General Montgomery's staff. After the war he rejoined his firm, the Commercial Union Assurance Company, soon to become its managing director, and then its chairman, with a thoroughly well deserved knighthood thrown in for good measure.

Troops at my disposal were a mixed lot. The most valuable because of their training and mobility were troops from the reconnaissance training centre at Lochmaben, some 1500 of them, and an Australian forestry company, also mobile and longing for a scrap. There were a varying number of Norwegian and Polish units, though not under my immediate control. The Polish soldiers were enthusiastic florists and would drive about the countryside with their vehicles lavishly decorated with flowers of every kind plucked from local gardens. Many of them perished later in their gallant assault on Monte Cassino. We were host in the area to a number of commando units and regular army formations undergoing intensive training. Among them were various units of the Brigade of Guards. It was a great pleasure to welcome them and to see old friends again, above all when the 1st Bn Irish Guards were stationed for some time at Ayr. Not long afterwards the battalion took part in the landings in North Africa where it was to distinguish itself in fierce encounters (during which a remarkable Victoria Cross was won by Sergeant Kenneally), as later at Anzio early in the Italian campaign.

My first year was a very busy and rewarding one, for by its end the sub-district was well organized, defensive and ambush positions had been dug and wired, and the troops and the Home Guard in the area had been fully trained and exercised. It was heartening to join the Home Guard at weekends and see the enthusiasm with which in their so-called leisure hours they tackled every task allotted to them, from digging positions to training with new weapons and to carrying out arduous exercises. All forces had plenty of opportunity of learning to use their arms, for I had lost patience with the endless red tape of officialdom in constructing new ranges and appealed to Walter Buccleuch for help; without hesitation he gave me permission to build a range on his ground near Drumlanrig. No doubt if there had been an accident on my unofficial firing range I would have been drawn and quartered, but no one was shot and our men learned to use their weapons effectively.

I had enjoyed my time in Dumfries, near which Rosemary and I had rented a very pleasant house, but once all was in order and the stimulus of threatened invasion past, I badgered the War Office on my infrequent visits to London for a posting to an area of conflict, or at least to one that might liven up. In due course I was posted to the Middle East and appointed to command in the Lebanon, with my headquarters in Beirut. Though I had sought it, this appointment happened to materialize at a highly inconvenient moment from my point of view. My father had died quite unexpectedly within days of my posting. I had to rush over to Ireland to be with my mother, to attend his funeral and deal with matters concerned with his affairs. My general was most considerate, and offered to persuade the military secretary's office in Whitehall to cancel the appointment, whilst advising me not to do this if it could possibly be avoided. There were important legal decisions to be made, for fighting a legal case from a distance of thousands of miles and in wartime seemed impossible. I had little choice in the matter and the lawyers were given their head for better or for worse; from my point of view they proved unimpressive and incompetent.

My father's funeral took place on a calm sunny day, attended by many friends and by a turn out in full regalia of all the Irish members of the Sovereign and Military Order of the Knights of Malta, of which he had been one. He was laid to rest beside his parents in the family vault. As a kind, very gentle and charming person he was admired and mourned by many, and very deeply by me. I realized in full at his death what I must always have known in my heart, that in him I had had a true, patient and loving friend. No doubt life held its frustrations and disappointments as for many another, but they never embittered him. He had little worldly ambition. Perhaps he regretted not having accepted a diplomatic opening offered to him by influential friends and colleagues of my grandfather's on the latter's early and unexpected death; but he had just married and was, one must suppose, not anxious to launch out so soon on a career, having no compelling need to adopt one. In retrospect this had been a profound mistake, for he was particularly well-fitted for diplomacy, with exquisite and courteous manners, a strong sense of humour – which sometimes got the better of him when dealing with the pompous – and great tolerance. Alas the opportunity was allowed to slip by. He later became a member of both the English and Irish bars, but never practised at either. Inevitably he got caught up for a time in politics, in the area of Irish affairs, but events in that graveyard of high hopes and lofty ideals disillusioned and sickened him. In truth his heart was never attuned to the sterile political game; the humbug, insincerity and ruthlessness involved in it were utterly repugnant to him. It is to be hoped that his reward is in heaven. There, we are led to believe, seekers after truth and justice possessing the qualities of love, constancy, compassion, gentleness and charity rate higher than those seeking worldly achievement and acclaim. Should we not say Amen to that?

I was not allowed to tarry. Having helped my mother as best I could and having attended to most essential business, I returned to my headquarters in Scotland. There I handed over my command to my successor, and spent a short period of embarkation leave at Penicuik in Midlothian with Rosemary and her parents. My last days at home were sad ones for us all, as my father-in-law Sir George Clerk was seriously ill, and as it happened, like my own father, he had died before the year was out. Soon I was at sea in a convoy bound for Alexandria.

Chapter Fourteen

The Lebanon

I found myself embarked on the 'flagship' of the convoy which consisted of about a dozen vessels, and was one of the first to pass through the Mediterranean, by the end of 1943 relatively secure. Even so our escorting warships were very active, and on several occasions we watched the spectacular eruption of depth charges when a submarine alarm had been given. With my usual luck, I found that the commodore of the convoy was Admiral The Honourable Sir Reginald Plunkett-Ernle-Erle-Drax, a cousin of Rosemary's and a kind host with whom I dined several times. Those retired admirals who had volunteered for convoy duty were superb, for it was a responsible and often hazardous task, always an anxious and exhausting one for men no longer young.

From Alexandria to Cairo for briefing at GHQ, and then within two hours I was in the air, headed for Beirut, where the officer I was replacing, John Barraclough, handed over to me. He had no liking whatsoever for the French, whose Vichy-controlled forces in Syria he had had to fight as a battalion commander, suffering heavy casualties in the process. He departed, with obvious pleasure, the following day. He joined the Control Commission in Germany after the war where he had the distinction of sacking Herr Adenauer from the post of Mayor of Cologne. As Adenauer himself said later, 'Had it not been for Brigadier Barraclough, I should never have become Chancellor of Germany.'

My headquarters were established in a modern building on the northern outskirts of Beirut. It had been a very well-appointed Italian school for girls and was known as *L'école des jeunes filles*. Now alas not a single jeune fille remained, their lively places taken by a large body of British officers who made up my staff. My first days were spent in meeting them, attending to essential matters and planning for the future. It was a great change from the well ordered life I had led so recently in Scotland to find myself translated to a strife-torn area of political turbulence and of potential conflict.

The staff I had inherited was more than five times as large as that which had served me so well at home. The permanent ration strength of the area was in the neighbourhood of 30,000 men, liable to be increased substantially at any time by an influx of troops from Egypt for specialist training or for temporary rest for the battle-weary. There were some 2000 officers under command, the proportion of officers to men was unduly high because many units were technical. Among 'other ranks' were a number of highly intelligent, skilled men doing valuable work. Michael Stewart, for example, was then a sergeant in the Army Educational Corps. When I asked him what he proposed to do after the war he said he intended to go into politics – he did, and within a few years had become a member of the Cabinet and British Foreign Secretary.

A major base had been built up in the Lebanon as soon as that became feasible, to counter a possible German thrust through Turkey aimed at a seizure of the Suez Canal and the disruption of British communications with India. Great dumps had been established in the area to accommodate enormous stores of every kind, ranging from mechanical monsters to clothing, boots and medical equipment, and caves had been drilled into hillsides to form emergency hospital accommodation.

To my delight I found that I was to work under the command of my friend and earlier divisional commander General Sir George Holmes who had taken over command of the British IXth Army from General 'Jumbo' (later FM Lord) Wilson and occupied a headquarters at Aleih in the mountains 2800 feet above Beirut. He wasted no time in getting into touch. Another staunch friend was Ronald Scott, now in command of an intelligence unit with sophisticated equipment; this was a welcome and unexpected bonus. The British minister was Sir Edward Spears whom I had known well when he had been Member of Parliament for Carlisle; I also knew Lady Spears – Mary Bordon, a writer of distinction. I was thus at home on the diplomatic front, which was a help, for relations between the IXth Army and the Spears Mission were often strained; as 'pig in the middle' I did what I could to reconcile conflicting views and to patch up rifts when they occurred, on the whole with some success.

In Beirut I got to know my opposite number, the local French general, General Humblot, and a number of his officers, some of whom I would meet lunching at their club, *Le Cercle des Officiers*, where the food was good if expensive.

Meantime I got round my area, stretching from the Turkish to the Palestinian border. It was a fascinating, varied and beautiful territory for which I was now responsible. Its coastline washed by Mediterranean waters ran for one hundred and twenty miles with villages and small towns on or close to the sea, many two thousand years old, some recorded in biblical history and in that of the crusades: Tyre, Sidon, Beirut, Byblos, Tripoli, Latakia, Aleppo. Inland from the coast rose the Lebanon and Anti Lebanon mountain ranges, with between them the Bekaa valley in which stood Baalbek whose fabulous ruins could be compared with those of Palmyra and of Petra.

One great 'dump' was established in the valley. A high wire fence surrounded it reinforced by a minefield, designed to discourage raids by bands of thieving Arabs. On one occasion a major raid took place mounted by skilled and determined thieves when large quantities of clothing were stolen to be carried off into the mountains and into the desert lands about Damascus. A goodly number of goats and camels were driven through the minefield, losses of beasts and possibly of men being accepted from exploding mines. The operation was carried out with determination and great efficiency.

My work pleased, and the country delighted me, it was so varied and I was given a very free hand, there was so much to see, so much to do and none of it dull. My large staff was quite capable of handling matters of routine and of straightforward administration. Once satisfied that this was so I was only too thankful to let them get on with it without interference. If difficulties arose I was always available to make decisions and to accept responsibility. I held conferences occasionally and a very brief daily conference for heads of departments, the purpose of which was to ensure co-ordination of effort, a clear understanding of objectives and the method by which they were to be achieved. Mistakes though regretted could be forgiven, but unimaginative working in water-tight compartments could not. We worked from eight till lunch time; owing to the heat and to local custom afternoons were free; work started again at five and went on till nine – in my case till all was done, whatever the hour. My afternoons I spent riding through olive groves and along the Mediterranean shore on a delightful little mare I had selected from remounts and had called Alouette. Bathing at an establishment known as *Le Bain des Officiers* was agreeable, but often too crowded for my liking.

I did not have to wait long before a lively political crisis blew up. At the conclusion of the Great War, with Turkey defeated, Great Britain, ever a glutton for punishment, had accepted a mandate over Palestine, its reward loss of face, loss of treasure, loss of life, though goodness knows our intentions were above reproach. The French on the other hand with both eyes fixed on the main chance were delighted to accept a mandate over Syria and the Lebanon, now freed from Turkish rule. The Lebanon was a prosperous land and its inhabitants, long used to oppression and divided amongst themselves, were ready to welcome with open arms any newcomer who promised a measure of justice and stability. So along came the French, bringing with them many good things, giving much to the Lebanon – order, a measure of justice, employment – so that the small country flourished under a benevolent suzerainty. For those Frenchmen who had chosen to live and make their careers in the Lebanon, it had been a paradise.

As the Second World War drew to a close the somewhat bogus attachment of the great ones to the principle of self-determination decided them to end the mandate. The cry went up 'Lebanon for the Lebanese', to be followed in due course by elections to a Lebanese house of representatives. This was an absolutely rotten idea from the point of view of the resident French population, who for over twenty years had enjoyed a free ride with easy prosperity, comforts, power and the trappings of a superior culture. They were not unnaturally hostile to a change in status guaranteed to threaten interests long established and entrenched. Egalité held no charms, Fraternité went into hiding. So it was that when I reached the Lebanon the political climate was explosive. It was further complicated by a serious division of loyalty between those who followed the Free French, and those whose loyalty was to Vichy, and feelings were deep and bitter.

Political tension reached breaking point within a fortnight of my arrival. I woke up one morning to be told that French militants had swooped by night, dragged the Lebanese Prime Minister out of bed together with his wife, seized a number of his ministers and had carted them off under cover of darkness to imprison them on the outskirts of Sidon. This high-handed action led to a lively day of threats and counter-threats and to acrimonious diplomatic exchanges. It also led to a great deal of noise and some demonstrations; one such took place after dark on waste land opposite my headquarters where I was trying to work peacefully against a background of cries, shouts and rifle shots. The British minister rang me in the middle of the hullabaloo to ask what was happening in my neighbourhood. I said there was a frightful lot of noise and shooting into the air, but thought little of it, having been treated to the same thing in Constantinople some years before; neither Turk nor Arab had ever been silent protesters. He said 'You are taking things very calmly'; 'So, Sir, I hope are you' was my reply, for I had satisfied myself that the legation guard was adequate.

A considerable diplomatic row blew up over the affair, the imprisoned ones were released and disciplinary proceedings commenced against the offenders. General Georges Catroux, the French C-in-C, was ordered to travel from Algiers to sort things out, and discipline his rebellious militants. He arrived, and everything calmed down, though things were boiling away under the surface, and the lid was ever ready to blow off the pot.

At times it was far from easy to keep the peace, frequently I was forced to confine all British troops to barracks to avoid clashes with ill-disciplined French troops. This was a hardship for our men, arising through no fault of their's, but they understood the need and responded loyally. For a short time the feeling was so bitter that machine guns had been mounted in sand-bagged posts in defence of certain establishments. All this between troops supposed to be allies: but had we not been deserted years before in Turkey in time of peril? *Plus ça change, plus c'est la même chose.*

Most troops under command were concentrated about the capital or larger towns, others were scattered widely, and it was my duty and pleasure to visit every unit of size. Some had taken part in local battles in which British and Free French troops had wrested the Lebanon and Syria from the Vichy French, some had been engaged in North Africa. A ski school was established high in the mountains near Tripoli at 'the Cedars' where individuals were trained as ski instructors, and later whole battalions of infantry were sent for training in snow conditions. A visit was always exhilarating, for the road climbed some 3000 feet, clinging as by magic to the mountainsides. I had encountered hairpin bends elsewhere but never before so acute or in such numbers, each in turn a hostage to fate, but hazards were worthwhile, for the superb views were breathtaking. It was from 'the Cedars' – those splendid trees now greatly reduced in number – that the timbers for the Temple in Jerusalem had been cut and brought down the mountainside, dragged to the small port of Latakia and towed by sea to a Palestinian port.

Another unit located in those mountains was a training school for mountain warfare, where I looked in whenever I could. Passing by one day I got out of my car to watch Gurkhas engaged in rock climbing; a few of these cheerful and formidable little men were gathered about a comrade who had just fallen and broken a leg, possibly two. This was an occasion for merriment, all about him were roaring with laughter as was the injured man himself. These small tough men, a terror to their enemies, seemed oblivious to pain.

Little more than a month after my arrival I was asked by the brigadier general staff and the chief engineer IXth Army to accompany them on a reconnaissance of roads and approaches leading southwards from Turkey into Syria. A southern thrust by the Germans aimed at Suez through Turkey and Syria was still considered a real possibility. Turning east from Aleppo we worked our way by bad tracks through a rough country, following the general line of the Turkish frontier, and for two nights rested and fed at small British Intelligence outposts. Eventually we reached Mosul and put up at an hotel, when a signal arrived from IXth Army headquarters, repeated by my own, to say that the newly appointed Commander-in-Chief Middle East was to visit my area within thirty-six hours. Back I had to go, breaking all rules of desert travel by journeying unaccompanied, and what a drive it was.

Desert tracks were notoriously uncertain and sometimes obliterated by blown sand. I had a compass but taking a direct line over rough deserted country was inviting trouble, and bad trouble in case of mechanical breakdown. I decided to follow the line of the river Euphrates which would in due course lead me back to civilization or what passed for it in those parts. The ancient river followed a very irregular course, twisting and turning in endless bends; at each bend teal, duck and other waterfowl rose from the marshes bordering the river. This was too much for me, and Commander-in-Chief or no Commander-in-Chief, I just had to have a go with my gun, shooting a number of birds at each stop. I shot two duck which fell into a bed of tall rushes, suddenly a Marsh Arab was beside me, having arrived in absolute silence. He was the only human being I had seen all day. In no time he retrieved both birds, handing them to me with a friendly smile; proud and unspoilt, he refused to accept the reward I was glad to offer him, nor would he accept the duck. I reached Aleppo in darkness and torrential rain, thence through Hama and Homs to Beirut, arriving at dawn. It had been a very long and trying journey, since my driver-batman was unwell, lying sprawled in the back of my car with our luggage, unable to drive. There was just time for a hot bath, a change of clothing, and breakfast before driving to the station to greet the C-in-C on his arrival from Cairo.

I had known him as C-in-C Home Forces, having met him in Scotland in the course of duty, and years earlier between the wars at the house of mutual friends. I had a great admiration for Sir Bernard Paget, particularly for his extreme devotion to duty as he saw it, he never spared himself or others, and worked ceaselessly, without rest, at the task of raising and maintaining the efficiency of all troops serving in the United Kingdom. It was said that his posting to the Middle East had come as a disappointment to General Paget, for it dashed his hope of selection as commander of British forces in the assault on Europe for which his recent work had been unstinting. He was a formidable personality and certainly not one to trifle with; to him the war was a crusade and no laughing matter, his outlook appeared Cromwellian and wholly uncompromising. It was said that he had sacked a charming popular friend of mine, commander of the 51st Highland Division, because that general had suggested an afternoon's fishing by way of recreation and had invited the C-in-C to join him. Aware of this, it behoved me to greet the great man in person on his first visit rather than be required later to explain why I had found it necessary to run about the desert after Arabs and waterfowl, when engaged in a struggle to the death. Sir Bernard saw all he had come to see, appeared fully satisfied, and in due course took his leave.

The American University at Beirut was a refuge of sanity and peace, in contrast to the state of bedlam that prevailed outside its gates. It drew students not only from the Lebanon, but from Iraq, Iran, Cyprus, Transjordan, Palestine, the Yemen, Syria, even from Saudi Arabia. At its head stood President and Mrs Bayard Dodge, a most charming, cultured and friendly couple of whom I saw a lot and from whom I received much hospitality, and on occasion sound advice in dealing with civilian matters. This splendid pair had stayed at their post during the shooting, and kept open house twice weekly for officers and men of our IXth Army, who could swim, play tennis, read, write or sit in the exquisite grounds in a friendly atmosphere. The university had been founded as the Syrian Protestant College in 1871. Its first president had declared 'This college is for all conditions and classes of men without reference to colour, nationality, race or religion. A man white, black, or yellow, Christian, Jew, Mohammedan or heathen, may enter and enjoy all the advantages of this institution and go out believing in one God, in many Gods, or no God. But it will be impossible for anyone to continue with us long, without knowing what we believe to be the truth and our reasons for that belief'. It was a noble challenge. Students were expected to go out to combat disease, organize anti-malaria campaigns, to teach under-privileged children and generally to serve the needy before returning to their homelands. The university had already turned out over a thousand graduate doctors for work in lands where medical care was desperately needed.

The Lebanon is old. It had been the home base of the Phoenicians, those far-ranging sea traders who cast their influence throughout the Mediterranean. Tyre and Sidon were great ports in those days, now decaying but still fascinating centres of Arab life. Learned men of Byblos, whence the word Bible was derived, constructed the first alphabet, adding to the power of men to transmit ideas beyond the slower capacity of cuneiform, of hieroglyphs and the word symbols of other, older cultures. I found the Lebanon a land of surpassing beauty as well as immense interest, with its snowy mountain ranges and great number of streams, for water meant life. Through centuries of prodigious labour, there were terraced hillsides and much cultivation in the valleys – grain, grapes, bananas, tobacco, some cotton and an abundance of fruit. Under the Ottomans the Lebanon had been allowed a large measure of autonomy up to the time of the First World War, when the Turks in a desperate frenzy killed off over a third of the population.

Camels, motor cars and hand carts, men and donkeys bearing loads, all jostled one another in the streets of Beirut, where Arab clothes vied with Parisian chic. Old and new ways of life were ever present; Turks, French, Arabs, Armenians, Jews and men of the Troupes Speciales, together with the British and French soldiers, crowded the cafes and bars. Inevitably there were explosions of temper resulting in fights, which my military police coped with speedily, efficiently and – given a chance – with good humour.

I enjoyed visiting outlying villages, many perched high on mountainsides. One such was Beit et Din where a group of palaces and gardens had been developed into an amazing exhibition of Arab decoration and architecture. It stood 3000 feet above the sea and had been erected 150 years earlier by Emir Behchir, a powerful Druse leader. It was in this region that Lady Hester Stanhope, an intrepid Englishwoman, had ruled over a tumultuous mountain people for some forty years in the last century. Deciding to live amongst them, she became a queen with absolute authority, who exercised the power of life and death. In one of the buildings at Beit et Din which used to be the court-room, there was a hole in the floor. I asked what purpose it served. The grisly answer was to drain away blood – a service it had been required to render frequently, since apart from executions for more serious offences, any one found guilty of theft would have the offending hand cut off without further ado.

In religious matters the people of the Lebanon were divided between Muslims and Christians, the latter in a majority. The Christian population consisted of Eastern Orthodox, Armenians, some Catholic Uniates, Roman Catholic Maronites and a growing number of Protestants. The people showed a welcome measure of religious tolerance, believers with violent convictions having adjusted themselves to one another in a manner unique in the Middle East, where faith could often be a killing matter.

Wherever you went in the Lebanon you were reminded of days long past. Travelling north from Beirut to Tripoli where the road hugs the shore, you come to the Dog river where there are no less than forty-five memorial markers or tablets covering a period of over three thousand years. No spot on earth has more remembrances of campaigns, for this route had been a bridge between Asia, Europe and Africa since before recorded history. Nebuchadnezzar left four elaborate markers in that grimly contested passageway. One of these memorials was to be found on an old road leading to the Moslem bridge. It bears the name of Emperor Caracalla of Rome (AD 211–217). Another of considerable length commemorates the victory of Esarhaddon the Assyrian king over the Egyptian pharaoh Tirhakah, while others even more ancient are much-weathered Egyptian records of campaigns against Syria of Rameses II (1300–1234 BC). In modern times a memorial recorded action by French troops in Syria and the Lebanon under Napoleon III (1860), and several others, more recent still, recorded action by Lord Allenby's forces in the First World War and by the French as late as July 1920.

I had to make a number of duty trips to Palestine, and in the course of these liaison visits saw most of the country, from the grim mountains of Moab to the pleasant hills covered with wild flowers in their season, round the Sea of Galilee. I paid several visits to Jerusalem which I found more fascinating every time I went there, in particular the two Christmases I was able to spend in the city. In contrast to the crowded streets was the complete isolation of the monastery perched on and partly hewn out of the very rock of a mountain face above Jericho, with a superb view commanding the Jordan valley, the Dead Sea and Moab – the site, it was claimed, of our Lord's temptation in the wilderness. A different sort of occasion in Palestine was a visit to Lydda, where Lord Gort (Governor and C-in-C) had discovered that the English alone had done nothing to honour the memory of their patron saint – for St George is reputed to be buried there. He had commissioned the Royal School of Needle-work to furnish him, at his expense, with a banner of St George, which was handed over, at a service of dedication, to be hung in the church alongside the banners given by other nations in the saint's honour.

I was rung up from Cairo one day by my friend Brigadier Anderson – Education Chief at GHQ Middle East – to say that a mutual American friend, George Stewart, was anxious to pay me a visit, could I have him? Indeed I could, and so that remarkable man arrived. An old friend of the President of the American University, he was invited to stay there. I carried him off to visit Damascus, a town claimed with Byblos and Baalbek to be the earth's oldest city; unlike the other two it has never suffered a major decline and after five thousand years it is still an important metropolis. I had made several visits to Damascus, for we had a small headquarters in the city and a diplomatic presence both of which then concerned me.

It took some four hours to Damascus by car from Beirut, driving over the backbone of the Lebanon Range. Fat-tailed sheep fed on good grass in the valleys, and we passed a number of camel trains coming from Kirkuk, lots of birds of many varieties, storks, teal on the wing and waders in wet places. There were caves not far from the road where snow was packed away against the thirst of summer, and lemonade sellers in Damascus had for centuries cooled their drinks with it. George Stewart suggested that it was probably from these caves that the courtly Saladin sent gifts of coolness to the fever-racked Richard Coeur-de-Lion when that valiant lay sick in Palestine on his tragic crusade.

Political and racial tensions in Syria centred on Damascus, and were at this time highly charged. As an aftermath of British and Free French forces having taken over from the Vichy French, there were serious misunderstandings which were reflected throughout Syria. There was a growing distrust, even hatred, for the United States because Washington gave aid and comfort to Zionists who were openly preparing to take over Palestine to the detriment of the Muslims. The air was electric with political intrigue, and the flaring-up of violence in Damascus was then sudden and frequent. The city and its environs are really an oasis, beyond it for five hundred miles stretches unfriendly desert until one reaches the wide valleys of Mesopotamia. Whilst Beirut was cosmopolitan, Western and in many ways European, Damascus was truly Arab. In Beirut there were a number of educated men to give quieter counsels in a period of passion and growing nationalism, but in Damascus there were none.

One of the great sights of Damascus is the Ommiade Mosque near the 'street called Straight'. A mosque of great beauty, its decoration has been enriched by many rulers and caliphs with superb tiles and lovely saracenic stone work. A sarcophagus within its walls, a Mullah claimed, contained 'the true head' of John the Baptist, whilst one of the three tall and graceful minarets was named after Jesus. Muslims, we were told, believe that our Lord on Judgement Day will descend here to confront and subdue the Antichrist. Like most such great mosques, it was a sort of university of Koranic studies.

Near the Mayeb Square is the large Souk Hamiedieh, where at that time corrugated iron, pierced by shrapnel bullets and well rusted, formed a roof over the narrow street. Small shops lined either side for nearly half a mile, where soldiers and others would bargain with merchants for bracelets, rings, necklaces, lace, rugs, shoes, leather bags, copper vessels and souvenirs for home. Not far off were other more specialized Souks. Of these the Souk Es Sagha offered everything from the cheapest costume jewellery to as fine gold and silver work as can be bought, strikingly beautiful pieces, more exotic than those to be found in Bond Street or in the Rue de la Paix, but as well done. In the Souk El Harn silks and brocades were sold, where on one visit I bought an exquisite brocade to place behind the altar in a chapel I had created within my headquarters in Beirut. There were smithies still turning out the famous Damascus steel made by welding together alternate thin laminated strips of iron and steel.

Finally there was the Souk Hudhat Pasha – the 'street called Straight' of the Acts of the Apostles. Here it was that Saul of Tarsus after his conversion became Paul the Apostle, found asylum in the house of one Judas, and was baptised by Ananias. I took my American friend to visit the small church of St Paul built directly into the city wall. As related in the Bible, hostile Jews waited to kill the Apostle but his friends, under cover of darkness, let him down over the wall in a basket, and there was some sculpture on the wall picturing the escape.

George Stewart seemed fascinated by stones, their size and weight appeared unimportant. He had planned to build a chapel at his home in New England where they were to be set into or form part of the structure. As we left the outskirts of Beirut one day he noticed two enormous stone pillars lying near to the road side; said he 'Could I have those?' I promised to find out to whom they belonged, if they could be bought and for how much. Transport to America did not seem to be a consideration, for in the end he got his pillars. Arrived in Damascus one day just before lunch, he decided he must have a stone from St Paul's church if possible, so before taking him to eat, I told my driver to secure a suitable stone from the nearest wall or ruin and lock it in the boot. I was conspicuous in full uniform and could not be seen engaged in acts of sacrilege or vandalism; my Welsh driver did well in securing a very convincing relic, and honour, such as it was, was satisfied. A number of other places yielded an assortment of masonry, trophies from Baalbek, from two or three Crusader strongholds, and from the Krak des Chevaliers, one of the finest examples of medieval military architecture – Carcassonne alone equals it in sheer magnitude and grandeur. This massive collection of stones great and small (some were very large indeed) was stored in the grounds of the American University, there to await the war's end and transportation to the New World. They finally reached their destination; fashioned by pagan hands centuries ago, they were to become part of a Christian chapel on the other side of the world.

My main preoccupation was French-Lebanese relations, for these were very far from happy. Tempers on both sides required cooling down at frequent intervals, this was no easy task and called for patience and tact. From time to time there were ugly incidents, often small in themselves, but vicious, which gave rise to understandable fury. Two small examples may suffice. One day two British soldiers walking peacefully along the esplanade close to the Hotel St Georges had grenades thrust down the front of their battle-dress blouses and were killed by the explosions, the attack was in broad daylight and quite unprovoked. The second incident took place at night and resulted in the death by bullet wounds of a medical officer and a British nursing sister returning to their hospital after dining in Beirut. French Colonial troops had set up an unauthorised and invisible road block in the middle of the night; when the hospital's car, unchallenged, failed to stop, they opened fire from ditches at close range. There was a hullabaloo about this, my report on the incident was sent to GHQ in Cairo without amendment by IXth Army. There were other incidents leading to loss of life. The French apologised, but for political reasons these ill-disciplined troops were not disbanded as in my view they should have been.

Another ghastly lot was a battalion of Palestinians, masquerading as soldiers and used for labour. My staff rightly urged me to get rid of them, and I had pressed IXth Army to do so several times; nothing had been done, no doubt again for some political reason. We caged them into a camp surrounded by high wire, but one night a lot of them broke out and played havoc in that area of the town, forcing their way into a convent and assaulting its nuns, also of course into other premises. I was at an evening party in our Legation at the time and the Minister when told of the incident was much upset. We rounded up these men in due course, locked them up, and after a week, the unit was removed and disbanded in Palestine, and I was rid of that riotous and useless lot for good.

The most violent storm of all blew up when some French started shooting into a gathering of Lebanese under the very balconies of the British Legation, these unfortunates had gone to petition Sir Edward Spears about some quite ordinary matter, so it was a most extraordinary thing to do. The British Minister, a witness of this wicked folly, was outraged by it, and was on to Downing Street within minutes. He was a personal friend of Winston Churchill's, neither was said to mince words, so I imagined the wires were red hot between London and Beirut. The upshot was that General Catroux was ordered to fly yet again and at once from Algiers, and General Paget from Cairo, to meet in Beirut the following day.

I was ordered to meet both generals at the airport, and to 'take it from there'. All the senior French officers in the Lebanon, including three ancient generals, were to be on parade to receive a ticking off, which they deserved. General Catroux was the first to arrive, Paget following from Cairo soon after, his aircraft escorted by fighters, quite an impressive arrival. Our C-in-C was in a fine rage and looked it, he shook hands with General Catroux, ignored and glared at the line of French officers. To me he said 'Take me to French Headquarters'. I said 'What about an interpreter?', to which he replied 'You are the interpreter'. This set me back on my heels somewhat, but there was nothing for it but to do as I was bid. Arrived at French General Headquarters to be greeted by much noisy saluting, we were shown into the Frenchman's office, General Paget was still in a fury, with his Chief of Staff beside him; the situation from my point of view was mildly perilous and quite ridiculous. General Paget said a great many very discouraging things about French discipline, lack of control, lack of every military virtue, shameful behaviour of an ally and so on and so forth, and there may have been threats of punitive action. All this fell from the lips of an outraged man in the grip of real passion and I was quite sorry for my useless old friend and fellow citizen of Beirut who wilted visibly – he was of course quite gaga. Well, I had to live with him and the C-in-C had not, so I did what I could and dared to misinterpret and water down the most passionate demands and denunciations, attempting to pour oil on troubled waters, without prejudice to the essential points my Commander-in-Chief had raised or in any way side-tracking the conditions he had laid down as a guarantee of future good behaviour by the French. I was relieved when our uncomfortable interview was ended, and the two generals parted somewhat icily. I have never yet discovered whether the C-in-C or his Chief of Staff guessed what I was up to. Perhaps their knowledge of French was even more limited than my own, or perhaps they were grateful that the more passionate outbursts had been conveyed to the senile Frenchman in more acceptable terms? However that may have been, I heard no more about it, and General Paget thanked me for my efforts before taking off later for Cairo. Relations between British and French grew rather happier and more settled after the flare-up.

Later I called on my old battered colleague, this time on a mission of peace. I wanted him to join me in a blitz on blowers of car horns who disturbed the peace of the city by day and by night, a quite unnecessary irritation to everyone. Though well received, I failed to extract a promise of support because he said he had tried to do this ten years earlier and had failed miserably. I took action unilaterally in the area of my headquarters, all cars were halted (except those bearing flags) two hundred yards short of where I worked, ordered to drive past in silence, failing which steps were taken to ensure the maximum delay and inconvenience. I hoped that this demonstration of enforced peace might spread; it did not, for the Arab's love of noise is deep-seated, but at least all was quiet about *L'école des jeunes filles*.

Despite the trouble they gave me I got on well with and liked the French individually and enjoyed their company; I did not trust them a yard of course, for many were insincere, but they were civilized and fun. Once over drinks in the *Cercle des Officiers* I tried laughingly to translate 'double cross' into French, I failed, but they understood perfectly, were in no way offended, roared with laughter, and doubtless agreed with my diagnosis, for it was after all a national pastime. Their politicians were past masters at the game, played I suspect as much for fun in a battle of wits designed to infuriate their less volatile allies, in which exercise they invariably succeeded. Unless the offence was quite outrageous I found it best policy first to anticipate, then to deal calmly with the most senior officer I could find, hoping that the affair might be resolved quickly and without fuss, and it nearly always was. I had ever believed in face-to-face encounters as the best and simplest means of resolving a problem, dealing only with the man at the top; lesser mortals had little authority, carried no weight, were often timid, incapable of decision and bound hand and foot by red tape.

On my birthday in late January of 1944 I reverted to boyhood, took a day off work and entertained myself actively. My idea was to take part in as many healthy distractions as the country offered, and they were many. Out of bed long before light, I drove over the mountains to the Bekaa valley to flight duck at dawn, then breakfasted with a guard unit stationed there, before driving back to Beirut. Having brought skis I spent some time amidst the snows as we recrossed the mountains. Back at Beirut for a bath and second breakfast, I set out to ride Alouette, then to swim in the sea at the *Bain des Officiers*. After that the senior RAF commander flew me to Damascus for a birthday lunch. In the evening I gave a dinner party in our mess, followed by a dance and a moonlight bathe in the Mediterranean for the hardiest, with bacon and eggs soon after sunrise. Quite a day, twenty-four hours of varied activity and no bed. On my next birthday in 1945 I managed to ride, swim and ski, but it took so long to get up to 'the Cedars' where the ski school was located that some other activities such as sailing had to be foregone.

Several big exercises were held, run by Headquarters IXth Army for troops under command, and in these I was always cast in the role of chief umpire. They were quite interesting and generally lasted about three days. One very big exercise indeed was laid on by GHQ Middle East; it lasted more than a week. A very large number of units came from Egypt and elsewhere to take part, and I was appointed chief umpire of attacking troops. Most of the activity took place in and about the Jordan valley, where it was necessary to lay bridging over the Jordan, to exercise the engineers, gunners and the like who had to cross the river in darkness and in silence. Broadly, the idea was to force our way on to the Transjordan plateau which Lord Allenby had not been able to do in 1918. He had sealed it off successfully and pressed on to take Damascus. It may be that we had more troops engaged in the exercise than Lord Allenby could spare for the task, we certainly had more modern equipment, aircraft and artillery. However that may be, we forced a passage all right after about five days of action.

When all was over, the Commander-in-Chief required me to call on King Abdullah who had established a camp under the foot-hills on the east bank of the Jordan. This tented camp was in three sections grouped at a short distance from one another, the largest section comprised the king's quarters, reception and dining marquees and accommodation for his ministers and senior officials. In the second were stabled his horses and those attending to them, in the third were housed his wives, poor souls, and their handmaidens. My instructions had been to explain to King Abdullah how much we regretted the disturbance our week's activities must have caused him, with particular reference to his horses. Not a word of solace or apology to his wives, who must have suffered just as much as the horses from the explosions that shattered the still of each night and the calm of each day. As ordered I called on the monarch, was graciously received, offered apologies on behalf of the British Army and was asked to dinner. This was to me a dreadful idea, but though I tried there was no wriggling out of it.

Taking an officer with me as ADC, and well ginned up, we returned to the king's encampment at the hour appointed. He greeted me kindly and in due course we went to dine. It was a most lovely night of full moon, as we followed some paces behind the little king as he made his way from the reception to the dining tent. I had had visions of sitting cross-legged on the ground, required to swallow sheep's eyes and other oriental delicacies. It was therefore with a tremendous relief that I saw tables were laid in European fashion. I was placed in King Abdullah's right, he carried on a triangular conversation with me throughout the meal. Opposite sat, let us suppose, the Lord Chamberlain, with what looked like an inverted wastepaper basket on his head. The king, looking squarely at me, would say something in Arabic which the Lord Chamberlain would translate. I would answer the question still looking at the monarch, and back would come my reply in Arabic from beneath the waste-paper basket. I found this all rather trying and highly ridiculous, for King Abdullah had I think been to England on several occasions and I suspected knew our language quite well. However, I was his guest and it was not for me to question this strange practice. The meal over without disaster, we returned to the reception marquee and after a time I took my leave. I was not to see him again, for he was assassinated by a fanatic a year later outside a mosque where he had gone to pray. It was a sad end for one whom I must say I liked, and who had been a good friend to us throughout his life.

From time to time I was called upon to cope with unusual situations, some serious, some absurd. One of these involved the disarming of a Greek battalion, believed to be politically unreliable, in camp south of Beirut, which was peacefully accomplished after I had moved troops by night to surround them. Another involved a search for arms in the area of a mountain village. Here intelligence had it that many weapons had been stored or buried, but only a few well-rusted, quite unserviceable arms were found. It was easy to see why; for political reasons the French had had to be told and no doubt the Lebanese had heard all about the plan in lots of time for the village to be warned and for all arms and ammunition to be carried off for storage or burial elsewhere in the mountains. It had been a good night exercise but otherwise a nonsense.

We were concerned with the suppression of the drug traffic, though it was primarily a matter for the Lebanese gendarmerie, some of whom alas were not above being themselves implicated. Someone had the bright idea that our mobile army bath unit might have been exploited and used for this traffic, for it passed freely and frequently through army posts at borders on its cleansing missions. The bath unit was halted, the young officer in charge interrogated, vehicles examined, the large boiler searched: no hashish but, hauled unceremoniously out of the boiler, was a Syrian dancing girl. So much for the young officer who deserved promotion for his initiative. The incident amused me, and the mobile laundry, free once more and complete with its Syrian, went on its way.

One day a crisis arose in Transport Control – railways, docks and so on, important to us because of supplies and freight from Egypt to feed and equip my hordes of men. An agitated staff officer reported trouble. Told to explain, he said that there was a woman dressed as a major on the control staff who spent much of her time 'brassing up' elderly officers of lower rank for their failure to salute her. I said 'Well done' and rejoiced that someone was livening things up. The staff officer did not agree, for he claimed the work at the base was being put seriously out of joint. Could I talk to the turbulent woman? 'Certainly' I said, 'and who on earth is this tigress?' 'She calls herself Lady Sidney Farrar' said the officer. I could not believe my ears, but directed that a car be sent for her at once so that she could be brought before me without delay and calm restored. She was a cousin of Rosemary's and when I last saw her over twenty years previously she had been a young debutante, pink, white and soft, elegantly dressed and living in rich and elegant surroundings, so it was a shock to find myself confronted by a woman tanned by the African sun, a little grim and unsmiling. She put up with a gentle reproof; though I had sympathy for her case, I explained the obvious, that all these old soldiers had given twenty or thirty years service to the army, many plastered all over with Good Conduct and Long Service medals. As her juniors they should certainly salute her, but for my sake please not to 'gum up the works' by rubbing them up the wrong way. She lunched, and over drinks I even made her laugh and later we went for a drive, when I extracted a promise of good behaviour before parting. All went well for a couple of months, or if it did not, I was kept in ignorance of the fact. Alas, an uneasy peace was in time to be shattered by further explosions, so I was forced in everyone's interests, not least her own, to invite Cairo with regret to recall her to duty in Egypt.

Then came VE Day, when it was agreed that celebrations should be held to mark the occasion. I had written a few lines of congratulation that were to appear in the programme, selected an officer and sent him to Jerusalem with orders to have thirty thousand programmes printed, not to come back until he had carried out his mission. In two days he returned and they were distributed to units. The president of the Lebanese republic (at that time Bishara Khalil el-Khoury) sent me a congratulatory message and later issued a more formal one for wide distribution. The sentiments expressed were admirable, and VE Day was ever to be remembered in the Lebanon as a national day of rejoicing.

As for my Victory Day programme, it advertised a wide variety of entertainment, and on an inner page I took the opportunity, as area commander, to address a personal message to all under command:

> My sincerest congratulations to you all on this great day.
> Since those dark months in 1940 when you stood alone, the
> eyes of the world have been turned upon you in gratitude
> and admiration.
>
> So now, when the powers of evil, against which you have
> battled, have crumbled and collapsed, let us give thanks with
> all our hearts for the strength then given us to persevere, and
> for the gallantry and sacrifice that with God's help have
> brought us the victory.
>
> Throughout the world our allies rejoice with you. They
> know that through the six years of a terrible conflict, you
> have marched steadfastly towards this day.
>
> Now, as in battle, so in peace, let us marshal all that is best in
> us, and pray for courage and wisdom to face up to the great
> opportunities and inescapable responsibilities that are ours.
>
> We can lead, we must lead, the world back to sanity.

Understanding, steadfastness, self-discipline and the ability
to make sacrifices are the qualities that will be demanded of
us, and we must not be found wanting.

We had high hopes then of better things to come, of a kindlier and
more enlightened world. Alas, we were soon to be disillusioned, as
was perhaps inevitable, but at the time our spirits rode high and our
aspirations were lofty. It seemed just possible that a larger part of
mankind would at length face up to the challenges and seize the
opportunities that the coming of peace afforded. To our shame, such
ideas found no place in post-war thinking. Expediency, irresponsi-
bility, greed and the 'soft option' were in; humility, effort, personal
responsibility, self-discipline out. The downward drift created confusion, strife, frustration and a despairing lack of purpose. These ills
are still with us, for our minds seem set on transitory unworthy things,
to which increasingly we have become slavishly attached. C. S.
Lewis, in youth an atheist, made the profound remark that 'All that is
not eternal is eternally out of date'. This suggests that, unfashionable
as it now is, we would do well to give priority to those things so
despised by pseudo-intellectuals and their disciples, and with confidence return to admire those qualities that are basic and vital to life,
progress and happiness. This is no pious cry, but sound practical
common sense.

At our sports meeting on VE Day, I thought I should give a lead,
and ran in a race in which I was soundly beaten by a tall Indian less
than half my age. Dressed in running shorts and still panting from
unaccustomed exertion, I was horrified to be told that the French
general and his staff had arrived to present their compliments and to
offer their official congratulations. Needless to say, they were res-
plendent in uniform and full regalia, I had been spotted and there was
no escape. Compliments were exchanged and the elegant Frenchmen departed. What they made of this meeting goodness knows.
Probably they had decided long ago that all British officers were
crazy, and not altogether responsible for erratic behaviour.

This view may well have been reinforced some days later when the
French paid me another more formal visit at my headquarters. Over
drinks, ever interested in their reactions, I showed them a 'game
book' recording the vast number of flies executed with my fly swat
over a period of months! *Mais que c'est magnifique, formidable, fantasti-*

que, said they politely as empty glasses were refilled.

Towards the end of my time in the Lebanon I was invited to call on the Lebanese president who said he wished to present me with the Lebanese Order of the Cedar for my efforts over two years to keep the peace. This was a kind thought, and I expressed my gratitude. Such matters have to pass through diplomatic channels, and after two months I was informed by IXth Army with regret that London had decided that I could not accept the decoration unless my opposite number, a French officer, was similarly rewarded. Naturally the Lebanese at that time flatly refused to honour a Frenchman, so that was that. At a further interview with the president this was confirmed, accompanied by his regrets, apologies, and the presentation of a silver salver with a suitable inscription in Arabic.

I was ordered to perform one last duty before going to Cyprus. This was that of making all administrative and other arrangements connected with the opening of a Middle Eastern Staff College at Haifa in Palestine and outside my area. It was the brainchild of the Commander-in-Chief who attended its opening to address its staff and the first batch of students. Happily all went well. General Paget seemed very pleased and thanked me cordially for what had been done to launch the new seat of learning.

When it became clear that within months my large headquarters building would be de-requisitioned and returned to the Lebanese, I made arrangements for the contents of my chapel, the church furniture, carpeting and lovely brocades to be given to the Anglican Bishop in Jerusalem, who was happy to accept them.

The war in Europe over, the area soon began to be run down very quickly, for it was important to repatriate to the United Kingdom many of the highly skilled men and specialists who had been serving under me. All were to be sent home for demobilization and redeployment in British industry so as to get the wheels turning again and fast. Thus it was that, when my strength had fallen to some 10,000 or so, I was appointed to command British troops in Cyprus.

Chapter Fifteen

India and Cyprus

I had long had an urge to visit India, to see something of its people, millions of them, made up of numerous races holding to strange creeds and customs. I had spent two years doing what was possible to keep French and Lebanese from flying at each other's throats and was overdue for local leave. My application to visit India had been turned down politely by my Commander-in-Chief in Cairo who invited me to consider whether the area now covered by Middle East Command was not big enough to satisfy my curiosity? He had a point, for it was indeed vast, covering all North Africa, Egypt, East Africa, all Asia Minor outside Turkey and much more. Yet India remained my objective, the question was how to beat down opposition; the method chosen was a flank attack and a measure of harmless blackmail by my American friend George Stewart who was then in Cairo. He had for years done superb work for British forces in every command, all generals of importance acknowledged this, consequently he had some influence with them. Clearly he was my man, and entered into the plot happily enough, for he had not yet visited India himself. Within a week – *mirabile dictu* – he rang up to say that a visit to India had been agreed to, for I had said airily that if he could extricate me from Middle East Command, I would look after everything in India.

Two years before in Scotland I had made friends with John Colville – later Lord Clydesmuir – who had been a member of Parliament and Scottish Secretary. He had been appointed Governor of Bombay and had pressed me to visit him there though such a prospect at the time seemed remote. Now I was urged to get there as soon as I could and bring George too, for John Colville had already met him, knew of his work and admired him.

Official papers arrived at my headquarters approving my leave, the documents must have been drawn up by a very unimaginative and humourless staff officer. I was given three weeks from door to door, no travel at public expense, which ruled out cadging a lift in an RAF aircraft even if flying empty; was I to swim? I contacted George who said 'Sure, I'll fix it with our airforce general' and did within twenty-four hours. So it was in a USAF Commando plane that we flew from Cairo to Karachi, and in an RAF Dakota to Bombay.

We landed at Santa Cruz airport to be met by an ADC and were driven twenty miles through Bombay to Government House on Malabar Point. We were housed in state and comfort in The Point Bungalow which stood on the edge of Malabar Point, seventy feet above the sea, with a splendid view over blue water to the city of Bombay, the hills of the Western Ghats beyond for the background.

In no time the governor arrived to greet us, it was good to see him again, for we had much to talk about. I plunged into the sea from the rocks just below my rooms before changing for dinner, when I happened to mention this I was astonished to be told that no one had yet been known to bathe off these rocks – so conveniently near, and taking you straight into deep water. We were waited on hand and foot by dignified, decoratively clothed bearers to a degree that was slightly embarrassing, George found it irritating and was rather shocked. There were dozens of men scattered about the place in scarlet and gilt uniforms, a scarlet flash in each white turban. The military secretary told me that his pay roll at Government House and at Poona was over two thousand.

Michael Scott, one of John Colville's ADCs, was a friend of my young cousin Francis Stuart and had been with him three days before his death, when his Commander-in-Chief, General Auchinleck, in person had pinned the Military Cross to his jacket and testified to his gallantry in action. Francis was one of the most delightful boys I have ever met, and I had felt his loss keenly. As for Michael, he was an unusual person, for he had wide interests and lofty ideals, and was courageous about the multiple wounds he had suffered from an exploding mine on the Lincolnshire coast, when serving with his Coldstream battalion.

Flowers in the gardens were beautiful as indeed they should have been with an army of gardeners to attend to them, and thousands of gallons of water showered daily upon them and on the green lawns. Birds and butterflies were varied and numerous, flying foxes came into roost each evening in trees near the shore. I had never seen such creatures before, with fox-like masks, prick ears, and substantial wing span. Cranes, kingfishers, sand pipers, terns and gulls inhabited these shores where all found peace and sanctuary. The only unhappy creatures I took to be the humans, who had a pathetic yet dignified air of resignation about them that was touching. The human problem was immense and it can never be solved whilst a caste system continues in force, yet no one can visualize its destruction.

In sharp contrast to the slums of Bombay was an afternoon at the races. It was hot in the paddock but cool, with comfortable chairs, in His Excellency's box, where I met a number of celebrities. A charming good-looking Maharanee and I went into partnership, pooling our winning tickets for the daily treble. Describing that afternoon George Stewart wrote: 'I have never seen greater beauty of form and face or of garb; the sari, at home in this climate, too ephemeral for cooler climes, was a perfect dress for the fragile beauty of the Indian women. Astounding colour, never worn well by paler women, contrasted perfectly with darker tones of handsome faces from Kashmir, Sind, the Princely states, the North West Frontier, and from Ceylon and the cities of the South. It was the high season and everyone in society was at the races. Bodices skilfully woven of purple, blue, green, dark indigo, black, snow-white, gold, silver and carmine, saris draped by some magic over glistening black hair, gave the atmosphere of a pageant, only this was real. Not a woman but had fine eyes and perfect white teeth; not a one but was immaculate. As they passed, heady perfume came from their flowing garments. Jewels flashed in the sun.'

A visit to the island of Elephanta was one of the highlights of our stay in Bombay. Tree clad to the water's edge, its vast cave-temples are dedicated to Siva in his many aspects; the isle was rich and important long before the Portugese had founded Bombay. Some buildings, and some of the hand-cut caves 130 feet deep, are said to be fifteen hundred years old.

Very different, and far to the north, was our next stay, at Peshawar where Sir George Cunningham, Governor of the North West Frontier Province for the last nine years, kindly put us up. The train journey had been full of interest, the scenery changing dramatically as we passed through the Punjab and into the North West. At the stations we had noticed small brick huts labelled 'Drinking Water for Hindus' and 'Drinking Water for Moslems', but everyone helped himself from a running tap that stood midway between these exclusive hutments. Near Peshawar the people at the stations included groups of striking-looking men all carrying rifles, the butts studded with brass nails. Some carried shining axes with slender shafts, and I couldn't decide whether they were weapons or domestic implements.

Government House in Peshawar was charming, not too vast, not populated by a horde of servants and filled with flowers – roses, stocks, violets and great sprays of a most beautiful deep pink prunus. The pear orchards round the city were a closely woven carpet of white blossom, but Sir George told us that the fruit itself was horrible. He arranged for us to visit the Khyber Pass under the guidance of a senior political officer.

At the entrance of the famous pass we had to show our credentials on entering tribal territory, all administration within it being carried out by the tribes themselves. The British only interfered in major disputes, but did insist that tribes were not to fight each other within 50 yards of the only road, and that sniping should not take place across it. Local levies called Khassadars were enlisted to guard the road, railway and caravan routes. The highest point on the road is a little below 4000 feet. Railway, road and caravan routes cross and re-cross at intervals, each signposted by drawings of a train, a motor car, a camel; since few could read, this was practical. Thirty miles of rail ran from Peshawar to a border terminus at Landi Kotal passing through more than thirty tunnels bored out of the rocky hills. The last station was surrounded by fortress-like walls for defence against raiders. Numerous small forts and block-houses perched on top of commanding hills dominate the road.

Tribal villages were small, all were surrounded by high fortress walls of mud and stone, with loop holes and watchtowers. We asked our guide why there had been so much trouble through the years. 'Sometimes', he said, 'the outer tribes are hungry, or just want other people's things. Sometimes there is a feud. Generally they just get tired of peace and want to do some shooting'. Down near the river women were washing clothes on rocks by the water. They left off work for a time to watch a procession of men carrying a long bundle rolled in red cloth – it was the funeral of an Afridi woman, men being wrapped in black cloth. Only men attended funerals.

Buses to and from Kabul ran regularly down the Khyber, crowded with tribesmen whose sheep, dogs, skins, carpets and baggage were lashed to the top. One swayed past us at hazardous speed, carrying Afridis, Afghans, Turcomans, Bashkirs, Kalmucks from far off Russian Turkestan, and slant-eyed Mongoloids from behind the Hindu Kush. Beyond the Afghan frontier to the north east lay ever more desolate, jagged miles of lesser peaks; the Hindu Kush stood out among the world's great mountains. Towering up into the clouds, their white heads struck awe even at great distances, and beyond them lay some of the world's most inaccessible lands.

On the 2nd March we flew south again to New Delhi, where we were fortunate to attend a splendid Viceroy's Parade (there were not to be many more of them) under the ancient walls of the Red Fort. The occasion was the presentation of five Victoria Crosses. We were given excellent seats as it happened just behind Oliver Leese, then Commander Land Forces South East Asia, and Bridget Carlisle, then Head of the ATS in India, and had a lot to say to both. Immediately in front of us were the two survivors to be decorated, and the families of the three who were dead. Bands and Guards of Honour from each Training Centre of the regiments to which the recipients of the Victoria Crosses belonged were drawn up in the centre of the immense grassy square.

Along the sides of the rectangle detachments of troops were formed up. Soon after nine the Chief Justice of India, members of the Executive Council and other dignitaries arrived and five minutes later the Commander-in-Chief General Auchinleck, finally the Viceroy, Lord Wavell. A Gurkha band was an amazing combination of pipes, brasses, trumpets and drums. Nowhere else could one find pipes mixed with other instruments save the traditional drums, but the Gurkhas seemed to manage it, and in the course of the inspection played in a peculiar, slow and rhythmic manner 'Believe me, if all those endearing young charms'. Following the inspection Lord Wavell stood whilst an Indian officer read out each citation, and the first recipient of this most coveted decoration stepped forward to have it pinned on his breast, then exchanged a few words with the Viceroy. The rifleman who followed was a Gurkha. The next three awards were made posthumously, two to widows, one to a mother. One of the widows, a young seventeen-year old seemed in a trance – I thought she would swoon; when Lord Wavell placed the cross in her hand she returned to her seat, and immediately her little son, four years old, took the precious medal and put it in his mouth.

The most moving award went to Lachrum Kumri, the aged mother, who had walked many miles over Himalayan trails to a village whence a British officer had provided for her journey and accompanied her to Delhi. The old lady stood before Lord Wavell, straight and grey, her face deeply wrinkled by sun and wind, the peculiar nobility of the pure in heart shining from her eyes. No one in the vast concourse possessed more natural dignity. Wavell, himself a great man, stiffened, for he knew he faced a person of kindred mettle. He waited for the reading of the citation with a smile of admiration, then handed the cross to the mother who returned to her seat. The band played, troops marched past, the parade was over.

How, we asked, were transport, special food, sleeping quarters and clothing arranged for these women from afar? 'It is all carefully laid on', we were told. 'Officers who speak the language are sent to the villages, clothing is bought, and these people are personally conducted, they are housed and fed in such a manner that no religious custom will be broken. The conducting officers have no other duties until the families are returned to their homes.' We expressed our admiration for such careful preparation.

We were rather disappointed with Lutyens's New Delhi, apart from the ornamental use of water, and visits to the Red Fort and the remains of the six earlier Delhis were more rewarding. Back to Bombay, where we spent three restful days (apart from the large luncheon parties that appeared to be almost a daily occurrence at Government House) and after taking leave of the kindly Colvilles returned to the Middle East as we had come.

It was not difficult to guess that the British departure from India would not be long delayed. Our short stay showed us that on the whole the British achievement in India was one to be proud of – something with which many distinguished Indians agreed. If we had stayed, we should have been blamed for obstructing self-government, however patiently we continued to educate and guide its peoples, so diverse and rent with caste and religious differences: alas, our unavoidable abandonment of responsibility led to the partition of the sub-continent and to murderous excesses on a hideous and massive scale.

I had enjoyed my visit to India, had seen and learned much from it; but when I landed at Beirut on the 11th March, the snow-capped mountains of Lebanon were a beautiful and welcoming sight, even though I was so soon to bid farewell to them.

Appointed to command in Cyprus, I considered how I should approach and take over my small kingdom, for unlike Richard Coeur de Lion I was not faced with the need to rescue a queen. He had paused briefly in his crusade against the Saracens to recapture Queen Berengaria from the King of Cyprus whose galleys had taken her prisoner. None could enlighten me as to the site of his landing so many centuries ago, but a glance at a map of the island convinced me that the place had been Kyrenia, a small fortified port, and one of the most beautiful places in that lovely island. Right or wrong, I planned to make my landing at Kyrenia, and the Royal Navy, ever ready to assist, agreed to convey me there in style in one of His Majesty's destroyers.

So I took over my command on the beach at Kyrenia, was met on landing by members of my new staff and driven to our headquarters in the capital, Nicosia. Some days were spent in getting to know the staff, making friends with the Governor and District Commissioners, visiting army units and bases and generally summing things up. I took over about a brigade and one armoured regiment, and in addition miscellaneous specialist and administrative units, and other troops for duties in camps, posts and bases.

We ran an efficient Infantry Training Centre for Cypriot forces, where NCOs were trained in considerable numbers. It catered for Greek and Turkish Cypriots alike, for at that time there was no friction between them.

As in the Lebanon, Syria and Transjordan, there were many evidences of past civilizations. When I had time I visited ancient sites and ruins, most of them of great interest, some dating back to 3500 BC: Neolithic, Hellenistic, Greco-Roman, Roman, Byzantine, Saracen. Whilst nothing remained in Cyprus that could be compared in size and grandeur to the spectacular ruins of Baalbek, yet there was one quite outstanding Crusader castle that struck me as even more splendid than the fabulous Krak des Chevaliers in Syria, this was St Hilarion, a truly fairy-tale castle. Once a royal house of the Lusignan dynasty, established by Richard the Lion-hearted, it is built on lofty crags, joined by battlements, with turrets, towers, storage rooms, armouries, ramparts for defence, cisterns and catchments for a year's supply of water. It had been one of the most formidable of the Crusaders' strongholds, its outer walls enclosing several acres of land. The architects and engineers of the day had laid out sleeping quarters, kitchens, guard rooms and battle stations with amazing skill. From its walls large sections of the island lay spread out like a map, and on a fine day, across the waters of the Mediterranean, the coast of Asia Minor was plainly visible. The mountains of the Lebanon, clothed in snow, formed the limit of the eastern horizon. Far below this splendid fortress which dominated the small port of Kyrenia, and a short distance from its harbour, stood the ruins of the Abbey of Bellapaise, strikingly beautiful with the mountainside reaching up behind it into the sky. I was so impressed by both of these ruins and by their romantic settings that I got an artist of some distinction to paint me water-colours of them, and guided him to the point from which he was to work. These and other water colours of Cyprus now hang with those of Turkey, Constantinople, the Bosphorus, Jerusalem and Palestine, in our house, colourful reminders of travels in distant lands.

Richard Coeur de Lion seized Cyprus in 1191 on his crusade to the Holy Land and had there married Berengaria of Navarre in the town of Amathus near Limasol, where she was crowned Queen of England. A year or so later King Richard, after negotiations with the Knights Templar regarding the ownership of Cyprus, gave the island to Guy de Lusignan, formerly King of Jerusalem. The Lusignan dynasty held Cyprus for three centuries from 1192 to 1489. Later the island was held by Genoese and Venetians who erected many buildings, especially at Famagusta, the site chosen by Shakespeare for the Cypriot scenes of *Othello*. Following the Venetians came the Turks, who gave the Orthodox Church a measure of autonomy, but let everything fall into the decay and corruption that was the general order of the day under the rule of the Ottoman sultans. Britain took over Cyprus in 1878 and made it a Crown Colony in 1925.

The administration of the island was now the responsibility of the Colonial Office who appointed a governor and a number of district commissioners. Under the governor they saw to the general welfare, to the establishment and the maintenance of justice, and to law and order within their districts. As area commander it was my duty to support and to work in close cooperation with these experienced, hard working civil servants. There was no problem, for all were kind, helpful and ready to give useful guidance on civilian affairs when these impinged on matters military. On a previous visit to Cyprus I had stayed with one of the island's commissioners – Mr Percival – and had gone on a tour of his district. We stopped at a rural coffee-house where soon most of the village joined us; whilst the schoolmaster acted as spokesman, everyone felt free to express his views on crops, prices, the war, shortages, education and health problems. All were discussed face to face with the utmost candour. Our commissioners were greatly respected, and fully justified the confidence reposed in them by all sections of the community, for they dealt wisely and sympathetically with all matters brought to their attention. In local disputes conflicting views were if possible reconciled; if not, judgement was given which was accepted and seen to be just.

In my time, Cyprus – some years later so turbulent – was at peace, for I had the means and determination to keep it so. The economy was small – small farms, small vineyards, yielding good wines and brandy, small fisheries and small trade. The British Army, the RAF and Royal Navy installations then based in the island brought much money to the civil population and considerable employment. Civil and military in Cyprus were on friendly terms, the only tensions lay in the realm of politics, which changed from day to day. Rumours and cross-currents ran so fast that no one could keep abreast of them, and I personally made no attempt to do so. Every small difference in political views in Greece was reflected immediately in Cyprus, for like Greeks on the mainland Cypriots were mercurial in their attitude toward any regime. The Pan-Hellenic movement was strong despite the fact that the island had never been united with Greece in modern times, but it never erupted into violence as it did so tragically some years later.

We had long had a military presence in the island in times of peace, usually one company detached from a battalion stationed in Egypt. A small house had been built high in the tree-clad mountains of Troodos, where it was always cool, sometimes very cool at night, for it stood high under Mount Olympus. The little house had long been a retreat in hot weather for officers of the small garrison, so I took it over and spent a number of agreeable weekends there. A short distance down the mountainside was the governor's summer residence to which he would repair when the heat in Nicosia grew oppressive. I got to know and like him and on several occasions dined with him in his house amidst the pines. He was doing a splendid job despite difficulties and frustrations. He was enthusiastic about forestry and re-afforestation, but goats, as everywhere in the Middle East, were a curse, de-foresting large areas, though the government was making headway in replanting. Goat-herders were uncooperative, and often a greater menace than their flocks, for deprived of free access to the grazing in young woodlands because of new protecting fencing, they occasionally set fire to plantations. The governor was eager to improve the island's ports and harbours, and considered dredging necessary, but suitable equipment was non-existent; where we or the Navy were in a position to help we always did so gladly.

Cypriot archbishops were always politically motivated, as were most of the Greek Orthodox clergy, the administration tended to mistrust them so there was little contact. My American friend George Stewart, staying with me for some days, sought leave to visit the archbishop. I thought it proper to invite the governor to agree to this, for it was a civilian administrative matter. Permission was given, though we were to be accompanied by the commissioner for Nicosia. So off we went to visit Archbishop Leontios who lived in a monastery in the hills at Stavrouvuni perched on the peak of a conical mountain some fifty miles from my headquarters. During the troubles of Sir Ronald Storr's administration when Government House had been set alight, Leontios had for a time been banished to Jerusalem, as later had his successor Makarios, that thorn in the side of Britain. The governor – later Lord Caradon – doubted whether the archbishop could speak English, but George was able to reassure him, for he had been partly responsible for Leontios' education and training in America after completing which he had returned to Cyprus via the Lambeth Conference.

Despite the fact that Greek bishops were ancestrally called upon by their people to be political leaders, and that politics were as ever in a highly volatile state of confusion, we found the archbishop welcoming and moderate in his views. As a result of this contact a meeting with the governor was arranged, and soon took place, it was appreciated by all concerned and relationships became more cordial. Leontios really cared little for politics, he wanted to train and lead an educated clergy, to provide social services, schools for the people, and other projects of like nature. Alas, parties used him, then deserted him, and a few years after the war he died. He was succeeded by that 'turbulent priest' Archbishop Makarios, who was to become president of Cyprus.

George Stewart's passion for collecting masonry did not run riot as it had done in the Lebanon and in Syria – perhaps he did get hold of a large stone or two from St Hilarion or from Bellapaise? However he ordered a very large and elaborate tapestry to be made in Nicosia by a Madame Johannides, widely famed for her needlework. Careful instructions were given, the tapestry was to depict saints, apostles and Christian martyrs. When it eventually reached America, to be hung in George's chapel, it was seen that there was nothing Christian about it. Beautifully executed, there stood out a fine collection of pagan gods, goddesses and numerous figures of Greek mythology. Having a strong sense of humour, George nevertheless hung it in his chapel, though somewhat removed from the altar that was to have been its resting place.

I missed the daily rides along the Mediterranean shore I had so enjoyed when in the Lebanon. Recreation was now confined to bathing in the sea from many splendid beaches, and to long walks and uphill climbs, particularly in the pine forests around Troodos. I got to know Cyprus well and made every effort to do so, visiting units scattered throughout the island or located in the four small ports of which Kyrenia in the north, Famagusta in the east, Larnaca and Limasol in the south were the most important. From time out of mind they had been centres of Levantine seaborne commerce, and were all of absorbing interest, with native craft built on the shore, their sails right out of Phoenician times, resting beside modern liners, freighters and troopships. I drove my car about my little kingdom with King Richard's emblem, the lion rampant, flying at its bonnet to remind me, and all who saw it, of that valiant and legendary monarch.

Before leaving the Lebanon I had been invited to take on responsibilities in a much wider field covering the whole vast area of the Middle East Command. I had flown to Cairo to discuss the matter and had given it much thought before reluctantly deciding to turn it down. Had I been a free agent I would certainly have accepted the appointment, for by doing so I should in the course of duty have seen something of many new lands, Ethiopia, Kenya, Somalia, Iraq and all the countries of North Africa amongst them. However, the war had ended and I was under pressure from my family to get home as speedily as might be.

Life had not been easy for Rosemary who had had to bear all the problems and anxieties of difficult wartime conditions, which were in no way relaxed with the advent of peace, and she had had to cope alone with our children's education. So one way and another, it was time to get back as soon as I could be released.

It had been kind indeed of General Paget, the Commander-in-Chief, to offer me that new appointment, and I fear he was less than pleased by my rejection of it, for he sent his Chief of Staff to press me afresh. However that may have been, when I did eventually leave Cyprus I dined in his mess as I passed through Cairo, and he was a kind and gracious host who seemed interested in my future plans.

The following day I flew to Tripoli, spent the night there, and the next morning saw me on the last leg of my journey home. The welcoming sight of those tall white cliffs I found moving after long absence, they seemed to stand as guardians of so much that I held dear. I could not take my eyes off them, and as we approached and flew over them a little wave of patriotic fervour (never far below the surface) washed over me, reminding me of Sir Walter Scott's verses learnt in childhood, that spoke of the returning exile. We landed in mid-afternoon on an East Anglian airfield. The Customs examination was brief, and no time was lost in contacting my sister who then lived in Essex. After two nights under her hospitable roof, I travelled to Scotland to rejoin Rosemary then staying with her mother, Honor Lady Clerk, at North Berwick. It was a joy to be at home again.

Chapter Sixteen

'Wars are Over'

My second war ended, to which should be added a near miss in Turkey in 1923, I was quite prepared to face up to a third. Many thought that the disastrous outcome of the Yalta Conference, leading to the enslavement of Eastern Europe and to the isolation of Berlin, had sown the seeds of conflict which would lead inevitably to a war of devastating proportion. Nearly forty years on, those dark threatening clouds still hang over us, and only a precarious 'balance of terror' shields us from disaster.

And so I gave myself two years' leave, the first months spent in visiting friends throughout the United Kingdom. My demobilization was delayed for a time as there had been some question of my joining the British Military Mission in Washington whose leader was General Sir Henry Maitland Wilson – 'Jumbo' to his friends – an outsize, benevolent figure, whom I was later to see much of. The plan came to nothing; the war at an end, the mission's services receded, its numbers were reduced and in due course it was dissolved.

Our Scottish home, The Barony House at Lasswade in Midlothian, had been leased to a senior naval officer stationed at Rosyth, and it was late in December 1945 before we could move into it. It was a cold winter of fuel shortages but happily we had plenty of 'blown' timber to cut into logs. I was never idle. A formal garden of some size had been neglected which called for much labour to restore to some semblance of its former elegance; overgrown timber had to be felled, an orchard replanted, yew hedges trimmed into shape, small avenues of lime trees pollarded and many colourful shrubs and trees planted whose blossom would in spring be a delight. Later to save unnecessary mowing I planted many thousands of daffodil bulbs, massed in a relatively small area, which year after year give an impressive display.

On the 29th June 1946 our second son, Robin, was born in the room which had been Sir Walter Scott's bedroom when he had been lent the house – then known as Lasswade Cottage – from 1798 to 1804 by his friend Sir John Clerk of Penicuik, Rosemary's forebear. It was here that Scott brought his bride when they were newly wed, and it was in what is now our dining room that he wrote *The Lay of the Last Minstrel*, a poem which I have always loved since as a small boy I learned much of it by heart. It speaks to us today of values which we would be the better for remembering –

> Breathes there the man, with soul so dead,
> Who never to himself hath said
>   This is my own, my native land!
> Whose heart hath ne'er within him burn'd,
> As home his footsteps he hath turn'd
>   From wandering on a foreign strand!
> If such there breathe, go, mark him well;
> For him no Minstrel raptures swell;
> High though his titles, proud his name,
> Boundless his wealth as wish can claim;
> Despite those titles, power and pelf,
> The wretch, concentred all in self,
> Living, shall forfeit fair renown,
> And, doubly dying, shall go down
> To the vile dust, from whence he sprung,
> Unwept, unhonoured, and unsung.

We paid frequent visits to London to see friends and to visit our elder son, Stephen, first at Eton and later when he was doing National Service training in the Brigade Squad at the Guards Depot. This was followed by Sandhurst before he was commissioned as a 2nd lieutenant into the IXth Lancers.

An eccentric friend of those days was John Heaton Armstrong, a Herald whose charmingly medieval title was Rouge Dragon Poursuivant. A room in his large flat near the Albert Hall was festooned with wires on pulleys along which cardboard pheasants, partridges, grouse and ducks would fly. In another smaller room he established a miniature rifle range, a great pile of old telephone directories stacked high against a wall making a satisfactory bullet stop. Having dined we were always required to exhibit our skill as marksmen, not always a reliable test, for his delightful French wife laid scrumptious meals before us and John saw to it that excellent wines accompanied them.

They were both delightful and great fun. John's heraldic career culminated in his appointment as Clarenceux King of Arms and a knighthood.

In Scotland we saw much of Rosemary's grandmother, Aymée Lady Clerk, who had a charming house in North Berwick. Visits to her were always rewarding, for she was intensely interested in everything up to the day of her death aged 94 in 1947. She thought profoundly and recorded some of her thoughts and conclusions in writings that she was to bequeath to me. In lighter vein she took the view that good food and wine helped stimulate witty and intelligent conversation. What guest, however dim, would quarrel with that? So it was always fun and never dull to sit at her table.

One of her great friends in North Berwick, though utterly different in character, was Margot Lady Asquith, whom I had met previously in Paris and London, and with whom I was now occasionally commanded to play golf. For me it was a highly entertaining exercise, though infuriating for serious players behind, since oblivious to their existence Lady Asquith would frequently miss the ball, was in no hurry to finish the round and talked ceaselessly, her ever-active mind set on other things. Her friendship with Rosemary's grandmother was remarkable and deep. Lady Asquith wrote an appreciation of her friend, but died first; her appreciation nevertheless appeared in *The Scotsman*:

> Her hospitality and generosity, as well as her many tastes, in gardening, golf, and devising plans for the amusement of her guests, made her a lovable companion. She had a happy life – since all who are as much loved as she was are happy. Her fidelity in friendship was rare; nor have I, in a long acquaintance, ever seen her out of temper. She loved life, and no one who knew her as well as I did could think of her as old. I think no one who retains the power she had of loving so many people and so many things of beauty can ever grow old. Although she was not an artist in the strict sense of the word, she was an artist with no achievements. She was never tired of showing her love for all that was beautiful, and all that was good. Such a woman as I have tried to describe need never be mourned. She should be emulated.

We spent some weeks in Ireland every summer with my mother, as we had done in pre-war years. It was always a delight to be back in Donegal and to see once more the family retainers – a sadly dwindling band as the years took their toll, and now reduced to a single old friend, nearly a hundred, who used to be a nursery maid.

In 1948 I was persuaded by Joe Airlie, then commandant of the Army Cadet Force in Scotland, to help with its reorganization and to build up an independent Scottish Headquarters in Edinburgh designed to cover the whole country from the Shetlands to the Borders. It was a challenge, for much was in disarray, and remote control from London at that time was ineffective. I started from scratch, for there was no headquarters, no staff, no furniture, no typewriters, no telephones and only £360 in the kitty. However, I embarked on this unpromising adventure and found modest headquarters within a stone's throw of the New Club to which I could repair to meet people and feed. I bought bare essentials, installed two splendid, self-sacrificing girls to run the office, able and willing to do so for pin money, whilst I got about Scotland to see how best to plan developments.

The object of the Army Cadet Force as defined in its charter is to develop the cadet's character and powers of leadership; to instil in him the soldierly qualities of discipline, initiative and self-reliance, and to teach him the duties, obligations and responsibilities of a good citizen. This last seemed to me the most important and enduring lesson to be learnt. Our cadets ranged in age from 14 to 18 when National Service, then obligatory, claimed them.

My early visits to units were enlightening, some were dreadfully bad and many ill led. In one county for example all that could be salvaged of two battalions was one platoon on which to build afresh. Scottish Command approved of my recommendations for reductions and disbandments. Leadership was, as always, the key to better things, but good officers were hard to find and I sought them everywhere. All ACF units were administered by the Territorial Army as then established, with drill halls and headquarters in every county. The cadets were affiliated to Scottish regiments, wearing their badges and proud of their traditions. Help and encouragement were given me by Scottish Command, by Territorial Army Associations and by Lords Lieutenant, all of whom took the keenest interest in our work.

I formed various committees, an executive committee the most important. On it a number of my more influential friends agreed to serve, amongst them Airlie, John Colville (now Lord Clydesmuir) and his brother-in-law Lord Bilsland who had been Commissioner for the West of Scotland during the war when for two years I was commander in his region, and in civilian matters his subordinate. Sports and finance sub-committees were brought into being and a religious advisory panel representative of all denominations to guide us in spiritual matters. Thus our work got under way, and apart from finance prospered.

A day came when Airlie, whilst remaining a member of the executive committee, sought to resign as commandant so I set about finding a successor. Many were consulted and offered suggestions, but it was my American friend George Stewart, then staying with me at Barony, whose choice was General Sir Richard O'Connor who had just retired from the post of Adjutant General. O'Connor had been a splendid fighting soldier and amongst other exploits had with very limited resources routed an entire Italian army. He had himself been taken prisoner in the desert. In captivity in Italy he escaped thrice, and was recaptured twice: his third attempt was successful, and on his return to England he was appointed to command British armoured forces in the invasion of Europe. With such a record he was clearly my man. I consulted General Sir Philip Christison, then C-in-C Scottish Command. He approved, wrote personally to O'Connor and soon General O'Connor arrived in Edinburgh to go into the matter, and eventually accepted. It was to be a red letter day for the ACF in Scotland, since not only were they blessed to be led by a man of extraordinary modesty and tact but by one with an impressive record of military achievement. His personal qualities and unassailable integrity, clear for all to see, were of the utmost importance to a movement dedicated to the service of youth. His splendid example and dedicated application to the work won him widespread affection and respect. His service as commandant covered a period of some twelve years, and saw the movement in Scotland firmly established on solid foundations.

We travelled much of Scotland together paying visits to units and camps; when these happened to be in the far north I was invited to stay at his home at Rosemarkie in the Black Isle. He and his wife were both charming hosts – sadly they had no children of their own, though Sir Richard adopted the son of his wife's previous marriage, who now bears his name. We went to conferences and meetings several times a year in the south; we were attending one of these in London when King George VI died. A great sadness descended on us, for there were none who did not feel deeply the loss of one who had, with his splendid and courageous Queen, given such devoted, brave, unselfish service to his country and its people throughout the war, and in the difficult years that followed. With my general on our way to an appointment at the Scottish Office close by the Houses of Parliament, I remember running into Leo Amery walking distractedly, head down and hatless, perhaps in tears. We both knew him quite well, but he scarcely seemed to recognize us, acknowledging our presence with a slight wave; I was touched by his evident distress and sense of loss, which was shared, less dramatically, throughout the kingdom. It was the end of an era, and what the future held for us no one could yet foresee, but our King had set us a noble example of simple faith and courage.

That evening I had gone to Sandhurst to stay with my friend Steven Anderson, then Chief Instructor at the Royal Military Academy, for Stephen's 'passing out' parade the next day. Like other events it was cancelled, to be replaced by a splendid and moving service in the chapel. Stephen was duly commissioned into the IXth Lancers and joined his regiment in the British Army of the Rhine within days.

A new reign about to begin, the nation was enchanted by the youthful Queen's grace and beauty, and deeply touched by her personal declaration of service and dedication to her task. It was suggested to the Queen that she might like to carry out an inspection of Scottish cadets of all three services when at Holyrood in 1952, and to that Her Majesty agreed. I was made responsible for all the planning. The Queen's Park was chosen as the site. I wrote all the orders concerning the form and conduct of the parade, movements, drill and so forth and was required to go through them in great detail with Michael Adeane at Buckingham Palace and get the Queen's approval. Scottish Command and Territorial Associations responsible for administration and travel arrangements for their contingents could not have been more helpful and co-operative. Mercifully the 28th June was a fine day and all went well. When the affair was over

Joe Airlie insisted on presenting me to the Queen who had a few kind words to say.

The 1950s were sad years. Hugo Gough, of whom I was very fond and whom I had known all my adult life, died at his home near Inverness in 1951 and I was required to represent the Irish Guards and Field Marshal Alex at his funeral. He was a strange but attractive character and there will have been few who served with or under him as I had done for many years who can have been other than touched by his eccentricities; and they were many. It may be that they prevented him from rising to high rank, for officialdom does not take readily to the unorthodox. On his dressing table stood four miniatures of his immediate forebears, all distinguished generals of whom two had won VCs. I had the impression that somehow he felt he had let the family down by failing to rise above the rank of lieut. colonel and having no VC! This was absurd and I would not have had him other than he was, brave, kind and entertaining. He had been severely wounded and taken prisoner in August 1914 and lost an arm. He was recaptured when the British over-ran the hospital in which he lay, in the forward thrust following the retreat from Mons.

Then Lord Camrose died in June 1954 and I went to London to attend the impressive service at St Paul's. The great cathedral was packed with mourners, his friend Winston Churchill amongst them. Of the many tributes paid to him at his death, most were concerned with his achievements, but I was touched by one in *The Sunday Times*: 'It is not the scale of Lord Camrose's attainment that shines as an example to youth: it is rather the fact that it was founded upon qualities which all may emulate; the hardest of hard work, complete business integrity, a courage and confidence which neither obstacles nor reverses could confound, and a determination to apply in his chosen world of journalism the highest standards of cleanness, reliability and truth. He never stooped to a shady thing, nor shirked to do a hard one.' Then there was a poetic tribute from A. P. Herbert of which I quote two lines: 'He had an armoury, of heart and mind, Wise, and courageous, friendly, calm and kind.'

In February 1956 I attended an investiture at Buckingham Palace to receive a modest award from the hand of the Queen Mother. Tim Nugent and Sidney Fitzgerald, now courtiers and members of her entourage, deserted their posts to offer congratulations and to have a talk. Visits to London were always enlivened by meetings with friends; an unusual one was an old comrade, jester, and exuberant Coldstream friend, Norman Gwatkin who had become a courtier and a KCVO. If we met, usually in Berkeley Street near our club, he would gather me into a bear-like embrace to the surprise of those admirably conducted men with their biscuit-coloured bowler hats who stood guardians at the entrance to the Berkeley Hotel. Norman was a most entertaining person and full of life. As a courtier he must have enlivened many a dull moment for those he served and lightened their burden on pompous occasions. Alas, an early death was soon to claim him.

Not many years later I was destined to lose Tim Nugent and Sidney Fitzgerald. On Tim's death Sidney had written 'You may like to know that Tim always had a great fondness and admiration for you!' I was touched, for I felt the same sentiments for both those loyal and valued friends whose unwavering support and comradeship had lasted for more than half a century in war and in peace.

> Beauty, strength, youth, are flowers but fading seen;
> Duty, faith, love, are roots, and ever green.

> George Peele (1558–97)

In 1956 Lady Airlie to whom I had long been devoted died. I had looked in on her at Airlie from time to time and in 1951 she had sent me a biography she had written for, I imagine, her immediate family. It was the story of Patrick and Mabell Ogilvy from their earliest days. In the flyleaf she had written 'In token of a *shared* remembrance of two very wonderful people, Airlie Castle, 22nd October 1951'. I was greatly touched, had the little book specially bound and it is one of my treasures.

I will always remember Mabell Airlie with the greatest admiration and with deep affection. She was in every way a quite remarkable woman, interested in everything and in people, brave, wise and warm hearted, an inspiration and an example to all of us lesser mortals.

My eccentric godfather Rosslyn Bruce also died that year, his devotion to all animals, which he himself described as 'Divine Beastliness', unabated. He would I think have approved of our attachment to dogs of which throughout our lives we have had many. Now that we had come to live on the outskirts of Edinburgh we no longer kept large shooting dogs, for the problem of exercise became increasingly difficult. When in time old age claimed them we turned

to King Charles Cavalier spaniels, elegant, affectionate little creatures. They towed Rosemary about when twice daily she exercised
seven of them on leads outside our gates – twenty-eight paws to two
small feet. She became increasingly interested in the breed and has
been for years President of the Scottish Cavalier Club. I have never
regretted bringing them into our lives. King Charles II was devoted
to them and had been painted holding one in his arms. They enjoy
being talked to. When one sings gently into their silken ears they
listen politely, until they move determinedly off a lap to rest on a
comfortable sofa or armchair and promptly go to sleep. They are
great ones for sleep: how wise to shut out the world and its cares
which are of small concern to them, for as befits royal dogs – and they
seem to know all about that – everything is provided for their comfort
and delight.

Twice daily we feed a motley collection of birds and beasts,
including a cock pheasant and his four wives, magpies, two crows, a
multitude of smaller birds and two squirrels. Our garden has now
become a sanctuary where all are free to nest or succour their young.
One is never surprised by what one may encounter, from a roe deer
disturbed from sleep under a clump of wild roses to nesting
pheasants and partridges, even one year a duck and her brood quite a
distance from water.

For years I had been considering giving up shooting and did so on
my seventy-fifth birthday – perhaps I had at last grown up? It had
been a lengthy process. I abominated shooting hares and had long
refused to do so, for if wounded they cry pitifully. Some Highlanders
are said to believe them to be reincarnated grandmothers, though I
never met a Highlander who would admit to such a belief, but it is an
agreeable thought, for it allows the hares to gambol unmolested
about the hillsides. Looking back at earlier days, I am amazed at my
enthusiasm and energy, that devoted to other more worthy things
might have done some good. No shooting day was ever too arduous or
too long. The wheel has turned full circle, for now I am ashamed and
disgusted with myself over such thoughtless destruction of bird and
beast. Nimrod, the mighty hunter, is no more, and glad of it. It is
shameful that man's dominion over the animal kingdom can be so
abused and exploited for ostentatious pleasure, worse still for greed
or profit.

The 1950s, though saddened by the loss of friends, had happier moments when Stephen returned to Scotland from Germany to be adjutant to the Lanarkshire Yeomanry, a regiment affiliated to his IXth Lancers, and when we made frequent visits to Robin at Maidwell and later at Eton. At both schools he was happy and at Eton did well as a 'wet bob'; I recovered some of my distant youth running with a crowd of others along the banks of the Thames encouraging his boat to excel, which it often did.

My mother died at her home in Ireland in 1957, which was a sad blow to us all, for she was a woman of strong personality and much wisdom. For ten years she had suffered from arthritis in her hips and when over seventy had courageously undergone an operation to put things right. For seven or eight years it had done so, but before the end she was crippled afresh. Throughout her life she had been unusually fit and active and this must have distressed her greatly, but she bore pain and disability courageously and without complaint.

In 1965 I was appointed a deputy-lieutenant for Midlothian. Early the previous year I had given up the secretaryship of the Army Cadet Force in Scotland, thus severing a last link with the army. An earlier link was snapped in June 1969, when Field Marshal Alex died under anaesthetic following a sudden heart attack. It was a deep blow to all who admired and loved him, and to the Irish Guards whose illustrious colonel he had been. Soon after his death I was asked by a friend to sum him up as man and soldier. It was no easy task, and I made no attempt to comment on the field marshal as a senior commander of great armies, for many others far better qualified than I have already written or spoken of his outstanding achievements. What I wrote and still abide by was this:

'Alex was a strong, entirely straightforward character, moulded by an unquestioning belief, a firm sense of duty, and by those standards of conduct and obligations that in our day were understood and accepted by all, in his case often softened by a sense of fun and a keen sense of the ridiculous. He was not a complex character, his was a sound well-balanced intelligence, with a quick grasp of essentials. In a crisis he had the ability to react correctly, swiftly and decisively. As to ambition? He cannot I suppose have been entirely devoid of some, but he never showed any outward sign of chasing down that sterile road – he really had no need to. His most outstanding characteristics as a soldier were a buoyant spirit and abounding confidence based on self-discipline; a great personal courage; unusual adaptability;

physical fitness; and an optimistic streak. He had an independent spirit and great determination – but he was never aggressive. His relationship with seniors and juniors alike was always kindly, interested, possibly at times slightly aloof. As a person he had great magnetism, he led by example, and rode us with the lightest of reins, so that we responded cheerfully to whatever task he set us. He never threatened or blustered; giving his orders, even in moments of stress, he did so calmly, simply and clearly, so there were no misunderstandings. No sacrificial demands were ever made by him of his subordinates in which he was not prepared to accept his full share of risk, and everybody knew this. His whole approach to problems, however exacting or frustrating, was gay and confident, this sustained the fearful and stimulated the lazy to give of their best. I do not ever remember him dejected even by battle casualties which were heavy in that first war, though – devoted to his men, as they to him – he must have felt losses keenly.

His characteristics made him, as they could not fail to do, a superb leader of men at every stage from subaltern (when I first knew him) to field marshal. It is fair to say that he enjoyed and was stimulated by the challenges of war, accepting its hazards with a contemptuous smile and with complete confidence in being able to cope, and this "rubbed off" on those about him. He thrived on challenges throughout his life, those of Dunkirk and Burma he took in his stride. Alex was a great, modest, and charming person; practising all the knightly virtues of courage, courtesy, compassion and endurance in adversity. He is one of my military heroes, the great Montrose and Prince Rupert the others. Alex combined a lot of both, the dash and unselfish service of Prince Rupert, and the superb and sustained heroism of Montrose. He had come cheerfully through so many perils that to me he seemed indestructible, and though I did know that his brave heart gave him trouble, his relatively sudden death was a very sad and unexpected blow.'

Only a year earlier he had shared my rug on a warm evening on the 4th June at Eton watching the procession of boats in which Robin was taking part, and later enjoyed the fireworks. He seemed happy and relaxed, so did Lady Margaret who sat with Rosemary – they had been together at a finishing school in Paris – and there was no sign of strain, anxiety or foreboding. I attended his memorial service on the 11th July at the Guards Chapel. It was a sad and touching occasion.

The hymns were doubtless of his choosing; they included *St Patrick's breastplate*, and *There is a green hill*, written amongst others by Mrs Alexander, a cousin of my mother's, and the wife of Bishop Alexander, a past Primate of all Ireland and one of his clan.

On my eightieth birthday I was treated to a splendid party at Penicuik, and for our golden wedding in 1978 to one at Barony. Having so much to be grateful for I happily count my blessings, ill-merited though they be, for they are many and enduring. They include a very happy marriage, the companionship we found in our daughter Bridget and two sons, Stephen and Robin, and our delight in a well balanced party of grandchildren, two girls and two boys. A happy band of godchildren and many splendid friends. As I grow older I look back as many another has on the freshness and wonder of my early years. I do not mean the familiar delights of childhood, nor the familiar regrets for them. This is no exercise in nostalgia, rather one of seeking enlightenment, for there seems to be a mystery and significance peculiar to childhood.

Could it be that in early childhood we have been accorded a momentary foretaste of a larger life, only to relapse into the prison-house? Some wise men subscribe to that view, and have something to say on the subject. The child, Wordsworth saw, is free of materialist prejudices imposed by later life, whereby the eyes of the adult are closed to the Presences which surround us, who watch and judge. The poet claims that the young child sees with special clarity, and he attributes to children a wisdom of their own, and a special nearness to God. I do not doubt that heaven does lie about us in infancy, or at least that it can and that children very often possess keener spiritual perception than any among their elders save the saintly.

Sadly, the special illumination of childhood, whatever it may be, is driven out by the onset of maturity, and by the necessity of self-adaptation to the circumstances of the world. The poet Henry Vaughan (1622–1695) in pursuit of this theme, wrote:

> Happy those early days, when I
> Shined in my Angel-infancy!
> Before I understood this place
> Appointed for my second race,
> Or taught my soul to fancy aught
> But a white, celestial thought;

When yet I had not walk'd above
A mile or two from my first Love,
And looking back, at that short space
Could see a glimpse of His bright face:
When on some gilded cloud or flower,
My gazing soul would dwell an hour,
And in those weaker glories spy
Some shadows of eternity. . . .

Then Thomas Traherne (1637–1674) wrote in a similar vein. Wordsworth says 'the thought of our past years in me doth breed perpetual benediction'. What he is acclaiming is the survival of memories which, though still 'the master-light of all our seeing are but a flickering shadow cast by the original experience itself'.

In his great *Ode* Wordsworth has this to say:

Our birth is but a sleep and a forgetting;
The Soul that rises with us, our life's Star,
Hath had elsewhere its setting,
And cometh from afar –

It is sad, if true, that men should, as they grow up, become distracted by the trials and trivialities of life and lose sight of 'the vision glorious'. I do not think that all do, and in this I am supported by the late Lord Elton who thought deeply and has written wisely on such matters. Is it too extravagant to suggest that our lives may occasionally be enriched by an awareness of this mystical involvement with the unseen force that can accompany, guide and help us throughout life, if we will only reach out to it? Whence come those rare and fleeting shafts of light that in peaceful moments descend as dew to illuminate the mind and warm the heart? They come upon us unsought without warning, anywhere, at any time and should be welcomed and listened to in wonder and with joy.

My interest in 'the human situation' which was first awakened at the age of fourteen has continued to fascinate me, but a long life of varied experiences has brought me no nearer to an understanding of it. 'Man's inhumanity to man' has if anything intensified this century, with atrocities on a massive scale throughout the world. To describe them as bestial would be to insult the animal kingdom, for man capable of rising to great heights has chosen to plumb the depths of folly and degradation. Walt Whitman in praise of animals says 'Not one is dissatisfied, not one is demented with the mania of owning things'. How great is this contrast with man's acquisitiveness, unbridled cruelty and greed. Has the time not come for a second flood? In the everlasting struggle between good and evil we must hope that what passes for good wins through despite imperfections, limitations, setbacks and a high cost in human misery. Vigilance is imperative lest we are suffocated by indolence, worse still by indifference. Our family motto is 'Vigilate et orate' and I have tried to live up to it. There is no monopoly in the phrase, and I urge others to adopt it as a bulwark against attack from without, and from the more dangerous and insidious assault from within.

What in a long life have I learnt? Quite a lot I think in one way and another. First, that ambition sought for personal aggrandisement may lead to an arid desert, for you cannot control the price you – and others – may have to pay to achieve your goal. It will almost certainly be far too high and is in any event unworthy. Motives matter desperately and should be examined critically. Meanness is despicable, in thought doubly so, and any betrayal of trust degrading. In life constancy is very important, for it endures hopefully and survives every disappointment. To show gratitude is important too, for both cement human relationships. Two Christian recommendations, to 'despise no man' and 'judge not that ye be not judged', are very sound and practical. *Tout comprendre c'est tout pardonner* is a noble and enlightened sentiment. I would like to accept it without reserve but then one thinks of Hitler and Stalin and other monsters of my time. The trouble, in the ordinary course of life, is that our very limited vision does not allow us fully to understand another's motivation from which actions stem. Thus we are in no position to judge, still less to condemn, and should resist all temptation to do either. Humility is important, particularly in relation to our fellows in distressing circumstances, even if brought about by their own action; self-righteous condemnation is shameful, a view endorsed by John Bradford (1500–1555) who was the first to declare 'there but for the grace of God go I'.

For the Christian there is a wealth of advice, encouragement and guidance. Though the road may be rough it is well worth following. There is a most moving writing by a soldier who fought in the

American Civil War embossed in the Hall of the Institute of Rehabi-
litation in New York, that reads:

> I asked for strength that I might achieve,
> I was made weak that I might learn humbly to obey.
> I asked for health that I might do great things,
> I was given infirmity that I might do better things.
> I asked for riches that I might be happy,
> I was given poverty that I might be wise.
> I asked for power that I might have praise of men,
> I was given weakness that I might feel the need of God.
> I asked for all these things that I might enjoy life,
> I was given life that I might enjoy all things.
> I got nothing that I asked for but everything that I hoped for,
> I am among all men most richly blessed.

This is to me a wonderful affirmation of faith and realization of
eternal values, not beyond the reach of most of us. To the non-
Christian this man's revelation will make no sense at all.

As I approach the end of a long and happy journey in the course of
which I have received so much, and to my shame contributed so little,
the best advice I can give to those who follow would be to seek the
truth, be just, and ever compassionate; to give thanks whenever, and
to whomsoever, it is due; to avoid bigots, for bigotry in any form is not
only extremely unattractive but often positively ridiculous. So
thought Dean Swift:

> We are the chosen few
> All others will be damned.
> There is no place in Heaven for you
> We can't have Heaven crammed.

I am confident that we will discover Heaven capable of infinite
expansion to embrace in time all men travelling hopefully towards it
by many different roads, and that there will be plenty of room for us
all. Better still, that we will be well received. Consider St Paul's
splendidly virile and encouraging letter to the Romans, chapter 8,
verses 35–39, for therein lies hope for even the meanest and least
deserving creature.

To the young about to embark on life, I would say 'Do not hesitate
to follow the wise guidance of your heart as opposed to your head in

regard to generous impulses, and do not be put off from doing a service to anyone in need because of a false pride, lack of sensitivity, fear of ridicule or rebuff. Go forward cheerfully in confidence and trust and all will be well – if obstacles obstruct your path overcome them courageously, you have great reserves of strength to call on and may do so with confidence'.

True and lasting happiness has to be worked for day after day and calls for dedication and often for some self sacrifice. The philosopher Carlyle may have contributed something in saying 'To read, to think, to love, to hope, to pray, these are the things that make men happy'. They are indeed, but there is a lot more to it than that. We are, each one of us, on our own to make or mar our lives, and a poet has put it this way:

> To every man there openeth –
> A way, and ways, and a way
> And the high soul climbs the high way
> And the low soul gropes the low –
> And in between on the mighty Flats
> The rest drift to and fro –
> But to every man there openeth
> A high way and a low
> And every man decideth
> The way his soul shall go.

The choice is ours and inescapable – do not be a drifter, for that shows a shameful timidity and lack of purpose. Faith in something and enthusiasm for something make life meaningful and worthwhile. It is not life that matters but the courage we bring to it, and there is no case for gloomy foreboding, but the strongest possible case for robust decision, continuous action, and daily application.

As for myself, who in the nature of things must soon be called away, there may be something to be said for critical self-examination, a depressing exercise, but I have never been much given to introspection which to me suggests too great a concern for an ego that is frankly unimportant.

This business of living is worthwhile when one may yet learn something of value every single day, when all things of beauty meet an eye as yet undimmed, and an ear happily still sensitive and responsive to the sound of music, a child's laughter and the songs of birds. The scents, colours and design of flowers a constant wonder and delight.

Our life span measured against the scale of millions of years is immeasurably brief, to compare it to a single day is to be generous. I end with a poem that appeals to me, written by A.E., a friend of my childhood, long disappeared into the sunset to greet a morning of unimaginable brilliance and loveliness. It is called *The Great Breath* and speaks of the ending of a single day:

> Its edges foam'd with amethyst and rose
> Withers once more the old blue flower of day:
> There where the ether like a diamond glows,
> Its petals fall away.
>
> A shadowy tumult stirs the dusky air:
> Sparkle the delicate dews, the distant snows:
> The great deep thrills – for through it everywhere
> The breath of Beauty blows.
>
> I saw how all the trembling ages past,
> Moulded to her by deep and deeper breaths,
> Near'd to the hour when Beauty breathes her last
> And knows herself in death.

Index